IMPERIAL SUNSET

Books by R. F. Delderfield

Napoleon's Marshals
Imperial Sunset
Retreat from Moscow
The Golden Millstones
Napoleon in Love

God Is an Englishman
Theirs Was the Kingdom
Give Us This Day

The Dreaming Suburb
The Avenue Goes to War

Too Few for Drums
Farewell the Tranquil Mind
Seven Men of Gascony

A Horseman Riding By
Long Summer Day
Post of Honor
The Green Gauntlet

Diana
To Serve Them All My Days
Return Journey
Charlie, Come Home
Mr. Sermon
On the Fiddle
All Over the Town
There Was a Fair Maid Dwelling
The Adventures of Ben Gunn

IMPERIAL

R. F. Delderfield

SUNSET

The Fall of Napoleon, 1813-14

𝔖𝔅

A SCARBOROUGH BOOK
STEIN AND DAY / Publishers / New York

FIRST SCARBOROUGH BOOKS EDITION 1980

Imperial Sunset was originally published in hardcover by
Chilton Book Company and is reprinted by arrangement.

Copyright © 1968 by R. F. Delderfield

Designed by JoAnn Randel
Printed in the United States of America
Stein and Day/*Publishers*/ Scarborough House, Briarcliff Manor,
N.Y. 10510

Library of Congress Catalog Card Number 68–31696
ISBN 0–8128–6056–X

For SIR ARTHUR BRYANT, C.H., C.B.E.

*In friendship and appreciation
of his unique contribution
to the history of this period.*

Acknowledgments

THE SOLE OBJECT of a bibliography is surely to facilitate the studies and leisure reading of readers sufficiently interested in the subject matter to go exploring among the author's sources. To further this object is a pleasure to anyone who, like myself, has derived so much enjoyment from reading contemporary accounts of the First Empire.

The task of citing every reference however is quite impossible, inasmuch as it represents forty years in the wilderness of the period, but the following list, subdivided, may be useful.

Fiction: It is not usual, in a history, to quote fictional sources but I make no apology for using background material contained in that excellent book *History of a Conscript of 1813* by MM. Erckmann-Chatrian. I first encountered this as a French exercise at school. It can be read in English, excellently translated by Russell Davis Gillman. As stated, the authors collected all their material from Napoleonic veterans and if one compares their work with contemporary accounts it will be seen that they have written with a very careful eye on the truth. Theirs is a moving account of what it was like to be a private soldier in the Grand Army.

Memoirs: The age is rich in personal memoir. Chief among those consulted are:

Mémoires et correspondance politique et militaire (Eugène de Beauharnais); *Mémoires* (Comte Beugnot); *Memoirs of Napoleon Bonaparte* (M. de Bourrienne); the *Memoirs of Carnot* by his son; *Correspondence and Despatches of Lord Castlereagh,* edited by C. W. Vane; *Souvenirs sur Napoléon* by Comte Chaptal; *Mémoires de Bonaparte* by Chateaubriand; *Journal des Operations, 1814* by C. N. Fabvier; *Manuscrit de 1813* and *Manuscrit de 1814,* by Baron Fain; the *Commentaries of H. de Jomini; Memoirs of Madame Junot; Memoirs and Commentaries* of Labaume; *Memoirs of Surgeon General Larrey; Memoirs of Marshal Macdonald; Memoirs of Marshal Marmont; Souvenirs Historiques* by Baron de Méneval; Napoleon's own memoirs dictated at St. Helena to Generals Gourgaud and Montholon; *Memoirs of La Maréchale Oudinot; Commentaries on Campaign of 1813* by J. J. G. Pelet; *Memoirs of Baron de Marbot; Memoirs of Captain Barrès; Histoire et Mémoires* by Comte de Ségur; *Buonapartis Reise von Fontainebleau nach Fréjus* by Waldburg; Wellington's Despatches, Correspondence and Memoranda; Private Diary of Sir R. Wilson, 1812–14; *Memoirs of Queen Hortense;* Maj. Gen. Napier's *History of the War in the Peninsula;* Kincaid's *Random Shots of a Rifleman.*

Histories and Commentaries (other than personal memoir) published in the last century-and-a-half concerning the campaigns of 1813–14: *Life of Napoleon Bonaparte* by W. M. Sloane; Emil Ludwig's *Napoleon; Napoleon, His Rise & Fall* by J. M. Thompson; *Decisive Battles of the Western World* by Maj. Gen. J. F. C. Fuller; J. B. Morton's *Marshal Ney;* James Kemble's *Napoleon Immortal;* Jean Savant's *Napoleon in His Time;* Margery Weiner's *The French Exiles, 1789–1815;* Sir Arthur Bryant's *Years of Victory* and *The Age of Elegance;* Michael Glover's *Wellington's Peninsular Victories;* Michael Lewis' *Napoleon and His British Captives;* P. W. Sergeant's *The Burlesque Napoleon;* Carola Oman's *Napoleon's Viceroy;* Macdonell's *Marshals of Napoleon;* Jean Robiquet's *Daily Life in France under Napoleon* and Lenôtre's *Memoirs of the French Revolution.*

Letters: Napoleon III, the Emperor's nephew, served twentieth century historians well by publishing his uncle's vast correspondence and this edited edition was supplemented by Lady Mary Lloyd in 1898. Since then that meticulous historian, J. M. Thompson, F.B.A., F.R.Hist.S. has translated and edited a carefully selected edition that has proved a godsend to writers on the First Empire. Thompson estimates that Napoleon wrote or dictated ten to twelve letters a day during his fifteen years' rule, a total of something around 60,000! Of these 41,000 have been printed in books from which Thompson made his selection.

Contents

1

SPRING, ALWAYS ANTICIPATED in northern Europe
more eagerly than in the softer south, was never more welcome
on the Baltic coasts than in 1813, for it brought not only the
promise of sunshine and shorter nights but a strong hint that great
events were impending. In the months ahead, it was felt, freedom
would return to the people of the ancient Hanseatic towns, the
uniquely personal and economic freedom that they had enjoyed
with few interruptions since the growth of the Hanseatic League
in the 13th century.

For the past seven years, ever since the Emperor Napoleon's
decisive victory over the Prussians at Jena, the towns of the
League—Hamburg, Lubeck and others—had been incorporated
into the sprawling French empire that now stretched from the
gates of Cádiz to the eastern frontier of the ancient kingdom of
Poland and from the north of Germany to the Straits of Messina
dividing the French-ruled kingdom of Naples from Sicily. Under
the pressures of the Emperor's economic blockade of Great
Britain, towns like Hamburg had withered, losing the greater part
of their trade in commodities ranging from furs, wax, honey
and pitch, to potash, charcoal, hemp, flax, grain, malt, wool, lead,
tin, cod and whale oil. French customs officials kept a jealous
watch on their sea traffic. A French garrison grew fat on local
levies. Smuggling was rife, and special trading licenses continued to fill many pockets, both French and German, but smuggling under the eye of old revolutionaries like Marshals Mortier

The Cossacks of the Elbe

and Brune was a hazardous occupation and licenses cost money in bribes. The old freedom to buy and sell in prodigious quantities had gone; so had the citizen of Hamburg's feeling that he was a specially privileged person in a Europe dominated by rapacious aristocrats. The population of the city shrank from 120,000 to 80,000 and the citizen looked into a bleak future where his orders continued to arrive by courier from Paris and his profits, when any existed, were strictly regulated. As long as Napoleon continued to dominate the Continent the residents of Hamburg could see no prospect of change in this unhappy state of affairs and yet, dramatically, the prospect of abrupt change presented itself in the month of December, 1812.

All that month rumors that had been drifting out of the east and the most astounding of them were suddenly confirmed in towns along the Baltic coast by the appearance of a flock of half-insane beggars, men with red-rimmed eyes and frostbitten ears, men moving slowly over the snow on feet wrapped in blood-stained rags, invalids arriving by sledge only to die in the town's hospitals and barracks. The burgesses peered at these human wrecks in astonishment. It was difficult to believe they were practically all that remained of the half-million men of sixteen nations that had made up the Grand Army of Napoleon six months previously and had crossed the Niemen to invade Russia as recently as last June.

In the sleigh tracks of this rabble came certainty that the Grand Army had indeed been annihilated, that all that remained of the mightiest host to tread European soil since the days of the Persian invaders of Greece, were a few thousand men of the Imperial Guard and about ten thousand veterans of the line whose hardihood and ingenuity had triumphed over the terrible Russian winter, months of starvation, and the lances of Cossacks that had followed them five hundred and fifty miles across the snow. To the men of the Hanse towns the pleasures of the past suddenly looked very near, almost within reach. No leader, they reasoned, could survive such a disaster and continue to exercise sufficient power to order their lives from as far away as the Seine. That they were wrong—at least temporarily so—is not an indictment of their judgment but proof of the genius of a short, plump man with a large head and a pale face, who had himself just accomplished the winter journey from Smorgini, on the far side of the Niemen, to his palace in the Tuileries, in fourteen days.

Among the first to adjust to the tidings that reached him out of Russia that season was Gouvion St. Cyr, the eccentric, violin-playing marshal of France, whose defensive talents had just won for him the coveted baton.

St. Cyr, wounded in the defense of Pultusk, had left Russia before the worst of the disasters had overtaken the French army, when the frosts were bearable and the tragedy of the crossing of the Beresina still lay ahead of the route. As commander of the Hamburg garrison he had with him some three thousand Imperial troops, plus a large number of customs men. As rumor after rumor of approaching Cossacks reached St. Cyr he made up his mind to retreat to the West. He was very far from being a craven—cowards did not exist in the upper echelons of the Napoleonic armies—but his vast military experience told him that he could not hope to hold a large and secretly hostile city against an army of the Czar with a few thousand men. In addition he was not unaware of the fact that the military pride of the Prussians, reawakened after a trance lasting seven years, was showing itself in the singing of the poet Korner's patriotic songs, in student riots, in forays by Lutzow's night raiders and here in Hamburg he was isolated at a storm center of this resurgence of patriotic enthusiasm. As news of the French rout was confirmed and skirmishers brought in reports of the presence of Cossacks as near as the village of Bergdorff, he formed the decision to evacuate while there was still time.

It was, as it happened, a foolhardy decision. The nearest Cossack hetman, Colonel Tettenborn, had no more than twelve hundred horsemen under his command but St. Cyr was not to know that. Stories of vast Russian armies moving towards the Elbe driving the frostbitten wreck of the Grand Army before them were repeated in the streets and quays of the old city every day and evidence of the appalling disaster that had overtaken French arms was before his eyes. Quietly, on March 12, 1813, he slipped away, leaving behind him a political vacuum.

II

When, in 1944, the Wehrmacht withdrew from the remoter provinces of France and the Allies delayed occupying billets used by the conquerors since 1940, the French provincials reacted in a variety of ways. The wise ones sat tight and waited. The cautious optimists came out into the open and glanced up and down the roads for the first signs of approaching GIs, or British Tommies. The impulsive hung out their flags and were often obliged to take them in again as detachments of Nazis marched through, en route for the Rhine.

Something like this happened in Hamburg in March, 1813, but, unluckily for the burgesses, the more vociferous voices, led by an exuberant pro-Russian, pro-British Swede called Doctor Von Hess, swayed the councils of the city fathers. As a result of their deliberations direct approaches were made to the Cossack colonel who was invited to march in and take possession of Hamburg in the name of the Czar, the Prussian King Frederick, and the old Hanseatic League. Colonel Tettenborn was assured over and over again that the French had gone but his brushes over the route from Moscow with iron men like Marshal Ney and Marshal Oudinot had taught him caution. He could not believe that a fighting marshal like St. Cyr had evacuated an important city without firing a shot and for a long time he undervalued his good fortune. At length, however, he came to believe that he was not being enticed into a trap. Having been given assurances that the city would be governed by its long dispersed Senate, and that he would be officially welcomed by the senators in their ceremonial robes, he gave orders to his men to saddle up and ride in. At four o'clock in the afternoon forty shaggy horsemen of the Czar trotted into the city, to be received, to their great astonishment, as heaven-sent liberators and feasted and fêted as they had never been welcomed anywhere in their unsettled lives. Yet this was no more than a token of the tremendous welcome Hamburg gave Colonel Tettenborn and his bearded warriors.

Fawning upon the Cossacks as though they had been jail-deliverers the citizens of the ancient trading center showered them with gifts, provisions and drink. Had they had more experience of Cossacks they would have known that generosity on this scale was misplaced. The average Cossack was the most accomplished freebooter in the world, not excluding a professional bandit, and would in any case help himself to anything he needed or coveted in his own country or anywhere else. This, inspired by the example of his commanding officer, is precisely what he did in Hamburg and within days the burgesses were beginning to wonder whether, after all, a French occupation was the worst that could happen to them. Even men like St. Cyr, who had paid his troops on leaving the town with a hundred thousand francs from the municipal treasury, had overlooked the post office, the banks, and the public offices, had not sold off every moveable object that came to hand and had left without pocketing the jewels and trinkets of private citizens, but apart from their cupidity what puzzled the reappointed Senate was the size of the relieving force. No columns of Russian grenadiers marched into the city and even the twelve hundred Cossack lancers began to disperse, searching out more loot in places like Lubeck along the coast. Within days there were no more than the original forty Cossacks left in Hamburg and the authorities began to be concerned with the possibilities of defense should the French counterattack.

To guard against this eventuality they formed a local militia. Together with other Hanse towns they raised and equipped a body of about ten thousand men and posted them on the crumbling fortifications and the islands adjacent to the city. The new companies were known as the Troops of the Hanseatic League but in a very short time they acquired another name, "The Cossacks of the Elbe." Recruited from the lowest classes of the city, an assembly of wharf loafers and ne'er-do-wells, they made the very best of their opportunities and the price of deliverance from the Imperial troops and bureaucrats rose a little each day. In the meantime the Senate was glad to speed Colonel Tettenborn on his way with a gift of five thousand gold Fredericks and the freedom of the city. It was observed by one onlooker that he was far more impressed by the money than with the honor of citizenship.

A fresh crop of rumors were reaching Hamburg, this time from the West and their purport was less reassuring. Napoleon, it seemed, had neither departed for Valhalla nor formed the decision to rule over an Empire bounded in the East by France's natural frontier, the Rhine. All the time Colonel Tettenborn, the Cossacks of the Dneiper, and the Cossacks of the Elbe, were being regaled by the Senate the French Emperor was, it appeared, hard at work raising a new army and was now on his way to rendezvous with the wreck of his battalions on the river Saale. Hard facts, all of them unpalatable to the men and women of Hamburg, soon confirmed rumors. By the first of May the new French army was fighting its way across the Saxon plains towards Dresden, recently occupied by the Russo-Prussian army, and the Hamburg Senators had cause to ponder the wisdom of the reckless hospitality they had shown the twelve hundred Cossacks from Bergdorff.

There was no question of reinsurance. Tettenborn and his horsemen were still in the vicinity, and so were the ten thousand loafers enrolled by the Senate for the protection of the city. Even so, it seemed unlikely that either force would avert retribution for fresh information arrived that General Vandamme was advancing from the southwest in force and Hamburg recalled that Napoleon had once said of this officer, "If I was to lose Vandamme I do not know what I would give to have him back again but if I had two such generals I should be obliged to shoot one!"

Vandamme was, in fact, the most hardbitten general in the Imperial Army and prospects of him taking a lenient view of the burghers' recent behavior were remote. Even this, however, was not the only threat that now hung over the terrified Senate. Behind Vandamme, and working in close co-operation with him, came Marshal Davout, known as the Iron Marshal, a tight-lipped martinet whose loyalty to Napoleon could not be purchased by all the gold Fredericks in Hamburg's coffers. And Davout had been designated the new Governor of the city.

There was nothing to do but make the best of it. At first sight of Vandamme's veterans the "Cossacks of the Elbe" fled and the real Cossacks followed their example. Taking with him his saddlebags of gold, memories of a pleasant stay, and the scroll confirming his honorary citizenship, Colonel Tettenborn rode away. With him went the Swede, Doctor Von Hess, on whose advice the Russians had occupied the city. Hamburg's liberation had lasted just seventy days.

The French re-entered the city without shedding a drop of blood. A column, consisting mostly of Danes allied to Napoleon, took possession of the fortifications and centers of communication. For a brief spell nothing was said of the rollicking parties Hamburg had organized on behalf of Tettenborn and his men but citizens who had felt the weight of Napoleon's hand in the past knew that this treachery would not be passed over. They were right. On May 7th, before in fact the city had been reoccupied, the Emperor had written to Berthier, his Chief of Staff, a summary of directions to be handed to Davout. "He is to arrest summarily all citizens of Hamburg who have served as 'Senators' . . . he is to court-martial the five chief culprits among them and have them shot. The rest he will send to France under strong escort, in order that they may be incarcerated in a State prison. He must sequestrate their property and declare it confiscated; their houses, landed property and so forth will fall into the Crown's domains. He is to disarm the whole town, shoot the officers of the Hanseatic Legion, and dispatch to France all who have enlisted in that regiment in order that they may be sent to the galleys."

This was still but a part of the punishment reserved for the city that had sponsored Colonel Tettenborn's convivial evenings. An indemnity of fifty millions was imposed on Hamburg and Lubeck; there were to be mass arrests and deportations of all who had in any way assisted the brief occupation of the Russians; and the city was to be put in a state of defense that would enable it to hold out, with a garrison of four to five thousand men, against any future attack from within or without.

Marshal Davout, disciplinarian though he was, did not carry out these reprisals to the letter although the punitive measures he did impose were sufficient to make the citizens of Hamburg reflect bitterly on the ease with which the talkative Swedish doctor, Von Hess, had persuaded them to open their gates to the Cossacks. From then, until the abdication of Napoleon a year later, Hamburg remained in French hands and Davout did not relax his grip upon the unfortunate city until he had been assured by a comrade-in-arms that the abdication was a fact.

Hamburg relapsed into sullen bondage, although whether the exactions of Davout were any more oppressive than the brief occupation of Tettenborn's Cossacks is difficult to say.

The story of what happened in Hamburg between March 12, 1813, when St. Cyr marched out, and the end of April, 1814, when Davout was finally convinced of Napoleon's fall, is interesting because it illustrates the ambiguous situation faced by rulers, cities, communities, duchies, principalities and even major powers like Austria during the final year of Napoleon's domination of Europe. Everywhere there was the same confusion, the same agony of divided loyalties and uncertain courses of action promoted by the sudden shifts and stresses of power. Initially these were brought about by the Russian debacle but they were tremendously complicated by Napoleon's resilience and astounding achievements in the four months between his escape from Russia and his barren victories in Saxony.

In the early spring of 1813 most people in Britain, Spain, eastern and central Europe thought of the French emperor as a spent force and his huge, sprawling empire as approaching the point of collapse. They had not taken into account the unique genius of the man, not only as a soldier but as an administrator. Their misjudgment in this respect was to cost Europe a million lives.

2

AT THE BEGINNING of the year 1812 the Duke of Wellington, poised in Portugal to make a dash to Madrid and unseat King
Joseph who had been foisted upon Spain in 1808, summed up
the situation on the Continent as follows: "Napoleon governs
one half of Europe directly and most of the other half indirectly."
This was neither a simplification nor an exaggeration. A single
glance at the map would have confirmed the Duke's summary
as fact.

The early victories of the French Republican armies over the
autocracies in the last decade of the eighteenth century had
possessed unique impetus, so much that France had overrun
her natural frontiers long before the twenty-six-year-old artilleryman from Corsica astonished the world with his victories
in Italy in 1796. After the conquest of the Italian peninsula
there was no looking back. Using new methods of warfare,
and united under the hand of a genius, the French volunteer
soldiers marched from triumph to triumph, overturning the professional armies of long-established dynasties with the ease of a
giant striding through an array of ninepins. What they did not
achieve by force of arms they won by propaganda as the dis-
ciples of égalitarianism, and the enemies of France were very
slow to profit by this manner of making war and the necessity
of coming to terms, in part at least, with the gigantic forces
released by the French Revolution.

For a long time—for at least fifteen years—they clung to

Joy in London

mid-eighteenth century fighting techniques and authoritarian concepts of governing people. They would not accept the fact that war is a year round occupation and that the gentlemanly business of going into cantonments for the winter months was outmoded. They were like a team of winded old carthorses competing with a young stallion and in all but two major clashes the issue was never in doubt. But their failure to learn the new techniques of combat in the field was not their only error, nor was it the most important. They could not or would not bring themselves to understand that the French Revolution, and its greatest single gain, the opening of avenues of advancement by merit rather than birth, was an international event of tremendous significance and not the product of a large scale riot initiated by the rabble of the Paris slums. For the most part their hired and conscripted soldiers fought without enthusiasm and without any prospect of political or material rewards. They were there in the field by royal decree, and fear of the firing squad or the lash, while enough to keep them at their posts, was not sufficient to enable them to compete on equal terms with Frenchmen who could expect to share in the glory of a victory, who could win promotion to the highest ranks in their new profession and also share in loot made available by conquest. In the armies of Napoleon were men who had risen from the status of farmhand and apprentice journeyman to that of duke in ten years. They had no equivalents in the musters of the Habsburgs, the Hohenzollerns, the Romanoffs or, indeed among the British where the social structure was equally rigid. It is this, as much as the technical ability of their chief, that explains victories like Marengo, Ulm, Austerlitz, Jena, Auerstadt, Friedland and Wagram.

By 1809, however, the autocracies were learning, although slowly. Until then the French had been fighting against hereditary rulers and governments but the war in Spain changed all this. The fanatical Spanish peasant was handled as roughly by Napoleon's seasoned troops as had been the levies of Austria and Prussia, but a victory over him did not end a war or even a campaign, as had happened after Marengo in 1800 and after Jena in 1806. He continued to fight in the hills, in the desolate mountain passes, in the reeking villages of Aragon and León. If

he survived he could always fall back on the disciplined troops
of a man who, if not a genius, was at least a very competent
and original strategist, who could exploit unlooked for opportunities and the possibilities of terrain as successfully as Napoleon himself.

But in 1808, the year of the first clash between Spaniard and
Frenchman, all this lay in the unforeseeable future. More than
four years were to pass before the most farsighted could discern
a resurgence of nationalism from Cádiz to St. Petersburg, from
the Hook of Holland to the heel of Italy. For this vast area,
during those four years, remained obedient to the Imperial will.
The one major attempt to challenge it, made by the Austrians
in 1809, ended as all previous attempts had ended, in the loss
of a major battle and a dictated peace by the conqueror.

It was not until the summer of 1941, a hundred-and-twenty
years after Napoleon died on St. Helena, that Europeans had
an opportunity to witness what one man and one nation could
achieve by a combination of brute force and guile. But even
then, measured in terms of square miles, the conquests of Napoleon exceeded those of Hitler and were, moreover, more soundly
based and better consolidated. By June, 1812, when Napoleon
was on the point of crossing the Niemen into Russia, almost
the entire continent lay under his domination. The Empire proper
extended from the Hanse cities down to the western Pyrenees,
and from the Franco-Spanish frontier in the south to the open
frontier between the kingdom of Italy and the French-ruled
kingdom of Naples. The western Balkans were also incorporated
and French customs were gathered as far south as the frontier
posts of the old Ottoman Empire. Spain, ruled by a Bonaparte,
was occupied by some three hundred thousand veteran troops.
The whole of what we now know as West Germany was a confederation of states ruled by French-nominated puppets, all
of whom contributed money to the French treasury and conscripts to the French army. Most of modern Poland, freed from
Russian domination and styled the Duchy of Warsaw, was dependent upon France for its existence although here there
was no necessity to bully or cajole the inhabitants, for the Poles,
almost to a man, were willing allies. Austria was prostrate after
many attempts to challenge Imperial policies. Wellington's army

was keeping Spain in a turmoil but without it Spanish resistance would have collapsed in a matter of weeks and even Wellington was forced to retreat before he could exploit his great victory at Salamanca. Holland had been incorporated into the French Empire, Denmark was an ally, and the Swedes had just chosen a French marshal for their crown prince. In the entire continent of Europe there were only two sources of anxiety for Napoleon; Britain, a country that continued to fight hard in one area and finance trouble elsewhere, and the great land mass of Russia, where the Czar ruled over millions of illiterate peasants. With these two exceptions, neither of them very threatening at that time, the catalyst of the revolution was unchallenged and unchallengeable. The conquest of Europe had been achieved in sixteen years. It was to crumble in a further twenty-two months.

The patriotic fervor of the war in Spain, that began in 1808 and continued unabated until 1814, was imitated in Russia in the year 1812 but on a larger scale. Here again the veteran troops of Napoleon found themselves involved with an enemy they could not pin down to a decisive action. The enemy melted away into the endless birch forests after brief, inconclusive engagements but was always out on the flanks equipped to murder stragglers, attack convoys, and, above all, to lay waste the surrounding countryside upon which every army up to the late nineteenth century depended for survival.

The Grand Army was not destroyed in combat, or even by thirty degrees of frost. It was overwhelmed by the vastness of Russia and the use made of the terrain by generals like Kutusoff. Supply depots had been built up over the long route between the Prussian garrison towns and Smolensk but an army dependent upon carts and beef on the hoof could not make use of these depots unless the roads connecting them were kept open. To achieve this over so long a route Napoleon would have needed not half a million men but two millions, for he was operating in a country where the forces of his enemy were augmented in direct relation to his own losses. His planned strategy worked reasonably well until he reached Moscow but the delay in that burned out city was fatal to his communications. By the time he was ready to march out his line of communications

had snapped. Links in what had been a 550-mile long chain
had been reduced to islets of French occupation. Stores were
pilfered, convoys attacked and broken up by Cossacks and
brigands, droves of cattle went astray or were sold off in drib-
lets, and within days the retreating army began to starve. Frost
only finished what distance and patriotic fervor had begun. As
the stricken column groped its way westward it advanced into
a white vacuum and the really astonishing thing about the retreat from Moscow is that any one man of the French or allied
contingents survived to recross the Niemen in mid-December.
No other European army at that time could have preserved
any kind of cohesion after the disastrous crossing of the Beresina
in November.

Thus the Moscow campaign was a military defeat of the first
order but it was more than that. It was an even greater political
defeat for it exposed the myth of French invincibility and revived the near-extinct patriotism of Prussia, Austria and some
of the more eastern German states. This, in the end, was to contribute more directly to Napoleon's downfall than his physical
losses on the icy road between Mojaisk and Kovno.

The remnant of the Grand Army trailed into the Prussian garrison towns in the last days of 1812, perhaps ten thousand men
capable of bearing arms and three times as many exhausted invalids who would eventually recover. Commanding them, and
utterly unfitted for such a demanding task, was Joachim Murat,
King of Naples, the Emperor's brother-in-law who had risen
from barracks to throne in seventeen years. Murat, one of the
most dashing cavalry commanders in the history of warfare, was
the worst possible choice among the survivors for a command
that needed ingenuity, patience and an unshakeable faith in the
future. Murat's skill as a soldier was limited to the art of maneuvering large masses of well equipped cavalry. He had never,
at any time of his life, possessed a moderate degree of patience
and his faith in Napoleon's future had been lost in the snow outside the empty revictualing magazines west of Smolensk. In
Naples his wife, the unscrupulous Caroline Bonaparte, was already contemplating treachery and her selfish determination to
keep the Neapolitan throne—in the event her brother lost his

—had been half-heartedly endorsed by Murat before he left Naples to rendezvous with Napoleon the previous summer. Of the two the man was the more trustworthy but it is not easy to find excuses for a professional soldier, who owed everything he possessed to the courage of the men he commanded, abandoning them to their fate as did Murat in January, 1813. Recoiling from the task of rallying what remained of the army he handed over command to Prince Eugène, Napoleon's stepson and Viceroy of Italy, and rode for Naples, announcing that he was ill. Sick or well he made the long journey in almost record time and at once resumed plotting with his wife, their intrigues adjusting to the prospect of Napoleon's overthrow within twelve months.

Eugène, the only son of Josephine by her previous marriage to Alexandre de Beauharnais, was thirty-one years old when he received the most difficult and thankless assignment of his military career. Intelligent, thoughtful, courteous and very courageous, he was one of his stepfather's most valuable assets. His loyalty to the Empire had survived the terrible test of seeing his mother set aside for a nineteen-year-old archduchess for reasons of state. Trained and schooled as a soldier since boyhood he remained a soldier to his death, steering his way through a maze of treachery without ostentation and without a thought of what he might gain or lose by changing his allegiance. He leaves behind him an almost unique reputation for loyalty and soldierly conduct and never was this more apparent than in the winter of 1812–1813. Uncomplainingly he set about the task of reorganization and considering his appalling handicaps he achieved a very great deal in the short space of time available. He was ably seconded by Marshal Macdonald, a stolid, unlucky officer, who also emerges from the record of the period as a man of honor and commonsense. Macdonald's advice was to write off the eastern extremities of the Empire at once, call in the garrisons in the path of the advancing Russians and concentrate on the Oder, or, failing that, as far west as the Elbe. Napoleon did not take this excellent advice and by mid-summer was to regret not having done so.

Macdonald's view was almost certainly formed by his recent experiences on the northern flank of the Grand Army, where a large section of his German auxiliaries had already deserted under General Yorck, placing him in a very difficult situation when the French withdrew from Russia. By keeping his nerve, and by moving at great speed, he extricated himself and what remained of his corps, retiring on Tilsit which he reached on January 28th.[1] By then the deserter Yorck, whose sovereign Frederick William of Prussia was still nominally Napoleon's ally, had been negotiating with the Russians for two months. The day before the French recrossed the Niemen he had signed an armistice with the Czar's representatives at Tauroggen.

This was how matters stood in the north-eastern extremity of the sprawling, patchwork empire in the first days of one of the most decisive years in modern history. Far to the south, where the Habsburg domains touched the southern frontier of the Duchy of Warsaw, they were even less promising when viewed from Paris. In the north there at least existed a holding force of a sort, as well as two French commanders who could be trusted. To the south, where Napoleon hoped he could rely upon the quiescence if not the loyalty of his Imperial father-in-law, Francis, there was an element of menace that was to increase day by day as spring succeeded winter.

When the Grand Army had pushed forward in a vast semicircle at the outset of the Russian adventure more than six months before its northern flank had been guarded by Macdonald and a mixed Franco-German force. The southern tip of the arc had been allocated to a corps composed entirely of Austrians, not the best fighting material at the best of times and almost worthless in the service of the man who had beaten them from the field time and again since the Italian campaigns of 1796.

They were commanded by an experienced soldier, Count Schwartzenberg, whose loyalty to Napoleon was even more doubtful, for Schwartzenberg was a sincere Austrian patriot and had behaved as one throughout the Russian campaign, refusing to engage his troops and even allowing Russian reinforcements to filter through his territory to join the advancing army of Kutusoff. Napoleon was not unaware of potential treachery in this quarter but he had no alternative but to ignore it both then and later. Schwartzenberg it is true was within range of the loyal Poles but Poland had been drained of recruits the previous summer and the finances of the Duchy of Warsaw were in no state to raise fresh forces. The Austrian was anything but a headstrong man. Perhaps influenced by a cautious nature, perhaps by advice from Vienna where Chancellor Metternich had already made up his mind to play a waiting game, the Austrian soldier committed no act of aggression towards the French or their allies but continued to do what he had done for the past seven months. He waited and watched as thousands of Cossacks, vanguard of the Czar's armies, crossed the Niemen into Poland. Only when they rode up to the gates of Warsaw on February 6th did he make his first decisive move. Quietly, without firing a shot, he withdrew into his master's domains. The southeastern flank of the French Empire was now wide open.

II

A month's ride to the West, in the heart of the Spanish peninsula, the death of the old year brought no cheer to King Joseph, the plump, amiable, nonentity whom family ties had raised first to the throne of Naples, then to the throne of Spain.

Joseph, who wanted nothing more than to be master of a country estate and one or two tame mistresses, had entered Spain with the greatest reluctance in 1808. The longer he wore the crown of the Bourbons the more it oppressed him. With less ambition but more prescience than his terrible brother he had foreseen that it would not be easy to win the loyalty of Spanish peasants, their proud grandees and their implacable priests. Spain, sunk in torpor since the great days of Philip II, had not proved difficult to occupy but it was proving impossible to pacify.

French armies, composed of veterans and conscripts in about equal proportions and commanded by some of the most talented fighting men of the age, occupied vast areas of territory, but in a country subdivided by mountain ranges, and having but one broad, paved highway, each unit was an island independently ruled by its military commander, none of whom paid the slightest attention to the edicts of King Joseph in Madrid. More often than not his instructions did not even arrive in their camps, the men who carried them having been ambushed in a mountain pass and murdered by partisans operating on both sides of their route. The fortunate among these dispatch riders had their throats cut. The unlucky ones were taken prisoner, boiled in oil, nailed to a tree, or slowly crushed to death under piles of stones. By the end of 1812 it required a body of five hundred men to convey a message from one corps headquarters to another. Detailed directions as to how to conduct war in Spain arrived from Paris from time to time. They were always two months out of date. News of what was going on outside the peninsula reached the French marshals through the medium of captured English newspapers.

In the summer of 1812 Wellington, emerging from his Portuguese base, had won a decisive battle over Marshal Marmont, the Emperor's oldest friend, at Salamanca and had entered Madrid in triumph. The king bolted for Burgos but Wellington soon ran into serious difficulties and after the British withdrawal Joseph cautiously re-entered his capital. The state of anarchy, however, grew progressively worse. Two columns of French went off into the mountains to hunt down some of the more dangerous groups of partisans. Another French army, under the command of Suchet, occupied Catalonia and Valencia, where Suchet ruled like an independent king. Various other contingents were scattered in other parts of the peninsula, most of them concentrated in the northwest through which ran the only really practicable road to France.

Of all the Napoleonic captains who fought in Spain only Suchet enhanced his reputation. The son of a silk merchant he possessed, as well as military talent, administrative ability of a high order. On St. Helena Napoleon was to say of him, "If I had had two Suchets I could have held Spain." But there were not two Suchets and there was only one Marshal Soult, who, as Commander-in-Chief of Spanish armies, paid even less attention to King Joseph than his juniors. Soult, who had once hoped he would be made king of Portugal, possessed a very considerable military reputation but his talents lay in defensive warfare and even Marshal Masséna, the most brilliant of the marshals, had been worn down, disgraced and defeated by the terrain and temper of Spain of which he said, "A small army is defeated and a large army starves!"

Bewildered by the bitterness of Spanish resistance, distressed by the sullen rejection of his well-meaning endeavors to improve the Spaniard's lot and coax him into the nineteenth century, and frustrated on every side by the insolence and selfishness of the men whose duty it was to buttress his authority, Joseph pinned his hopes on Napoleon's acceptance of his repeated offers to abdicate. Instead the Paris couriers brought him nothing but carping criticism and a stream of out-of-date advice.

Then, on January 6, 1813, momentous news did arrive in the form of the famous 29th bulletin, issued on the road to Vilna, a proclamation that had plunged France into mourning by telling the stark truth concerning the fate of the Grand Army. Five weeks later Joseph received a word of mouth account of the retreat from a survivor. To him it must have come as confirmation that his throne was about to collapse under the weight of disasters, far and near.

There was only one grain of comfort to be derived from the latest despatches. Marshal Soult was recalled to France and in his place, as Chief Military Adviser, came the amiable and less ambitious Marshal Jourdan, an old republican whose reputation rested on a victory won at Fleurus two years before Europe had heard the name of Napoleon Bonaparte. It was obvious that the British-Portuguese army would attack in the spring and spring was on the doorstep. Messages went out to every French commander in the field to concentrate on Madrid where Joseph had about fifteen thousand troops under his hand. If they obeyed, and lost no time about it, there was still a chance that the western bastion of empire could be held.

III

Eugène retreating in northern Germany, the eastern-European frontiers laid open by the withdrawal of Schwartzenberg, panic measures for large-scale defensive action in Spain. What were Imperial prospects in the south and center, the one held by King Murat, the other by an assortment of satraps including Napoleon's youngest, devil-may-care brother, Jerome?

Mention has already been made of the incipient treachery of Murat and his wife, Caroline. As the spring sunshine ripened the oranges and lemons in Naples some of the palace plots began to mature and the general trend of affairs in southern Italy did not favor the man who had elevated Murat to a throne. For more than a year Queen Caroline had been apprehensive of the future. Learning what had occurred in Russia she was convinced that the empire was on the point of toppling. King and queen, reunited, redoubled their efforts to come to terms with the Austrians, their nearest potential assailants discounting British men-o'-war lying off the toe of Italy, and Caroline proved an energetic plotter.

Letters between Naples and Vienna were sent and received, sometimes crossing one another en route, and on the whole prospects of a settlement seemed promising for it was very much in the interests of Chancellor Metternich to keep the Kingdom of Naples neutral in the forthcoming Allied advance over the Elbe. Hints were dropped that under certain conditions Murat and Caroline would be allowed to keep their throne and hints were all that Caroline needed. She had not, like her husband, watched her brother wrest success from failure on fifty battlefields and had no true conception of what his prodigious energy could achieve, or how surely and swiftly he could exploit a moment's carelessness on the part of his enemies. Murat, listening to the reports of his spies (the palace was thick with spies, some of them serving four different masters) was still hesitant but his wife, taunting him with cowardice, intensified her secret campaign. Then came Napoleon's summons to the field and Murat obeyed it, perhaps from habit, perhaps from fear or, very possibly—for he was not a vicious man—in response to stirring of principle notably absent in the heart of his wife. Slowly and glumly he rode north. On the way he was handed another letter from Vienna but it was in code and he sent it on to Naples to be deciphered. He had, it would seem, no talent for conspiracy. The letter confirmed the promise that Austria would support his claim to remain king when the French Empire was dissolved by the victors in the forthcoming war.

If there was some doubt as to the future in Naples it was duplicated in the capital of every other puppet state that spring. Dedication to the cause of Napoleon could be measured by the

distance between various German capitals and Paris, so that
the clamor for war crossed Europe like the throb of a drum,
loud when heard close at hand, faint when heard at a distance.
All the German states with frontiers running within a few days'
march of the Cossacks professed the warmest goodwill towards
the Czar and the king of Prussia. West of this belt of disenchantment German citizens counseled caution and waited upon
events. Territories within easy reach of Paris, however, could
display neither defiance nor caution. The doubts of their rulers
were resolved by stern Imperial demands for troops and for
money and one and all they obeyed orders, as they had obeyed
them since the Grand Army had destroyed the Prussian army
in twenty-one days six years before. Only the king of Saxony
maintained an unwavering personal loyalty to his friend Napoleon and was to continue on this course until the end. His
subjects, being within the orbit of the Russian army, decided
otherwise, welcoming the invaders with the same enthusiasm as
that shown the Cossacks by the citizens of Hamburg.

In his tinsel capital at Cassel, ruling over the bankrupt kingdom of Westphalia, Jerome Bonaparte hoped he was pursuing an
honorable course but he was finding life as a puppet king extremely wearisome. His realm had been stripped of troops, his
coffers were empty, and his debts, personal and municipal, were
enormous. Like Joseph he was receiving furious letters of advice from his brother. One of them urged him to put his fortifications in order but Jerome did not see how this could be
done when he did not possess sufficient money to pay laborers
to dig a trench or build a glacis. He wrote back saying that he
feared for his own safety and when this produced another angry
letter pointing out his shortcomings as a soldier, Jerome countered by kidnapping two recently raised squadrons of French
chasseurs that happened to be crossing his territory at that moment. The chasseurs were enrolled in his bodyguard, and Colonel Marbot, who had gone to enormous pains to raise and train
them, was so enraged by this appropriation that he carried his
contempt for Napoleon's youngest brother to the grave.

All over Western Germany there were shifts and vacillations
as news of a Russo-Prussian alliance hardened, and stories of
the advance of the Cossacks brought Wurttembergers, Rhine-

landers, Westphalians, Bavarians, Hessians and Brandenbergers face to face with the alternatives. Which choice, of the three open to them, should they make? To remain loyal to France, gambling on Napoleon's ability to win? To subscribe to the patriotic hysteria in the east and enlist as liberators of Europe? Or to follow the example of the crown prince of Sweden who, of all men in the Continent at that time, was best qualified (judged on past performances) to walk the tightrope of neutrality until everyone else had jumped down on one side or the other? For even now, in his capital at Stockholm, Bernadotte, once a Bourbon sergeant-major, later a French marshal, later still the heir to the Swedish throne, had not committed himself. He was still pondering the relative worth of Napoleon's bribe of Pomerania, the Czar's bribe of Norway, or a British bribe in cash.

Hamburg, Lubeck, Dresden, Berlin, Stuttgart, Frankfurt, Vienna; there was doubt, caution and procrastination in all of them. In Naples there was treachery within the family. In Madrid there was dismay. Only in St. Petersburg and in the camp of Wellington was there calmness and self-confidence on the part of Napoleon's enemies. In London, where bankers had been financing wars against France since Louis XVI had been tried and executed by his subjects, there was optimism of a kind that had not been experienced in a generation. The jubilant cry of *The Times*—"He's falling! He's falling!" had yet to be heard but other printing houses were busy, pouring out a flood of pamphlets and cartoons announcing that the overthrow of the Corsican ogre was all but accomplished.

Nowhere did the trade of the pamphleteer and cartoonist flourish more spectacularly than in London during the first decade of the nineteenth century. It was the heyday of the pictorial satirist, with the French Emperor and his brothers as their exclusive subjects. Lurid, grotesque and often delightfully vulgar, the work of these artists has left us a vivid picture of the average Englishman's conception of his traditional enemy. Flashes of Crécy and Agincourt can be seen in the arrogance and vigor of their caricatures. The Emperor himself is displayed in any number of guises—as a drunkard, a lecher, a vampire, a satyr, a ravening satanic beast feeding upon human flesh. With enormous cocked hat, protruding belly and spindly legs, he leers from the European map he bestrides, inhuman, implacable and merciless, the epitome of everything that is evil and degrading, and the words that balloon from his lips are keyed to his appearance. Crushed under his spurred boots is the carnage of a tormented continent and around him, in a variety of fawning attitudes, are grouped his brothers, his marshals, and his satraps. In the background, as often as not fleeing in panic before the serried ranks of Wellington's army, is a huddle of bluecoated infantry, the men who had marched into almost every capital in Europe since 1796, and to a middle-aged man of the present generation there is something familiar in the stridency of this paper campaign. Studying one of these cartoons it is not difficult to discover the inspirational source of their direct descendants that appeared in so many newspapers and periodicals between the years 1914–18, and 1939–45, when Kaiser Wilhelm, his son "Little Willie," Hitler and Goëring were vilified. For Britain, alone among the enemies of the Revolution, had never ceased to oppose the Napoleonic conquest of Europe, had never stopped believing in French vulnerability to a blockade from the sea or the power of gold to promote fresh alliances. In the twenty years between the death of the well-meaning Louis and the advance of the Cossacks into the Hanse cities, there had only been one short break in the war against France and even that was regarded by most Englishmen as an extended truce. There had been waverers in this unrelenting campaign. There were even men of influence who considered Napoleon Bonaparte might have something valuable to contribute to Western civilization but this minority had backed down when the Grand Army was poised along the Channel coasts in 1805 ready for a triple descent upon Sussex, the Isle of Wight and the Thames estuary.

The war had been resumed. The British purse was reopened and guineas fed the jealousies and resentments of Continental dynasties. The naval blockade kept station off Brest, Havre and Toulon, an indestructible fleet of three-deckers and frigates, captained by the best sailors in the world but manned, for the most part, by men shanghaied from seaports, fed on trash, and somehow converted into extremely competent seamen by the whistle of the cat-o'-nine-tails and the lure of prize money. Whatever was imminent on the Continent, Britain was always there in the offing, watching, waiting, encouraging and in the past four years she had done much more than this. Her small, highly trained army in the peninsula had met and defeated the veterans of Austerlitz and Friedland, darting out of Portugal when the occasion offered, withdrawing to impregnable lines around Lisbon when the prospects of victory in the field were bleak. Because of this army the Portuguese had not only rallied but built up an excellent force of their own and beyond the Portuguese frontier fortresses the debris of defeated Spanish armies had been able to coalesce and fight again.

And yet, for all its string of Allied successes, the Spanish peninsula remained a sideshow in the struggle for Europe. For one thing it was too far from the center of operations. For another the forces employed there were too small to do more than influence a clash that was to involve seven major powers and innumerable smaller states. The key to the door that would unlock the gates of Paris was not to be found in Lisbon or London or St. Petersburg. It was waiting to be pocketed and carried West from the throne room of Frederick William, King of Prussia.

Without Prussia's active support the armies of the Czar Alexander could not hope to penetrate far beyond the Elbe, and unless Prussia marched, Austria, beaten to her knees so often in the past, would continue to temporize, Prince Bernadotte in Stockholm would continue to sit on the fence, the smaller German states would make the best of what could not be altered, and exiled French aristocrats, pensioners and beggars since the days of the Terror, would continue their games of whist in British spas, supporting themselves by teaching languages and giving fencing lessons. Prussia, in the early spring of 1813, held the key, and the question in the minds of Napoleon's enemies was would Frederick William have the courage to use it and follow the example of his dead wife, Louise, whose patriotism had inspired Prussia's bid for freedom in 1806 and whose epitaph on that disaster had been, "We slumbered on the laurels of Frederick the Great."

In spite of the resurgence of nationalism in Prussia, and among Germans generally, an irrevocable decision was not easy to make. The King was a nonentity, mindful of the terrible lesson he had been taught in 1806, overawed by the majesty of Napoleon's reputation and, above all, robbed of the inspiration that had stemmed from his heroic wife. Forces of circumstance, however, were rapidly becoming too strong for him. All over his realm pressures were being exerted from below, from the student corps, from ambitious soldiers like Gneisenau and Scharnhorst, from young adventurers in the secret army of Count Lutzow who practiced assassination by night, from embittered old warriors like Blucher who hated Napoleon so much that blood rushed to his head whenever the French Emperor's name was uttered; above all from Baron Stein, the midwife of Pan-Germanism.

Of all the men ranged against France at this moment Baron Stein is the most interesting and certainly the most dedicated and singleminded. Exiled in 1808 as a threat to the security of Prussia he had gone first to Vienna and then to St. Petersburg, where he became the friend and adviser of the Czar. Resolute, passionately attached to the German landscape and the traditions and culture of the Fatherland, honorable, incorruptible, fearless for his own safety and unremitting in his determination to achieve the unification and independence of Germany, Stein had stood like a rock through all the alarms of the French invasion of Russia in 1812. When the Czar was disposed to negotiate it was Stein who advised him to ignore the occupation of Moscow and leave the invaders to the climate and now, with the French Empire contracting day by day, he saw the prospect of liberation as a wink of light at the end of a long tunnel. Patiently he drew together the threads of revolt. He cared nothing for the machinations of statesmen like Metternich and he despised the timidity of his own sovereign. In December he had written, "I have but one Fatherland and that is Germany. The dynasties are indifferent to me in this moment of mighty development." Now that the moment for concerted action had come Stein left his friend the Czar and hurried to Breslau to demand action on the part of Frederick William.

Already the states of Eastern Germany were mobilizing. The

secret societies were no longer secret. There were arms for every able-bodied man between the age of seventeen and twenty-four. Women converted their jewelry into money for the war chest. Professor Steffens, of Breslau, summoned the students of his university to arms and his call was heard by eager young men from Berlin, Königsberg, Jena, Halle and Göttingen. Soon the level of the patriotic tide had submerged Frederick William's prudence. On March 1st he conferred with the Czar. On March 17th he signed a royal proclamation calling out the army and formally declaring war. By March 19th his summons had been broadcast as far west as the Rhine and Stein was given authority to plan the structure of new governments in all reconquered territories. Germany, backed by the Czar's victorious army, was on the march. The key to the gates of Paris was at last in Prussia's pocket.

The war, however, would not be won by students' songs and proclamations. Neither could a genius of Napoleon's dimensions be thrown down by patriotic levies, however bold and self-sacrificing they proved under fire. What was needed in addition to money and trained troops was a leader capable of measuring himself against the greatest captain of the age and in this respect the new coalition was singularly handicapped. Kutusoff, "The Old Fox of the North" as Napoleon had called him, died in April. He had never favored an advance into Europe and would have been content to end the war when the last French invader had recrossed the Niemen, but his terrible exertions between July and December, 1812, had proved fatal to the old man and his place as commander-in-chief of the Russian army was taken by Wittgenstein, who was dedicated to a war beyond the frontiers.

Wittgenstein, unlike many Russian generals of the period, was a commander who combined enterprise and caution. Part of the cause of the long retreat of the Russian armies the previous summer had been intense rivalry between two schools of military thought. Barclay de Tolly, commanding the Russian central army, favored Wellington's scorched earth policy, tempting the French deeper and deeper into a ravaged countryside. Bagration, his rival, had been in favor of an offensive, hoping to draw the teeth of the invaders and make them double in their tracks to protect the Duchy of Warsaw. Kutusoff, who superseded both commanders halfway through the retreat, favored withdrawal but was tempted to make a single stand at Borodino, west of Moscow. On this bloody field his army had suffered fearful carnage (Bagration was among the fatal casualties) but the French had suffered equally and from then onwards Kutusoff remained on the defensive, at least until he considered the Imperial troops easy prey at Krasnoi, halfway to the frontier. In the meantime Wittgenstein, with a small army covering St. Petersburg, had acquitted himself well. Although he lost battles against Marshal St. Cyr he was never overwhelmed and was able to mount an offensive in the autumn and advance in sufficient strength to contribute to the French disaster at the Beresina.

Now, with the Czar's blessing, he had a chance to show what he could do in open country and with superior strength. From the moment he took command the Russian advance speeded up and the self-styled liberators were soon across the Elbe and in possession of Dresden, the capital of the Saxon king who still adhered to Napoleon. Wittgenstein also had an opportunity to display his talents as a propagandist. "Germans!" ran one of his pamphlets, "we open to you the Prussian ranks. You will find there the son of a laborer placed beside the son of a prince. All distinction of rank is effaced in these great ideas—the king, liberty, honor, country. Among us there is no distinction but talent, and the ardor with which we fly to combat in a common cause!" From the pen of a man whose master personified autocracy, and addressed to men who were in the habit of being flogged into battle by the canes of their NCOs, this appeal has an irony that has not escaped historians. It is proof, however, that Napoleon's enemies were learning more than battle tactics from their opponent. Throughout the entire campaign that lay ahead autocrats who recoiled from the word liberty used it very freely in their stirring addresses to the underprivileged. The men opposing Napoleon in 1813 and 1814 were not notable libertarians. They included, as well as the Czar and the King of Prussia, the Austrian Chancellor Metternich, whose attempt to put the clock back delayed social and political development in Europe for two generations, in some cases four generations, whereas the Russian serfs were not even free on paper until Napoleon had been in his grave more than thirty years. Austrian minorities continued to be oppressed until they helped to achieve the break-up of the Habsburg Empire in 1918, and as late as 1878 mass arrests were being made in Berlin "for speaking ill of the Kaiser." The lot of the Prussian peasant did not noticeably improve until the end of the century and, at a time when Bernadotte was accusing his former benefactor of despotism, French prisoners on Swedish territory had to listen to the howls of Swedish soldiers suffering merciless punishment for minor infractions of duty.[2]

When the battle was won and Europe was at the disposal of these unlikely converts to the creed of equality, it was a very different story. There was no more heady talk of laborers rubbing shoulders with princes. Instead, for the vast majority of people rescued from "despotism," it was the status quo. It required violent revolutions in almost every capital in Europe to force sovereigns to bestow upon their subjects rights that Frenchmen under Napoleon had taken for granted half-a-century earlier.

However, the pill worked and volunteers flocked to the barracks. In town and village the Russians were received as liberators. Everywhere the tricolor was torn down and burned. Alone among his subjects Frederick William of Prussia had reservations concerning the final outcome of the war. Calling out troops at the insistence of Stein, Blucher, Scharnhorst and the Czar, he said doubtfully, "Well, gentlemen, you force me to this course but remember, we must conquer or be annihilated!"

There was one other prominent German who lacked confidence in the outcome. Watching the rearmament of his fellow countrymen the poet Goethe remarked, "Shake your chains if you will; you will not break them. That man Napoleon is too strong for you!" In the event both king and poet were wrong but in the months ahead there were occasions when the leaders of the coalition were to question whether they had entered upon the war with an excess of optimism.

In Paris the new mood of Germany did not go unnoticed and neither did the assurances of freedom for all, proclaimed in the pamphlets of the allies. Learning of the Prussians' decision

Napoleon was philosophical. "Better a declared enemy than a doubtful ally," he said, and must have weighed the loyalty of princelings who had fawned upon him throughout the past ten years. The friendship of all but one was to prove worthless and in some instances betrayals took place under fire. Napoleon was never surprised by human fallibility but in his years of exile on St. Helena he was to remember the Coalition's manifestoes in the spring of 1813 and his own failure to implement the social gains of the Revolution in conquered territories. "Had I granted free constitutions to those who desired them and abolished vassalage," he said, "the people would have been content and the struggle would have been a mere contest of princes for supremacy."

Therein lay the true cause of his overthrow and it was Europe's loss as well as his. In 1813 hereditary despots temporarily embraced the language of free men. Had Napoleon demonstrated his basic intention to modernize Europe beyond the Rhine he would have had to contend not with patriots but hirelings.

3

DICTATING A MEMO to his friend Duroc, Grand Marshal of the Palace on February 23, 1813, Napoleon proved beyond doubt that he had learned some valuable lessons from the disasters of the 1812 campaign. "I intend to adopt a totally different plan as regards my baggage train from that followed in my last campaign," he announced. "I wish to have a much smaller suite, a reduced kitchen staff, and less plate—the bare necessities; not merely to save trouble but also to set a good example. Both at the front and on the march the meals, including my own, will consist of soup, boiled beef, a roast, and vegetables without any dessert . . . cut down the number of canteens to the same scale, have two beds in place of four, two tents instead of four and furniture to correspond."

Napoleon had never, at any time in his life, indulged in the pleasures of the table. Neither had he, at home or on campaign, set much store on creature comforts, but now, facing an ultimate challenge, he streamlined his personal equipment to match the rigors of the days ahead. "Come, my old friend," he said to his shockheaded Chief of Staff, Berthier, when he first set to work to repair the ravages of the Moscow disaster, "let us fight the campaign of Italy all over again."

He had less illusions than his friends or his enemies. No one was more aware of the appalling difficulties that awaited France in the coming spring. Even before news reached him of the alliance of Russia and Prussia, or the current situation in Spain,

The Bare Necessities

he realized that the campaign of Germany would be decisive and that the stake was no less than his Empire. He could assess with accuracy the military capacities of the Czar and King Frederick William, the holding power of Joseph's armies against the advance of Wellington, and the loyalty of men like Murat and his father-in-law Francis of Austria. He had not been making war for twenty years without learning how to equate superior numbers with military opportunity and it must have been obvious to him, as he sat far into the night wrestling with the complex problems of raising and equipping an army of over 300,000 men, that time was the vital factor in the approaching confrontation. The challenge of the Russo-Prussian alliance had to be met quickly, before the waverers took heart and enlisted in the ranks of his enemies, before Wellington could drive on the Pyrenees and convert the running sore of the Peninsula into a mortal wound but, above all, before the dynasties of Europe could recover their nerve after a generation of defeat.

Stores, guns, money, officers and men were desperately needed but an even more desperate need was time, time to replace the splendid cavalry that had melted away on the long march across the Russian plains, to consolidate French-held fortresses like Danzig and Magdeburg, to sort out the muddle of his affairs in Spain, above all, time to teach eighteen-year-old conscripts the rudiments of their trade. But there was no time, hardly enough to raise much less equip the host he had promised the men who gathered round him when he stepped into the sleigh that rushed him from Smorgoni to Paris in a fortnight. He had arrived at the Tuileries in mid-December and now it was March, and his enemies were already advancing into Saxony. By late April he would have to be in the field with the prospect of meeting and defeating the armies of three, possibly five major powers. It was a prospect that would have seemed hopeless to any man who did not think of himself as the mental superior to any conceivable combination of hereditary princes.

Yet herein lay his strength. Notwithstanding the recent catastrophe he retained not only his nerve but the confidence of his youth. He was a man who thrived on difficulties, who warmed his hands at the flame of enterprise, and he had the supreme advantage of two factors in the forthcoming trial of strength—his matchless reputation as a strategist, and his habit of attending personally to all but the most trivial aspects of the task on hand. Whereas the Allies were obliged to work as a team—and this does not come easily to autocrats—he alone was the co-ordinator of policy and this, to a very great extent, gave him the initiative. He did not have to consult colleagues and wait upon majority decisions. He issued his orders and expected instant obedience. Such was his personality and administrative ability that obedience was forthcoming. Within a few days of his return to a palace where he was unrecognized by his own servants he was the Napoleon of Rivoli and Austerlitz again, working, planning, improvising, assessing, with trained men speeding in every direction to do his bidding or face his wrath. In the history of war there was never a feat such as he accomplished in the three and a half months between his return from Lithuania and his advance east of the Rhine to contest the future of Europe.

Count Daru tells a story that illustrates the astounding physical stamina of the man at this period, when he was half-way through his forty-fourth year. Overcome by exhaustion Daru fell asleep while Napoleon was dictating to him and on awakening the embarrassed secretary saw his master seated at the desk completing the documents. The candles showed that Daru had been asleep a long time and when he stammered his excuses Napoleon said, quietly, "Why didn't you tell me you were tired? I don't want to kill you. Go to bed. Goodnight." Daru went to bed and Napoleon, showing no signs of physical stress, continued working into the night.

Some of the complex logistical problems Napoleon had to solve between December 18, 1812, and the day he led his new army into the field, can be compared to those facing the belligerent powers in 1917, the third year of the Western Front stalemate. In that year France, Britain and Germany were drained of men and were obliged to resort to all manner of shifts to repair the terrible attrition of the battles of First and Second Ypres, Verdun and the Somme offensive. And yet these powers, with huge populations and twentieth century technology at their disposal, had been fighting for less than three years. France, in 1813, had been at war, almost continuously, since 1792. War weariness was a national malaise from Moscow to Lisbon but nowhere was it more apparent than in a nation that had been in a turmoil since the day the Paris mob stormed the Bastille, in July, 1789.

The losses incurred by the French in the Russian campaign, probably about 150,000 trained soldiers (exclusive of allies), were only a small part of the sacrifice Frenchmen had made to overthrow their own autocracy and spread the Revolutionary creed across Europe. In 1813 there were few families in France that had not contributed towards the price paid for the Napoleonic triumphs in the Low Countries, Italy, Egypt, Bohemia, Poland, Germany, Spain and Portugal, to say nothing of her disasters at sea. Probably a million young men had yielded up their lives to enable Paris masons to carve the names of fifty victories on the half-completed Arc de Triomphe, and the maimed who survived to live out their remaining years as cripples, could be seen in any village street of Maine, Languedoc or Brittany, and in every French town between Lille and the Pyrenees. By 1813 the price of a conscript-substitute had soared to a figure that was unthinkable for all but the wealthiest families in the land. And yet, now that France was seen to be the target of so many enemies, the means to raise another host were not merely available but could be applied without endangering the internal stability of the state. Applied they were, and with an efficiency and ruthlessness that throws into sharp relief the astonishing popularity of a man who had raised France to the position of the most dominant and aggressive Continental power since the days of Charlemagne.

To appreciate this, to understand why, after so many sacrifices, France was willing to make still more to preserve the dynasty, one has only to read a report made to the Legislature by Montilivet, Minister of the Interior, on February 25, 1813. It goes some way towards banishing the popular conception of Napoleon as a military bully preoccupied with blood and conquest, and substituting, in place of this cartoon figure, an administrative genius whose achievements in the civil sphere were far superior to those of any previous despot. Montilivet declared,

"Notwithstanding the immense armies which a state of war has rendered necessary, the population of France has continued to increase; French industry has advanced; the soil was never better cultivated, nor our manufactures more flourishing; and at no period in our history has wealth been more equally diffused among all classes of society."

It would be easy to dismiss this as the lip service of a political puppet were it not for facts quoted in later stages of the report, or contained in a survey of civic achievements during the last decade-and-a-half. From the anarchy of a revolution that had bedeviled the population from July, 1789, until November, 1799, the hand of Napoleon had produced a modern state that compared with the most progressive in the world, not excluding her nearest rival across the Channel, untouched by war and civil strife. Rotation of crops was studied, cattle multiplied and their breeds improved, feudal tenures, tithes, mortmains, and monastic orders that had kept small farmers in a state of subjection for centuries were suppressed, the processes of law were not only simplified but speeded up, money was lavished upon buildings, seaports, docks and harbors, new roads ran right across the country, new bridges were built by the score, and millions of francs went into canals, embankments and drainage. "These miracles," says a contemporary writer, "were effected by a steadiness of purpose, talent armed with power, and finances wisely and economically applied." These achievements after centuries of oppression by a dissolute aristocracy, are an indication of why France was willing to renew the interminable war in 1813.

The annual yield of 140,000 conscripts provided a nucleus but with the plans of a mass offensive already forming in his brain, he was aiming at an army of half-million. The lists of the four previous years were scrutinized and a merciless combout produced 100,000 men. The yield of 1814 was anticipated to provide another 150,000. Four new regiments were formed from the ranks of idle sailors, others were conjured out of the National Guard and Gendarmerie, but this mass of men, by far the greater number of them youths who had never handled a musket or slept a night in the open, was useless without trained officers and NCOs to lick them into shape, or cavalry that could screen their movements and prevent their annihilation in open country. In both spheres the shortages were more acute than in that of recruits.

Over in Britain, dotted about the country and coastline in parole towns, in hulks, or in the recently built prison on Dartmoor, were some 41,000 veterans who would have been invaluable to Napoleon but the British Government had no intention of presenting its arch enemy with the means to train and lead his hotchpotch of farmboys and apprentices, particularly as France, at that time, held fewer than 11,000 British captives as a basis of exchange. To find instructors and company commanders Napoleon was therefore obliged to turn to the hard pressed regiments of the Peninsula, and the garrison towns of the Empire where hundreds of old campaigners had been skulking for years, congratulating themselves on successfully avoiding the risks and exertions of campaigns in Spain and Russia. Orders were despatched to recall every non-essential veteran on the muster rolls and reluctantly the professional loafers of the Grand Army made their way to assembly points. By the time green leaves were showing on the limes and chestnuts outside the barracks of a hundred towns in northeastern France, the old grognards were hard at work teaching the rank and file how to form square and receive cavalry, how to load and fire, and how to make bivouac in the dark after a twenty mile march carrying a kit load weighing eighty pounds.

In search of still more men the Emperor attempted to put into practice a project that had been dormant in his mind for some years, namely the absorption, into the new military hierarchy, of aristocratic families tempted back to France after Napoleonic order had succeeded revolutionary chaos. The plan, sound as it was in precept, was not a success and the formation of four regiments of high born Frenchmen who had somehow escaped previous conscriptions foundered on the twin shoals of prejudice and jealousy. Styled the "Guard of Honor," this formation found little favor in the hearts of men whose fathers and uncles had fled to avoid the organized massacres of aristocrats in 1792 and 1793, and it aroused the bitter hostility of the Imperial Guard. Aware that this corps was the backbone of the army Napoleon shelved the fusion of old and new for the time being.

Assembling a force of cavalry was another matter. From Moscow to the Niemen the French survivors of a 550 mile march had existed on horseflesh and the utmost the army requisitioners could achieve by April was a total of some 15,000 mounted men. To do this every farm in France had been robbed of its animals used for transportation.

An army—some kind of army—was in being. At home one-third of the able bodied men between the age of seventeen and forty-five were in uniform, and beyond the frontiers Prince Eugène, Viceroy of Italy, was regrouping the 40,000 men he had somehow assembled around the tiny nucleus of the Russian survivors. The finances of the realm were replenished by a variety of shifts, including, among others, a new issue of paper currency, virtual appropriation of municipal funds, trading licenses, fines, patriotic loans, and other expedients some of which belonged in the repertoire of the professional swindler. An attempt was made to lend this latest adventure some kind of sanctity by means of a new Concordat with the Pope (then a prisoner of France) and His Holiness was offered the bait of a promise to return Germany to the Papal fold. But all these endeavors and improvisations, brilliant and effective as some of them were, could not provide Imperial France with an instrument capable of fighting a war on two fronts and in planning for a bold offensive Napoleon was taking the only real course open to him. The southwestern backdoor would have to be left to take care of itself, at least until the main enemy could be brought to battle and destroyed. Austria and Sweden, potential enemies both, were still officially neutral, and most of the central and western German states were undecided. A crushing victory would help them to make up their minds and re-establish French supremacy as far east as the Oder. Turning aside from his immense labors in the fields of recruitment and supply the man who had initiated a system of war depending exclusively upon the attack, gave his full attention to strategical possibilities that were beginning to form a pattern on his war maps.

II

The far distant objective of the coming campaign as seen by Napoleon in early April, 1813, was the lower Vistula. To reach it, driving the Russo-Prussian forces before him, he would have to advance across the Rhine, the Saale, and the Elbe and concentrate his main striking power in the area of Leipzig. He would also have to guard against possible treachery on the part of his Imperial father-in-law, who was positioned to issue from the Bohemian mountains and fall on his right flank, and he would also have to dominate the cities of the Hanseatic League and guard against an attack by Sweden.

The curving line of French garrisons in the area where the main fighting seemed likely to occur was already contracting. It now pivoted on Bremen, Magdeburg, Bamberg, Wittenburg and Dresden, for in March Eugène had been obliged to abandon his new headquarters at Berlin and had fallen back on Leipzig. For a brief spell, with reinforcements moving in from the west every day, he held on but the forces of resurgent patriotism were too strong for him to do more than keep neighboring subject states outwardly loyal. In front of him isolated pockets of Imperial troops held their ground in fortresses of the quality of Danzig, Küstrin and Stetten, but Dresden, despite the King of Saxony's personal loyalty, welcomed the invaders and knocked a kingpin from the tenuous line of defenses that now divided Central Europe into two camps, east and Coalition-dominated, west and still nominally allied to France. Saxony, flooded by allied troops, was lost and its sovereign was a fugitive.

The future hinged upon the degree of territorial flexibility within the mind of the Emperor. Would he seek to re-impose his will on the entire continent west of the Russian frontiers, or would he, after a show of force and perhaps a few tactical victories, settle for three-fifths of a loaf and agree to contract? It did not seem, in that eventful spring of 1813, that he entertained the latter possibility and yet, studying his correspondence at the time, and his reflections dictated in retrospect, it is certain that at this stage he would have been grudgingly content to retain Italy, Holland and the cities of the Hanseatic League, and relax his attitude towards Prussia, Austria and, above all, Russia. That circumstances changed shortly after his initial victories was not only France's tragedy. It was the tragedy of a Europe that was to tear itself to pieces in the century that followed his death on St. Helena and again a generation later. World War I, the Hitler tragedy, and the Cold War that has divided Europe up to this very day, are the direct legacies of Napoleon's misjudgments and the mutual jealousies of the powers arrayed against him in the spring and early summer of 1813.

On April 15th, the day that Napoleon mounted his coach and set out for Mainz, the first major rallying point of his eastward journey, his situation was difficult but by no means desperate. Neither Russia, in arms against him, nor Austria, playing a waiting game, were resolved upon his banishment from the European scene. Their rivalries concerning the unification of Germany and the future status of Poland were far too tense to enable them to make common cause against the Titan. The Czar did not want to see the power of the Habsburgs enlarged at the expense of France, whereas Austria was by no means sure what might emerge from German unification and Prussia's rise to a position of equality. Baron Stein could dream of a Germany strong enough to dominate Europe, as France had dominated since its pestilential revolution, but Metternich, coveting a slice of Poland as well as the Illyrian provinces on the Adriatic, had dreams of his own. The men occupying the seats of power in St. Petersburg, Vienna and Berlin might prattle of liberty and equality but their principal concern in the struggle ahead was to insure that the balance of power was restored in their individual favor. Russia and Prussia had arrived at a satisfactory (if temporary) agreement, that of a senior and a junior partner in the bloody task of reducing Napoleon to size, but it was not in their interests to create a vacuum that would be filled by a Habsburg. There was also the future of Sweden to be considered and it was difficult to forget that the heir-apparent in Stockholm had once been a French marshal, and now saw himself as a possible successor to Bonaparte. And behind all these inshore cross currents was the heavy swell created by the British Navy with its undisputed command of the seas and a growing empire overseas promising enormous wealth in the decades ahead. It is not surprising that Napoleon felt reasonably confident as his coach rumbled across northeastern France to a rendezvous with the hard-pressed Eugène. He knew, better than anyone alive, the inconstancies and mutual suspicions of hereditary kings. For almost twenty years he had been using them as the spokes of a wheel of statecraft, its hub centered on the Tuileries and now it was in his interests to work upon them ceaselessly, to fight with promises, hints and assurances as well as with fieldpiece and bayonet. He was a past master of this particular exercise and for the moment he concentrated on Vienna.

Within a month of launching his offensive he was writing to his father-in-law, "I have made up my mind to die, if need be, at the head of all honorable Frenchmen, rather than become the laughing stock of the English or allow my enemies to triumph over me. Let Your Majesty think of the future. Do not throw away the fruits of three years' friendship, or renew the intrigues of the past, which plunged Europe into wars and convulsions whose issue might have no end. Do not sacrifice for meager motives the happiness of our generation and of your own life; do not sacrifice the real interests of your subjects, and (why should I not say it?) of a member of your family who is sincerely attached to you. For Your Majesty must never doubt my affection."

Metternich, reading the letter in the Schonbrunn, must have smiled. How could he or his sovereign fail to find satisfaction in receiving such assurances from a man who had occupied Vienna twice during the last eight years and, on the second occasion, had carried away a Habsburg archduchess to bear him a son who would, it was hoped, perpetuate his conquests?

The three great armies drew closer together. To Europe, watching, it was like a vast extension of the popular *retiarius* versus *secutor* combats of ancient Rome. Russia and Prussia held the nets, France the blade. North and south of the battleground Sweden and Austria hesitated to commit themselves to a trial of strength and skill. A fifth gladiator, Britain, was committed but was too far removed from the arena to play more than a diversionary part in the contest. Viewed objectively it seemed a very unequal struggle, three, possibly five, against one. But

to those involved it was not as simple as that. The man marching down on them had a reputation that more than offset his
numerical inferiority. There had been many previous trials of
strength and always it was he and not his adversaries who slept
upon the field.

4

THE GREAT PLAIN of Saxony, setting for the gigantic struggle ahead, is a pleasant, well-watered country. In 1813 it was largely pastoral, a place of meadows, farms, wide, undulating pastures and coppices of oak and chestnut, watered by tributaries of the Elbe that ran through its center. It offered the greatest opportunities for maneuver, particularly by cavalry, and was peopled by farmers, small tradesmen and craftsmen who had given the French so little trouble since their conquest that Napoleon said of them, "Not one of our soldiers was murdered there." In summertime it was a place to idle and dream, or raise fine crops and fat cattle. The towns were old and prosperous, the rivers placid and slow moving like the peasants. To the north lay the Prussian frontier and to the south the mountains of Bohemia, respectively the seats of German fanaticism and Austrian watchfulness, but on the actual battleground, along the route from Weissenfels to Lutzen and from Leipzig to the outskirts of Dresden, there was little partisan activity, certainly no situation comparable to the harassment that had brought about the westward retreat of Eugène from Eastern Prussia. The easygoing Saxon did not, in fact, give two straws who ruled Europe so long as he was left in peace to till his acres and give attention to his business, and the plight of his sovereign, now a fugitive from his own capital at Dresden, did not concern him overmuch. He had become accustomed to the march and counter march of Napoleon's armies and the billeting of men in all his

The Plains of Saxony

towns and villages between 1806 and 1813. The relationship between billeter and billetee was generally cordial. Looking back on these years the men of the Grand Army were to think nostalgically of their fat German hosts, veterans among them recalling years of garrison duty in a land where there was no danger and always plenty to eat, a pleasant contrast to the deserts of Egypt, Spain and Russia.

Napoleon left St. Cloud by carriage on April 15th and with him went his old traveling companion Caulaincourt, a man accustomed to receive his random confidences for he had shared the Emperor's epic journey from Smorgoni to Paris when Napoleon talked incessantly of whatever came into his mind. More confidences and aphorisms were on their way. As he settled back among the cushions Napoleon said, "I envy the poorest peasant in my realm. By the time he grows old he has already paid his debt to his country and can stay at home with his wife and children. I am the only person whom an inexplicable fate leads back ever and again into the field."

Caulaincourt was not impressed by this Imperial sigh. It is true that Napoleon, since his second marriage and the birth of a legitimate heir, had begrudged the demands made upon him by a campaign and expressed a yearning for the slippers and fireside of a bourgeois but basically he was, and never ceased to be, a man of action and the challenge facing him now did not daunt him. Notwithstanding the obvious shortcomings of his newly-raised battalions he possessed supreme confidence in himself. He had beaten his enemies so often, and so easily, that their military prospects in the coming campaign had no power to frighten him. He might be short of heavy artillery and trained rankers, and even shorter of cavalry with which to exploit a victory, but his subordinate commanders were the most experienced in the world and among them were men whose names were already legends among professional soldiers all over Europe, America and the Near East. Davout and Vandamme were on their way to recapture Hamburg and hold down the Hanseatic towns. Ney, hero of the retreat and idol of the conscripts, was already in the field, having left France in March, none the worse for his 550 mile walk from Moscow to Gumbinnen. Berthier was in his usual place as chief-of-staff, sleeping upright in the enormous war coach that had rushed to and fro across Europe like a devil's traveling carriage. Marshal Macdonald, and the veteran Marshals Mortier and Oudinot were there, and so was Victor, and around these men were grouped a hundred other soldiers all hoping to win a baton in the forthcoming war. Souham, Bertrand, Reynier and Rapp were only four of this select body of veterans. The Emperor's old friend and artillery expert Marmont was on hand, and Augereau was preparing to lead his Bavarians into the field. In Galicia was Poniatowski with his Poles, still completely loyal to the Empire, twelve corps in all and more than a match for Russians and Prussians under second raters like Wittgenstein, Schwartzenberg and seventy-two-year-old Blucher.

For all that Napoleon, settling into his coach and envying the poorest peasant in his dominions, might have spared a thought for his grave deficiencies in fighting material, for it taxed the strength of many of his youthful recruits to march as far as Saxony over a route signposted with well stocked depots. Most of them were under twenty years of age. They had been born during the years '93 and '94, when their country was torn by revolution and civil war and food was hard to find, so that they were not as robust as the men who had conquered Italy, marched across the Sinai desert and back again, and triumphed at Marengo, Austerlitz, Friedland and Wagram.

MM. Erckmann-Chatrian, who wrote the brilliant documentary novel *History of a Conscript of 1813 and Waterloo,* have left us a vivid picture of these sorely-tested boys. Both authors were born in 1822, and grew to manhood among survivors of successive Grand Armies, from whom they sought their material. Their hero, Joseph Bertha, is a domesticated young man with a limp and his accounts of the fighting in Saxony in 1813 are as accurate in detail as the memoirs of real heroes, like Captain Maurice Barrès of the 47th Infantry of the Line, or Major Marbot, the chasseur whose account of the Napoleonic wars, seen from the viewpoint of a junior officer, earned him praise and a legacy from the exiled Emperor.

Describing his first day in Mainz en route for the front Bertha says, "Some waggons emerged from the archway and we were told, first in Italian and then in French, that arms were about to

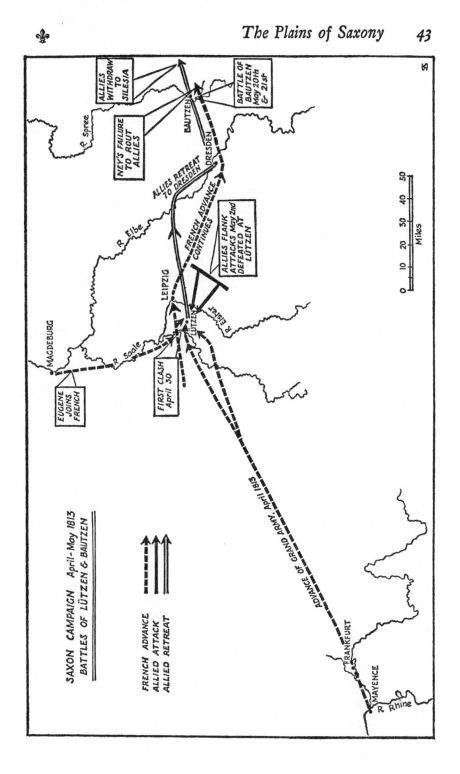

ALLIES WITHDRAW TO SILESIA

BATTLE OF BAUTZEN May 20th & 21st

NEY'S FAILURE TO ROUT ALLIES

R. Spree

BAUTZEN

ALLIES RETREAT TO DRESDEN

DRESDEN

FRENCH ADVANCE CONTINUES

ALLIES FLANK ATTACKS May 2nd DEFEATED AT LÜTZEN

R. Elbe

50
40
30
20
10
0

Miles

LEIPZIG

MAGDEBURG

R. Saale

R. Elster

LÜTZEN

EUGENE JOINS FRENCH

FIRST CLASH April 30

SAXON CAMPAIGN April–May 1813
BATTLES OF LÜTZEN & BAUTZEN

FRENCH ADVANCE
ALLIED ATTACK
ALLIED RETREAT

ADVANCE OF GRAND ARMY, April 1813

FRANKFURT

MAYENCE

R. Rhine

be distributed and each one had to step out when his name was called. . . . As each one came out from the ranks he received a sabre, a cartridge-box, a bayonet and a musket. These were slung over our blouses, or coats, or overcoats, and with our various hats and caps we must really have looked like a band of brigands. My gun was so heavy that I could hardly carry it, while the cartridge-box hung down to my knees, until Sergeant Pinto showed me the way to make the straps shorter; he was a good man. All these straps across my chest seemed terrible to me, and then I saw that our troubles were not over, as I had imagined. An ammunition waggon was brought and fifty cartridges were given to each man. Instead of telling us to break up, and sending us back to our lodgings, the captain drew his sword and cried 'Right file! Forward march!' and the drums began to beat."

Bertha had no illusions about his future role as a private in the Imperial army. Reminded of the prospect of glory he said, "The glory is not for us. It is for people who live joyously and who eat and sleep well; they dance and make merry and they get their glory into the bargain, which we win with our sweat and blood and by having our bones broken. Poor creatures like us are compelled to march away and we are lucky if we get back, able to work after losing a limb . . . ," and he went on to describe the attitude that civilians of all nations reserve for the soldiers who win their battles: "And when those who go to seek glory by killing others pass with stripes on their arms . . . and if, by chance, they have red noses from drinking wine to keep up their courage in rain and snow in long forced marches, they say, 'These men are drunkards . . . they are little more than beggars!' "

Bertha, more surely than any other figure in the literature of the period, is the prototype of the French conscript of the Napoleonic wars and his wry comments on military discipline will find an echo in the heart of millions of men of later generations who were encouraged by armchair patriots to seek glory in Flanders mud and the jungles of Vietnam and Malaya. "I learned that the corporal is always right when he speaks to the private soldier, the sergeant is right when he speaks to the corporal, the sergeant-major when he speaks to the sergeant, the subaltern when he speaks to the sergeant-major, and so on upwards to the marshal of France—even if he were to say that the moon shines in broad daylight, or that two and two make five. That is not an easy thing to get into your head, but there is one thing which is a great help to you, and that is a great notice-board fixed up in the rooms and which is read out from time to time to settle your thoughts. This notice-board enumerates everything that a soldier is supposed to want to do—such as, for instance, to return to his native village, to refuse service, to contradict his superior officer, etc., and always ends by promising he shall be shot, or at least have five years' hard labour with a cannon-ball fastened to his leg if he does it."

Bertha, of course, is a fictitious character but we do not have to look far to identify him in fact. Captain Barrès of the 47th, marching his conscripts into the first skirmishes of the campaign, records: "On the afternoon of 29th April, being in bivouac, we heard the guns for the first time during the campaign. A young soldier of the 6th, at the sound of this cannonade, which was apparently at some distance, went to take his musket from the piles as though to clean it, saying to his comrades as he moved away, 'The devil! There's that beastly sound already. I shan't hear it long,' and hiding behind a hedge he blew his brains out."

The orchestra, as the old soldiers said, was tuning up. Marshal Ney, "Le Rougeaud" as his men called him on account of his red hair, was already in the field and no better man could have been found to lead untried youths into action. Ney had been fighting almost continuously since he enlisted as a hussar before the Revolution and his battle honors went back to the days of Sambre-et-Meuse, when the young zealots of the Revolution threw back the professional armies from their frontiers. As a tactician Ney had few equals but he was a front line field officer, not a strategist. Once in touch with the enemy he could never be located by Imperial messengers. He was commanding an infantry square against cavalry, or defending a village with the bayonet. The men in the ranks adored him and, although his uncertain temper cost him the friendship of equals, every officer in the Imperial army respected his courage in attack and his staying power in defense.

It was Ney's troops, under the command of General Souham, who gave the French conscripts their first boost in morale. Probing towards Eugène's army on the lower Saale, Ney's corps came into collision with 10,000 Russian cavalry in ambush at Weissenfels. To their own astonishment they not only routed the horsemen but stormed up to a battery of six guns and captured them all. Ney declared that he had never seen newly joined recruits show so much dash and gallantry. That same day a squad of fifteen soldiers of the 13th of the Line beat off an attack by a regiment of Prussian hussars without losing a man.

In the meantime Napoleon, having assembled 180,000 men at Mainz, was approaching with his usual speed and was soon on the scene, throwing three bridges over the Saale and passing over with substantial reinforcements. It was here, in the defile of Rippach near the village of Poserna, that the Grand Army suffered its first major casualty in a campaign that was to account for many of the men who had dominated Europe for a generation.

Riding forward with some of the cavalry of the Guard, men he had commanded in twenty pitched battles, Marshal Bessières, once a hairdresser and a close companion of Napoleon since the days of the Italian campaign, rode into the range of a laid fieldpiece and was killed by a ball that shattered his wrist and chest. In almost exactly similar circumstances his rival Marshal Lannes had been mortally wounded at Essling, four years before.

Bessières was the second of the twenty-six marshals to die in action. There was to be one more death in battle and after that a long string of violent deaths, including two executions, a lynching and a suicide. The almost casual death of a veteran like Bessières cast a gloom over the army. He was universally liked as a quietly disposed and excessively polite man and the only one among the marshalate who had served the Royalist cause in the Revolution.[1] The Guard loved him and so did his chief. Captain Barrès saw his body pass, laid in a jolting wagon: "In him the Emperor lost a faithful friend, an old and valiant comrade in arms," he says, adding, "The death of this worthy marshal grieved me greatly for I had for a long time been under his orders; he was a charming and courteous man."

This comment, from a junior officer to a marshal, illustrates a hidden strength in the Napoleonic armies, the strong bond of personal comradeship existing between the highest and lowest in the Grand Army. It was unique at that time, even among the old soldiers of the Light Brigade in Wellington's Peninsula army, and contributed materially to the long succession of French victories between 1792 and 1814.

In the midst of the distractions of the opening stage of the campaign Napoleon found time to write to Bessières' widow in the following terms: "My Cousin: Your husband has died on the field of honor. The loss which you and your children have sustained is doubtless great but mine is still greater. The Duke of Istria (Bessières' title) has died the noblest death and without suffering. He has left a spotless reputation, the best inheritance he could transmit to his children. My protection is secured to them. They will inherit all the affection I bore their father."

But it was Ney, the dead marshal's comrade in the field, who spoke the real epitaph. Looking down on the body of the man he had fought beside since they were both junior captains he said, "C'est notre sort. C'est une belle mort," and rode away to lead his young troops across the plain towards Leipzig.

II

Eugène was now within close touch of the Grand Army and on the second day of May the two commands met near the obelisk raised to commemorate the death of the Protestant "Lion of the North," Gustavus Adolphus, King of Sweden, whose army had met and defeated that of the Catholic League at Lutzen in 1632.[2]

To get here and effect the junction Eugène had performed prodigies, not so much of valor but of improvisation. Ever since Murat had abandoned the wreck of the 1812 army on the Baltic coast in January, Eugène had been hard at work gathering his forces, holding off attacks, doing what he could to check the rise of patriotic fervor in Prussia and generally moving west and south as his position became untenable. He had discharged his responsibilities admirably, sending all his sick into the hospitals, and writing innumerable letters to parents who plagued him with inquiries concerning the fate of their relatives in the great retreat.

Established at Posen in late January Eugène held his first review. Round him, many of them dying and all of them physically and mentally exhausted after the terrible rigors of the retreat, were men who were his seniors both in age and experience but they submitted to him, much as the young Bonaparte had dominated veterans like Masséna and Augereau in Italy at the start of the '96 campaign. General Roguet was there, still the strict disciplinarian, and Generals Eblé and Lariboisière, respectively of the Engineers and Artillery of the Guard. Marshals Berthier, Lefèbvre and Ney were still with the army but all save Ney were tired and ailing men, suffering from what a later generation would call shell shock or battle fatigue. General Eblé, whose tremendous bridge building exertions had saved the army at the crossing of the Beresina, died in a hospital at Köenigsberg, and Lariboisière, who had lost his son at Borodino, died soon afterwards. Tough old Lefèbvre, who had once commanded the escort that returned King Louis and Marie Antoinette to Paris after their abortive flight to Varennes, was also mourning the death of a beloved son, and the brilliant Berthier was in a state of nervous collapse. These men held on but grumbled unceasingly. Eugène decided on a bold stroke. He sent all senior officers who could travel on leave, cutting himself off from a stream of unwanted advice, and after that some kind of order began to emerge from the chaos around him. Evacuating Poland he moved to Berlin and then to Magdeburg, where detachments and guns were added to his command and it began to look like a fighting force again. A stream of advice—some of it fatuous—still reached him from Paris, Napoleon writing "that if the Prussian towns behave badly they are to be burned!" Eugène was far too practical to court trouble in this fashion. He went on planning and improvising until he had around him something over fifty thousand men and one hundred and fifty guns. If the Emperor had followed Marshal Macdonald's advice, issued in the new year, he would have had a far stronger force. The Scots marshal had long foreseen a withdrawal over the Oder and the Elbe and perhaps as far as the

Rhine, and had counseled abandoning the fortresses of Danzig, Zamosk, Modlin and Pillau. His advice was ignored and veteran troops were left behind in all these places, together with the garrisons of Stettin, Thorn, Torgau, Custrin and several other strong points. In this way the Grand Army ultimately sacrificed a hundred thousand men who could have turned the tide in the autumn fighting. Napoleon, hitherto the champion of concentration, dug his army's grave by abandoning the precept during the retreat to the Rhine. A vast army of trained men might have been assembled to defend the frontiers of France had it not been isolated in fortifications all over Europe.

By April Eugène was on the lower Saale and his lonely ordeal was nearly over but by then the enemy had entered Dresden and were preparing to cast their net over the approaching main body. It must have seemed to them, as they marched out towards Leipzig, that one strong effort on their part would accomplish what the frosts of Russia and no previous Coalition had been able to achieve—the overthrow and capture of the man who had been turning Europe upside down since the spring of '96.

III

The new Grand Army came out of the west, heading across open country in the general direction of Leipzig, a vast straggle of 145,000 infantrymen, 372 guns but only 7,500 cavalry.

Ney's Third Corps occupied the center, a force of five divisions composed almost entirely of conscripts with a single day's battle experience, gained at Weissenfels. Issuing from Lutzen, where he established his headquarters on the night of May 1st–2nd, Napoleon and General Lauriston probed directly at Leipzig, expecting no major opposition and certainly no direct attack, for Napoleon was convinced the main body of the enemy was in the city. Marmont and Bertrand, with most of the Guard, were still west of the plain but moving up in support. Eugène, with Macdonald and another strong body of infantry, was further north marching on the Elster.

At nine o'clock on the morning of the 2nd the general movement on Leipzig began, Lauriston moving forward to within field glass range of the suburb of Lindenau. Ney's boys, billeted in a string of villages—Kaja, Eisdorf, Rahna, Klein, Gorschen and Gross Gorschen—were cooking their soup in pleasant, pastoral surroundings, a long string of cottages, gardens and enclosed pastures. By nightfall they were to be places of horror and desolation.

The Grand Army's acute shortage of cavalry had robbed it of its eyes. Napoleon, as it happened, was quite wrong concerning the whereabouts of the enemy. Within two miles of the Grand Army's center the élite of the Russo-Prussian army was assembling behind some low heights, having crossed the Elster at two in the morning.

The strategy of the allies was simple and direct and their opportunity to execute it unique. Under the nominal command of Czar Alexander and the King of Prussia, but actually led by the Russian Wittgenstein and the elderly Blucher, their object was to hold Leipzig with a detached force of 5,000 men and take the French in the flank from the north, cutting the army in two equal halves and driving the eastern, or more advanced half, into the Elster. This achieved they could then deal at leisure with the reserves pouring out of the west from the direction of Weissenfels and Naumberg.

The plan recommended itself very strongly to the impetuous old warrior Blucher. With him on that sunny May morning were his two famous lieutenants, Scharnhorst and Gneisenau (their names were to become familiar as elusive German battleships in World War II) and for Scharnhorst the plain of Lutzen was to prove the end of the road. Eighty thousand strong, and covered by a formidable artillery and a reserve of twenty-five thousand excellent cavalry, they formed up in four dense columns and descended on the unsuspecting III Corps, the battle opening with a terrible cannonade that tore lanes through the ranks of the French conscripts. By seven o'clock they were fully deployed and advancing on the villages at the double. By nine o'clock at the latest the battle should have been over and the new Grand Army destroyed at a blow. The fact that this did not happen and that the French were able, by the time dusk fell, to convert near disaster into limited triumph, was due to

two factors—the presence of a professional genius and the gallantry of a mob of boys undergoing a baptism of fire that
would have daunted an army composed of veteran soldiers.

Every eyewitness of the battle of Lutzen described the initial
cannonade as one of the most terrible of the Napoleonic wars,
and out here on the plain there was no protection from the
rain of projectiles sweeping down on the knots and squares of
the untried infantry. Men fell in dozens but none left the
ranks and after each terrible discharge the conscripts formed
up and moved slowly back to rally on the villages. Then, with
a third of their number dead or dying, the III Corps was called
upon to sustain and throw back a series of massed infantry
attacks and the charges of innumerable squadrons of cavalry.
Notwithstanding their desperate courage they could never have
survived had it not been for the walls and buildings of the
villages and hamlets to which their officers and sergeants led
them, still under a hail of fire.

By eleven o'clock every barn, every cottage and every cattle
pen and pigsty was a miniature fortress. Time and again Blucher's heroic infantry stormed up to the bayonets of the conscripts, fighting with sword and clubbed musket; time and
again the hussars and Cossacks dashed in with sabre and lance,
but although there was a slow withdrawal there was no rout,
and no hint of a rout. Gross Gorschen and Klein Gorschen were
taken, retaken and lost again, Kaja was overwhelmed, and the
hamlets of Rahna and Strasiedel on the western edge of the
perimeter were heaped with the slain. Two of the villages were
blazing, adding another horror to the wounded but still the
battle continued, an eddy of tiny triumphs and miniature disasters, where General Gérard, wounded in several places, refused to quit the field and hung on waiting for help that he
knew would come. Beside him, fighting with the valor of the
Guard, stood all that remained of twenty thousand boys who
had hardly mastered the art of loading and discharging a musket
but who now defied every attempt to drive them from the field.
Their valor, the legacy of the Revolutionary-Napoleonic tradi-
tion, saved the army.

IV

Napoleon was well on the way to Leipzig when he heard the roar of the Allied cannonade on his immediate right. His reactions were those of a much younger Napoleon, who had astonished the world at Lodi, Rivoli and Arcola. They had said of him in Russia that he was not the man he had been, that power, domesticity and middle age had sapped his vitality and blunted the fine edge of his judgment. They were wrong and in a matter of moments were seen to be wrong. Without the slightest hesitation, without waiting for gallopers to bring him reports of the situation, or the opinion of those within reach of him to harden a resolve, he made his decision. The Allies were attacking in full strength in an attempt to cut the army in two while it was strung out over thirty miles of road and plain. He would halt, wheel about and lead a counter flank attack in person, checking their onslaught on the III Corps until Marmont and Bertrand could sweep in from the right, Lauriston from the left and then Macdonald from the right. Meanwhile a coup-de-grace could be administered from the center by sixteen battalions of the Imperial Guard and their eighty pieces of artillery under the personal command of the Emperor.

In the meantime something had to be done to succor the III Corps and Ney was despatched at the gallop to rally the conscripts by his presence. "We have no cavalry and must do it with infantry, as in Egypt," Napoleon said, and began to issue detailed and precise directions to every commander within range. Aides-de-camp galloped off south, west and north but before any one of them had discharged his mission Ney was among his embattled recruits, scrambling from point to point and yelling defiance at the enemy in the voice he had used to beat off a hundred attacks on the rearguard moving across the Russian plains six months before.

The effect of his presence, says an eyewitness, was magical. "Le Rougeaud" was here and defeat or withdrawal was out of the question. Help was coming and Ney knew that if he could hold on the tables could be turned on the men who had already destroyed half his corps but he also knew that the encircling of the attackers by Macdonald, Lauriston, Bertrand and Mar-

mont would take time and that it would be early afternoon
before the Emperor could mount an effective counterattack
from the center. There was nothing to do but fight on in the
blazing ruins of the villages or the wrecks of squares constantly assailed by roundshot, lance and bayonet.

Captain Barrès, serving with a division on the extreme right
of the battlefield, has left us a graphic picture of what it was
like to officer one of the surviving squares throughout those
hours of trial. Pounded by roundshot and assailed between the
discharges by masses of cavalry, he steadied his boys as the
supply of officers shrank. In less than an hour's fighting Barrès,
as the fifth captain of the battalion, was commanding it. For
three-and-a-half hours the struggle continued without a moment's respite, the shattered battalion moving slowly back on
the hamlet of Strasiedel. By then his unit alone had lost forty-
three men and almost all its officers. He himself was wounded
in two places, one of the wounds being inflicted by the head
of a sub-lieutenant that had been hurled into his face. He
even recognized the man whose blood had drenched him,
". . . a nice young fellow who, having left the École Militaire
two months before, had said, 'At thirty I shall be a colonel,
or killed.' "

At this stage Barrès thought the battle lost but a major who
had just arrived from Spain assured him that it was nearly won
and pointed to the columns of the IV Corps under Bertrand,
and the V Corps under Lauriston, debouching on the extreme
left and right wings of the enemy. That man was a good judge.
In less than an hour the wreck of Barrès' battalion moved forward and re-entered the disputed villages, sustaining more
charges and more casualties on the way.

The net had been thrown but the cast had missed. By two-
thirty in the afternoon the movements directed by the Emperor
were achieved. Two hours later Bertrand and Marmont had
closed in from the right and Lauriston was hammering the enemy's right wing. Marshal Macdonald, unable to descend on the
plain without cavalry, describes the furious attacks on his Corps
by the frustrated Russian cavalry. All were beaten off with
heavy loss and General Latour-Maubourg[3] offered to counter-

attack with his pitifully small force of cavalry but was prevented from doing so by the cautious Eugène.

By 5:30 all was ready for the assault from the center. The Young Guard formed into four dense columns and in close support were the Old Guard and the Cavalry of the Guard. General Drouot brought up eighty guns and the whole column moved forward like a battering ram. There was no disputing its progress. Rahna, Gross Gorschen and Klein Gorschen were stormed and Russian reserves could do little to stem the tide. Yard by yard the enemy were pushed back on the Elster and only lack of cavalry on the part of the French prevented a rout.

Several men who observed Napoleon during this attack have left a record of his personal participation in the fighting and the heartening effect it had on his young troops. In twenty years in the field he had never exposed himself more recklessly but galloped from point to point with shot and shell bursting on all sides. Marmont, "subsequently no friend of Napoleon," pays tribute to his courage and enterprise and says that as he hurried by even the dying saluted him. There is no record of similar behavior on the part of the allied sovereigns, although Blucher fought with his customary gallantry and at 6:30 his lieutenant, Scharnhorst, received a mortal wound.

Conscripts lying among the debris of the ruined villages marked the progress of the Imperial counterattack by the advancing flashes of the Guards' artillery and by 7:30 all was over, the Allies retiring across the Elster, their retreat covered by cavalry. Pursuit was impossible and they withdrew unmolested to Leipzig and then to Dresden. For the French it was a Pyrrhic victory. Their losses in killed and wounded were upwards of twenty thousand men, by far the greater number from Ney's III Corps. The Allied loss was less, somewhere in the region of twelve thousand. Commenting on the gallantry of the conscripts Napoleon said, "In my young soldiers I found all the valour of my old companions in arms. During the twenty years I have commanded French troops I have never witnessed such bravery and devotion."

At daybreak on the morning of May 3rd the Emperor rode over the field. Friend and foe with a chance of recovery were carried into barns for a field dressing and transportation to hospitals at Leipzig and Weissenfels. Among those buried with military honors at the command of the Emperor was a young Prussian found embracing a flag he had given his life to defend. The flag was buried with him.

5

BETWEEN WEISSENFELS, WHERE the first shots were fired, and Breslau, where the first stage of the campaign was to end thirty-four days later, run ten rivers, three of them broad streams even at this time of year, the others fordable tributaries of the Saale or the Oder. The French army crossed them all, a plodding multitude of victory hungry horse and foot, veterans and conscripts, marching under the greatest captains of the age, spurred on by the battle honors of a generation, cuirassiers, dragoons, lancers and hussars, flying artillerymen dragging their light pieces and caissons, moustached grenadiers of the Guard and conscripts sweating under their packloads, all moving eastward but too slowly and clumsily to envelop the retreating armies of Czar Alexander and Frederick William of Prussia as they withdrew towards the Silesian border and the northern spur of the Bohemian mountains that marked the frontier of Austria. On the bloody plain of Lutzen Napoleon had triumphed but decisive victory had eluded him. What was required now was another Austerlitz, a triumph that would stun Europe into accepting the best terms it could wring from a man who, a few weeks ago, had been seen as a crippled giant ringed by enemies and traitors. Across the length and breadth of the Continent the neutrals and the satraps waited in an agony of indecision as the three armies maneuvered about the great central plain. Couriers galloped from capital to capital with proposal and counter proposal. In the camp of the Allies there was des-

"Not a Gun! Not a Prisoner!"

pondency and mutual distrust. In the courts of the German princes and dukes there was dismay and bewilderment. In Vienna Metternich pondered all the various possibilities in an attempt to find a solution for every eventuality. In Stralsund, where former marshal Bernadotte awaited his British subsidy, there was an uncomfortable doubt that he might, after all, have backed the wrong horse.

The result of the great battle of Lutzen had been political rather than military, a postponement rather than a decision, a false dawn of hope for both French and Allies. The armies had met and contended but although two of them were now in full retreat, and the other was advancing, all three were still in the field and each had been augmented by reinforcements that more than made good the gaps of the artillery salvoes, the cavalry charges and the murderous infantry encounters that had filled the ruined villages of the plain with dead. Austria, feverishly rearming, remained a potential mediator. Sweden, with its well-trained army, remained uncommitted. Wellington and his battle-hardened British and Portuguese were continuing their advance on the Pyrenees. Nothing had been settled; neither would it be until the plains of Saxony had been watered by the blood of a half-million men.

The issue of the battle of Lutzen had resolved the course of action in the mind of only one man, the king of Saxony, unique among the puppet kings in that he looked upon Napoleon as neither benefactor nor despot, but as a friend.

The king had fled to Prague when the Russo-Prussian forces marched into his capital, leaving his Dresden subjects to welcome them as liberators, but now the burghers were in the same situation as the citizens of Hamburg earlier that spring. The man they had thought of as a fugitive was at their gates with a victorious army. Luckily for them their sovereign was also present to intercede on their behalf. The beaten liberators moved back over the Elbe and over the Spree to Bautzen where they dug in, fortifying the ground behind the town with their rear resting on wooded heights and their left on the Bohemian mountains. Marshal Macdonald, probing forward with his 9th Corps, crossed the broken spans of the river bridges on ladders and pushed on to the banks of the Spree. Eugène, having written a politely phrased letter to the king of Saxony apologizing "for making war in His Majesty's realm," followed and after him came the rest of the Grand Army, two formidable striking forces under the command of Marshal Ney and Napoleon himself, who entered Dresden on May 8th, six days after the victory at Lutzen.

Tremendous exertions had resulted in a complete regrouping of the armies of the Main and the Elbe. Ney's northern force, consisting of the 2nd, 3rd, 5th and 7th Corps was led by Marshal Victor and Generals Lauriston and Reynier, and consisted of 80,000 infantry and 4,800 cavalry. Napoleon, advancing on a more southerly route, led the Guard, the Guard cavalry, the 4th, 6th, 9th and 12th Corps, respectively commanded by General Bertrand and Marshals Marmont, Macdonald and Oudinot, all first class soldiers with twenty years' active service behind them. This army now had a cavalry force of 12,000 and its line regiments, with the Guard, totaled 107,000 men.

Despite his temporary advantage in numbers Napoleon was still anxious to compromise if a compromise could be achieved by a minimum sacrifice of territory and prestige. With this in mind he welcomed an Austrian emissary into camp and sent his veteran negotiator, Caulaincourt, to the Czar. He thought it possible that mistrust of Austria, and dissension among the Allies, could now be exploited in favor of France.

He was overoptimistic. Although badly ruffled his enemies in the field were not yet ready to concede him victory whereas Metternich, gambling on imponderables, continued to hold out for what Napoleon considered an impossible price for Austria's neutrality—nothing less than the restoration to the House of Habsburg of Illyria and Dalmatia on the Adriatic, French withdrawal from Poland and the Lowlands, and the independence of the Hanseatic towns in the north. This was more than the price he would have been prepared to pay for defeat and negotiations along these lines produced nothing but talk.

At the camp of the Russians, behind Bautzen, the Russian diplomats would not even grant Caulaincourt an audience with the Czar but continued to insist that all approaches for a peace were made through Austria. The rift between the enemies of

France was not yet wide enough but Napoleon, assessing the current situation in Dresden, decided that one more resounding victory would solve his problems, bring about a break-up of the new Coalition, and isolate his arch enemy, Britain, for the third time since 1800. To that end he studied war maps and set his battalions in motion. If the Russo-Prussian army at Bautzen could be enveloped and rolled up he could dictate terms as he had dictated them at Tilsit, in 1807, and again after Wagram, in the summer of 1809. Driven in from the northwest by Ney's army, and hammered at the center by himself, the Allies would have no alternative but to retreat into Austrian territory and here his father-in-law's bluff could be called. If Austria was neutral the fugitive armies would be disarmed. If it was not, if Metternich persuaded the hesitant Francis to fight again, then the Guard would roll down on Vienna like a juggernaut and the whole of Europe, including Bernadotte's Swedes and the German princelings, would jump down from the fence. This achieved and Europe under control once again, the French veterans could return to the Peninsula and chase Wellington back to Portugal. One more effort and the thing was as good as done. The dynasty would be secured and the tricolor would fly from the Vistula to Torres Vedras. Orders were sent to Ney to detach two corps to cover Berlin and with the rest of his army to concentrate on Bautzen. In the meantime, with the Guard and his own four corps, Napoleon marched out of Dresden heading due east for the Spree.

II

Prince Eugène, Viceroy of Italy, had written to his adoring wife Augusta, daughter of the king of Bavaria, saying that he intended applying for a month's leave and expected to get it within eight days. In the event he got two months without making an application, for as soon as he arrived in Dresden he was sent to Italy to raise a new army. What Napoleon needed as much as men in this quarter was a vigorous demonstration and he was careful to insure that his stepson fully understood the situation. "Raise your troops openly," he said, "and make certain Austria knows your purpose." A new Italian army, recruiting on the western flank of the Habsburg Empire, would keep Metternich neutral while the fate of Europe was decided on the Spree. It was an excellent move but, having made it, Napoleon went on to commit a psychological error that was to cost him the campaign.

Aware of Ney's shortcomings as a strategist he sent him an adviser in the person of the Swiss military theorist, General Jomini. Having regard to Ney's temperament this was a particularly tactless choice. Ney did not take kindly to any theorist and no one was more likely to irritate him than Jomini, a man he distrusted and disliked.

The relationship of the two men had once been very close. It was Ney, indeed, who had made himself the patron of this clever mercenary officer, who had hawked his treatises on the art of war round the French camps in the days of the Consulate. Later they had worked together in Switzerland and later still, when the invasion of England was being planned, Jomini had been made Ney's chief-of-staff in the Boulogne invasion force. But since then marshal and general had quarreled violently and Ney now regarded Jomini's presence as a slur on his ability as an independent commander. Always jealous of his military reputation Ney sulked over the appointment. In the critical days ahead his attitude of mind was to have very serious results in the field.

Relying on prompt co-operation from its left wing the main body of the Grand Army approached the Spree where Macdonald, with the advance guard, had already had an opportunity to study the strong positions of the Russo-Prussian army. Awaiting the arrival of Napoleon the marshal had resorted to a time honored ruse to deceive the enemy as to the real strength of the French. He had caused innumerable watch fires to be lit on the left bank of the river, and deceived or not the Allied commander, Wittgenstein, took no chances. Reinforced at Bautzen by 16,000 Russians under Barclay de Tolly (one of the heroes of the 1812 campaign), and 11,000 Prussians under Kleist, the Allies sat tight in their entrenchments, making no more than a show of resistance when the French reconnoitered their position. It was then the 19th of May, seventeen days after the battle of Lutzen and twenty-one days after the first clash at Weissenfels.

Napoleon's plan of attack had the simplicity that characterized most of his grand offensives. Napoleonic strategy was rarely complicated in conception or execution. Mostly it was a matter of carefully selecting a point of attack, summoning the means to promote that attack with tremendous vigor, and catching the main forces of the enemy off balance at the weakest sector of their line. But in all the great Napoleonic battles timing was vital and never more so that at Bautzen, on May 20th and 21st, 1813. Here everything except timing went according to plan and the single flaw in the operation led back to two earlier errors, both in a sense Napoleon's. One was a miscalculation of distances for which Berthier, as Chief of Staff, must share responsibility. The other was the Emperor's casual appointment of Jomini as Ney's adviser. These comparatively minor misjudgments in an otherwise faultless plan of battle were to affect the course of 19th century history out of all proportion to their importance at the time.

Orders had been sent off to Ney canceling those instructing him to detach two Corps (Victor's and Reynier's) to threaten Berlin and urging him to march with the whole of his force on the Allies' right flank at Weissenberg, a small town in the enemy's right rear. He was instructed, however, to halt at Preititz, a point only a few miles from Weissenberg, and co-ordinate his descent on the Prussians here with Napoleon's central attack from Bautzen. If the plan succeeded—and there was no reason why it should not—the entire Russo-Prussian army would be forced into Bohemian Austrian territory, terrible terrain for an army in flight. Since Austria, at this stage, was neither able nor willing to succor them, the immediate result of their defeat could only have been a dictated peace. There would have been no Leipzig, no abdication, no Waterloo and no St. Helena.

But the plan did fail, and it failed because it did not take into account the original orders sent to Ney concerning the detachment of half his army to threaten Berlin. By the time Ney received his new orders Reynier's 7th Corps had been halted, and

Victor's 2nd Corps was at Senftenberg, fifty miles from Bautzen. Orders were at once despatched instructing both commanders to concentrate but in the meantime, with no time in hand, Ney had only half his men available. Nevertheless, being a man who always preferred to march to the sound of the guns, he set out at 4 o'clock on the morning of the 21st and reached Preititz six hours later, where he was at once engaged by an alerted Blücher and was soon locked in combat. If Reynier and Victor had been within striking distance this might have proved an advantage. They could have fallen on Weissenberg, in the enemy's rear, while Ney and Lauriston kept the Prussians occupied and in the end the Allies' right wing must have collapsed on to its hard-pressed center. But Reynier was thirty-five miles away at Hoyerswerda, and Victor was fifteen miles to the northwest at Senftenberg. There was no one to send behind Blucher who, fighting with his usual obstinacy and having the advantage of cavalry, fell back and eluded the trap Napoleon had baited for him.

In the meantime things looked promising for the French at Bautzen. There had been skirmishing as early as the 19th and on the morning of the 20th the main attack began, Marshal Macdonald storming across a repaired bridge over the Spree and Bertrand and Marmont following on trestles and pontoons. Bertrand ran into serious opposition under Barclay de Tolly but by 3 P.M. a firm footing had been won and the Allies, driven in at every point, fell back on their entrenchments behind the town. By 6 P.M. fighting ceased for the day but for Napoleon, working on the assumption that the next morning would see Ney's storming descent from the north, there was a night of complicated map work and dictation of orders. At 8 A.M. on the morning of the 21st, having made his dispositions down to the last detail, he issued orders for the assault to begin and lay down on a pile of skins in his tent to sleep.[1]

The second day's assault went even better for the French than the first. Czar Alexander, who was given to interfering with the dispositions of his generals, played into his enemy's hands by presupposing that Napoleon's aim was to drive him north, away from Austrian territory, instead of south and directly into it, and obligingly transferred his major strength to the center and left, leaving Blucher's wing very weak. Marshal Oudinot, whose fighting reputation was second only to Ney's (he was wounded thirty-four times in the Napoleonic wars) stormed into his center with the Guard, strongly supported by Macdonald, Bertrand and Marmont. There was no resisting such an onslaught and the Russians began to give ground rapidly. Now was the moment for Ney's descent from the north that would buckle the entire Allied line and force it into the Bohemian defiles. It did not come. Looking to their left the marshals could see no smoke from Ney's batteries and no sign of Blucher's wing crumpling upon the center. Instead there was a general movement backward. The hard-pressed Allies were on the retreat not southward, as had been intended, but directly eastward, towards Gorlitz on the river Neisse.

III

There was far more behind Ney's failure to close the jaws of the trap than his shortage of troops, caused by the detachment of Reynier and Victor on the far side of the Spree. That fateful morning he was in a sullen mood and his way of demonstrating his sulkiness was to maintain a strict adherence to orders, one of the most stupid things an independent commander can do when involved in combined operations in the field. Napoleon had told him to attack at noon and when Jomini urged that, in view of the center's spectacular success, he should attack at once with every man and every gun he could advance, he refused. Long ago, in the Jena campaign of 1806, he had been rebuked for over-eagerness and perhaps he remembered this but it is more likely his obstinacy stemmed from resentment at having a Swiss mercenary at his elbow giving him unwanted advice. He stuck to his orders, while becoming more and more involved with Blucher, until even that general, not renowned for military prescience, began to discern Napoleon's plan of action and prepared for rapid withdrawal. Looking south he could gauge the progress of Oudinot's attack on the left and center and soon it became obvious that there was only one hope for him, to withdraw as quickly as possible towards the Neisse.

For Blucher, who hated withdrawals of all kinds, it was not an easy decision. With the whole of his being he hated the French and his notions of strategy were confined to violent attack to his front so that he became known, in his own lifetime, as "General Vorwarts." But on this occasion there was no alternative but to break off the fight and pull back and this he was able to do because, unlike his opponent, he had plenty of cavalry. He went back and the Russian center and left went back with him, moving eastward along the Austrian frontier towards Silesia. By late afternoon the field was abandoned to the French but what could they do with the ground they had won? Their infantry was exhausted. They had no spare cavalry to harry the beaten enemy as at Jena and Austerlitz and Wagram. All they could achieve on the following day (May 22nd) was to send in the cavalry of the Guard under General Bruyère and at that moment a battery covering the Allied retreat scored three fatal hits in two shots.

The first ball mortally wounded Bruyère, a brilliant cavalry commander who had been seriously wounded in a similar pursuit after Wagram, four years earlier. The second ball was even more deadly. Ricocheting from a tree it killed General Kirchener and went on to strike down the Grand Marshal of the Palace, Duroc, one of Napoleon's oldest and best loved companions-in-arms.

Of all the legendary figures in the Grand Army Duroc is the most attractive. Kindly, mild mannered, utterly loyal and with a brave and honorable record that went back to the days of the first Italian campaign, he was loved and admired by every man on Napoleon's staff. They carried him, dying, to a small farm and the Emperor was summoned. Some twenty thousand men had fallen during three days of battle but no loss touched Napoleon more deeply than that of Duroc. The surgeon told him there was no hope of recovery and he turned away. "Ask me nothing until tomorrow," he muttered and sought his tent. In the early hours of the 23rd Duroc died and Napoleon paid the equivalent of £800 to the owner of the farm where the Grand Marshal's body lay, with instructions that one-fifth of this sum was to be devoted to the raising of a memorial containing Duroc's name. The rest was to be regarded as compensation for the damage the farm had suffered during the battle. Duroc's body, together with the body of that other popular soldier, Marshal Bessières, killed at Lutzen, was subsequently taken back to France for burial at Les Invalides but the money left for the memorial and repairs to the farm went into the pockets of the advancing Allies that autumn.

The death of his friend depressed Napoleon to a degree that surprised men to whom war had been a trade since their earliest youth and it may have had something to do with his agreement to a temporary cessation of hostilities. First Lannes, at Essling in 1809, then Bessières at Lutzen, and now Duroc. The old companions of Italy were disappearing at an increasing pace and when he surveyed the field, and added up the cost of yet another indecisive victory, Napoleon might have decided there must be an attempt to move from the battlefield to the conference table.

Meanwhile, the Grand Army pushed eastward, Napoleon commenting gloomily, "Not a gun, not a prisoner! These people don't leave me so much as a nail!" Oudinot was left behind to collect his men and march north to Berlin. The others, reunited with Ney, crossed the river Katzbach to Jauer as the Allies fell back beyond Breslau on the Oder. On May 29th news came that Davout and Vandamme had re-entered Hamburg and on June 1st, with his entry of Breslau, Napoleon decided to accept the offer of an armistice until July 20th, later extended to August 16th with the object of convening an all-round conference at Prague.

During the final stages of the advance the French army passed through the village where the Russian General Kutusoff had died in April, "The Old Fox of the North" as Napoleon used to call him. Napoleon never showed a lack of respect for a gallant adversary and although Kutusoff, more than any other man, had been responsible for driving him from Moscow to the Niemen six months previously, he felt no bitterness for the old warrior and ordered a memorial to be erected in his honor.

For the junior officers, NCOs and men trudging along the sunny, flower decked roads in pursuit of the Allies, the prospect of an armistice was welcome. Captain Barrès, of the 3rd battalion of the 47th Regiment of the line, marched cheerfully enough. At Borna, near Lutzen, two days after the battle, he had been asked to recommend men for decorations and on May 18th, moving eastward with Lauriston's corps, he was himself appointed Chevalier of the Legion of Honor, under the number 35,505. The cross was greatly coveted by the men of the Grand Army and had not, at that time, been cheapened by indiscriminate distribution. "Never did a reward give so much pleasure," records this estimable man but there was an ironic sequel to one of the rewards distributed to men of the 47th on that occasion. Barrès' sergeant-major was made adjutant and was still holding this rank when he was discharged the following year. "If he had been given a commission he would have remained in the army," says Barrès. "As it was he became a civilian clerk in a government department and by 1824 he had amassed a private fortune!"

Barrès played a strenuous part in the battle of Bautzen and was one of a storming party that scaled the walls of the town without the aid of ladders. He was heavily engaged in all the fighting on May 21 and 22 and his company suffered horribly from the enemy's artillery, losing twenty-one men killed and wounded. Barrès emerged unscathed and his luck held up to the time he advanced into the town of Jauer, on the far side of the Katzbach, for here he stumbled against a heavy object enclosed in a nosebag. Barrès had been marching and fighting with the Grand Army for nine years and his nose for loot or provender was as sharp as the next man's. He picked up the bag and carried it along, later discovering that it contained the largest trussed turkey he had ever seen. For Barrès and his comrades this was as good as a victory on the field. Officers with culinary experience were assembled, ingredients pooled and the bivouac scoured for vegetables. Soon the little group were sitting down to the best meal they had eaten since leaving Paris, the dinner being washed down with several bottles of excellent Moravian wine. "The pleasure of being gathered together and of eating, quietly seated, the products of our culinary friends," comments Captain Barrès, "enabled us to spend a few agreeable hours such as are rare in wartime."

In all the letters, diaries and memoirs of soldiers pages are devoted to similar incidents, a clear indication that the commissariat of Napoleon's armies left a great deal to be desired. Mostly the men were expected to forage for themselves. The fact that the French could fight and march on the products of their own acquisitions in the field goes some way towards explaining the comment Europeans made at the time, "Even the rats starve where the Grand Army marches."

Saxony had been cleared and a temporary halt called in the butchery but at what a frightful cost? All along the route between the Saale and the Oder lay the newly buried dead, perhaps 100,000 in all and 40,000 of them French. The hospitals at Weissenfels, Lutzen, Leipzig and Dresden housed as many sick and wounded. The Russians and Prussians had suffered even more severely but their losses could and would be made good by columns marching westward out of Russia and by a steady flow of patriotic young Germans from recruiting depots within easy reach of the Allies. The French lines of communications reached all the way back through Dresden and Leipzig to Mainz and the frontier depots of the Rhine, and France had been at war since 1792. It was surely time to call a halt and gain what terms could be secured on the basis of the startling but indecisive victories of the short campaign, to see what could be done to ferment strife between Russia, Prussia and Austria. The troops went into bivouac. The diplomats packed their portmanteaux and set off for Prague. Four weeks of fighting were succeeded by ten weeks of talking.

6

THE ARMISTICE DIVIDING the two Saxon campaigns
lasted fifty days and during that period every old trick emerged
from the diplomatic bags, together with many new ones.
Throughout the fifty days, and often far into the night, men
bargained and bluffed with a zest that was not to be repeated
round a conference table until the Powers assembled at Versailles one hundred and six years later. As an exercise in patience
and ingenuity the event was an astonishing performance. As a
manifestation of bad faith and double dealing it must have
prompted men of integrity on both sides to wish themselves
back on the battlefield.

The pivot of the conference was Austria. Would she throw
in her lot with the Allies, pocketing a half-million in British
gold and gambling on her ability to contain Russia and stunt
the growth of a German Empire? Would she continue to temporize and keep both Napoleon and her rivals in the north and
east guessing? Or would she exact vast territorial benefits by
siding (or threatening to side) with France, in an attempt to
prevent either Russia or Prussia from filling the power vacuum
that would follow a dismemberment of the French Empire? Nobody knew; not Napoleon, not the Czar, the king of Prussia,
the British envoys, or, indeed, Metternich himself at the opening of the conference. It was like a vastly complicated card
game where every player held what he considered to be a strong
hand. The result depended upon who made fewest mistakes
and whose nerve was equal to the challenge.

"Doubtful Permission to Exist"

Throughout the greater part of the nineteenth century it was fashionable to regard the 1813 campaign as a war of liberation. The Coalition powers were presented as a force contending with a man whom ambition had driven almost insane, but with the collapse of the Romanoff, Hohenzollern and Habsburg dynasties in 1917 and 1918 free access to the archives encouraged a shrewd reassessment of the earlier struggle. It was seen then, and has since been confirmed, that most of the men who gambled in the conference rooms of the Mascoline Palace in Dresden, or at the full dress conference that followed in Prague, were not what they seemed to be, crusaders who had agreed to sink their personal differences in a united attempt to overthrow a megalomaniac. They were professional schemers concerned, almost exclusively, in securing their own ends and furthering their own careers. Their collective object, if they had one, was to restore the old order in Europe where privilege was everything and meritocracy counted for little.

This is not to say, of course, that the aims of Napoleon in maintaining the struggle against his adversaries were democratic in the sense that we understand that word today. One has only to read some of his letters, dashed off at the time, to decide that in most respects he was as calculatingly selfish as his rivals but at least it can be said in his favor that he was concerned with the future rather than the past, with the vast possibilities that the new century offered rather than the conventions of an age that was already dead, even in the summer of 1813. As he was to reflect during his exile, "These wars arose out of a conflict of past and future," and when he considered, and ultimately rejected, the terms offered him by powers whom his army of conscripts had driven from the field, he concluded: "They offer me a doubtful permission to exist. . . ." As a footnote to these reflections he added that, whereas an established monarch might hope to survive twenty defeats and then return to his capital, such an inglorious end to a foreign war was not available to "an upstart soldier." He was very well aware that France longed for peace but he did not see a lasting peace emerging from any treaty signed by the hardfisted man who faced him across the conference table and in this view history proved him to be farsighted. The deliberations that followed his abdication within nine months of the armistice did nothing to moderate the rivalries of Russia, Austria, France and a newly-emergent Prussia. In point of fact they are still with us, after a century of repression, two world wars, and any number of smaller conflicts that preceded the two major conflicts. The dream of European federalization that inspired Napoleon's European conquests has only just shown itself in the Treaty of Rome and the price of that federalization is the same—French hegemony under De Gaulle.

At the heart of the Dresden and Prague armistice deliberations lay jealousy and bad faith. Because she had not been involved in the disasters of 1812, or in the subsequent campaign ending at Bautzen, Austria's position was stronger than it had been for more than a decade and she used her new bargaining power ruthlessly and effectively. With an army of 200,000 men assembling in Bohemia she had a formidable card to play and when Metternich met the envoys of Russia and Prussia on June 24th (three days before he confronted Napoleon at Dresden) it was he, and not the belligerent powers, who called the tune. His proposals were reduced to six main points and the stiffness of the terms underline Austria's fears that Napoleon would use the armistice period to revive the Tilsit balance of power that was a virtual division of Europe between Russia in the east and France in the west. The fear was real enough. The Russians, having driven the Grand Army in ruins from its territory, were half inclined to leave Western Europe to its own devices and had it been less certain that Austria would take his place as the arbiter of Prussia's future, it is possible that the Czar might have withdrawn to his own dominions and refused to prosecute a war so far west of his frontiers.

British agents, however, were busy with substantial bribes and there was also a strong temptation among Russian soldiers to give France, and particularly Paris, a taste of the fire and sword Napoleon had brought to Moscow the previous summer. Britain, despite her continuing successes at sea and in the Peninsula, wanted nothing better than to climb out of the European cauldron but only when the balance of power, her political cornerstone for centuries, had been readjusted to her satisfaction. Prussia's position in this whirlpool of intrigue was that of a sizeable pawn. The future of the ancient kingdom of Poland, that had never, despite many half promises, been resurrected by Napoleon, was yet another stake in the game.

Metternich's six articles were designed to restore Austria to her once dominant position in Europe. They included the extinction of the Duchy of Warsaw (Poland), the enlargement of Prussia by a slice of Poland and Danzig, the restoration to her of Illyria and Trieste on the Adriatic, the independence of the Hanseatic towns on the Baltic, the dissolution of the Confederation of the Rhine and finally, the restoration of the western borders of Prussia to those of 1806 before that power's defeat at Jena.

This was nothing less than an insistence upon France's withdrawal to her natural boundaries, the Rhine, the Alps and the Pyrenees. As to her presence in Italy, not specifically included in the articles, Napoleon was quite correct in assuming that any peace secured on these terms would be temporary. Austria's subsequent demands at the Vienna Congress, and her long exercise of tyranny in Venice and elsewhere in Italy, established this beyond any doubt. Her ultimate withdrawal from the Italian peninsula was only achieved at gunpoint more than a generation later.

They were terms he could not be expected to accept. No victor would have accepted them and even before they were drawn up Metternich knew they would be rejected. Napoleon, himself playing for time, and having no real faith in his ability to detach Austria from the Coalition or even count upon her continued neutrality, countered by offering Warsaw, Illyria and Danzig but mainly, one feels, as debating points.

Even so some kind of understanding might still have emerged between the two men (they had each taken one another's true measure) had it not been for the latest news from Spain, a bulletin that knocked the kingpin from French diplomacy at the outset of the conference. On June 21st, only seventeen days after the armistice had been arranged, word came that irretrievable disaster had overtaken King Joseph at Vitoria and he was now not merely a king without kingdom but a fugitive, scrambling back into France with Wellington and the British army at his heels. Hearing the sensational news the Austrian attitude hardened and the Russo-Prussian command plucked up heart and prepared to exact the utmost from the situation. Napoleon, who did not underestimate the damage Vitoria had done his cause, dictated a spate of vitriolic letters to his representatives in that quarter, after which he took what seemed to him the one step likely to prevent the British smashing their way through the back door of France while he and the Grand Army were holding the Coalition troops at bay east of the Elbe. He sent one of his finest defensive fighters, Marshal Soult, to take command of all military units left in Spain, at the same time dismissing the incompetent Marshal Jourdan and heaping scorn upon his inept brother Joseph who was henceforth forbidden to show his face in Paris.

II

The magnitude of the disaster at Vitoria had surprised everyone, including the victors. They had anticipated a victory, and a further contraction of French power, but not the hopeless rout that a single engagement had produced in the ranks of the enemy.

By June 4th, the actual day of the signing of the armistice, British-Portuguese columns, 81,000 strong, had concentrated north of the River Douro and were marching northeast towards the rivers Carrion and Pisuerga. Screened by cavalry the veteran army crossed the great plain of Old Castile in perfect weather and before its approach the French main army had no alternative but to retreat over bitterly hostile territory. First Valladolid, then Palencia, then Burgos, were evacuated and the line of march was cluttered by a rabble of noncombatants, French civilians, renegade Spaniards aware that they would be garroted within hours of capture, and innumerable harlots who had plied their trade in French camps for years.

The habit of loot was very strong in a Napoleonic army and even in flight the veterans among Jourdan's battalions would not jettison the valuables they had acquired in five years' campaigning in this pestilential country. The motley cavalcade struggled on towards the Ebro and such laggards as there were fell into the hands of Wellington's Light Division, that had spearheaded every British advance across the Peninsula since the forlorn campaign of Sir John Moore in the winter of 1808.

Toughened and tested by years of campaigning, Wellington's infantry had no European equals except in the Imperial Guard and even the Guard was inferior in terms of marksmanship and mobility. They were now advancing through a friendly country with no prospect of having to retreat, as they had been forced to withdraw before superior forces so often in the past.

Advancing northeast that June was Johnny (later Sir John) Kincaid, whose boyish high spirits were thoroughly typical of those animating the junior officers of Wellington's Peninsula army. "We were welcomed in every town and village through which we passed," he records, "by peasant girls with garlands of flowers and a peculiar dancing style of their own," but he goes on to say that, while the señoritas were entertaining one regiment, the preceding one was diligently engaged in pulling down their houses for firewood! In this way, more confident of victory than at any time in the long war, the British came up with the retreating French where King Joseph had insisted Marshal Jourdan make a stand. The final trial of strength took place in a plain twelve miles by seven, in the valley of Vitoria under the spurs of the Pyrenees, an army of 58,000 dispirited French facing three columns of 80,000 British, Portuguese and Spanish, who saw the end of the five year war within their grasp.

For the British it was a splendid moment, the culmination of years of effort. For King Joseph it was a final attempt to avert his brother's wrath. The army that closed with the French at Vitoria that sunny June day was the best equipped, the best trained and the best disciplined that had ever taken the field for Britain. It was not to have a successor of such quality until almost exactly a century later, when the British Expeditionary Force tried to check the march of Von Kluck's legions through Belgium and died, almost to a man, in the murderous battles of Mons, Château Thierry, First Ypres and Loos.

In the endless war against Revolutionary and Imperial France Britain's land operations had been at best frustrating, at worst inept, a dramatic contrast to her brilliant successes at sea.

Once firmly established in the Spanish Peninsula, however, her field force had become a formidable and seasoned army. At Busaco, Talavera, Albuera, Barrosa, Ciudad Rodrigo, Badajoz and particularly at Salamanca, eleven months before, it had shown itself superior in fire power and maneuverability to any French army in Spain and Portugal. Its target practice was infinitely better than that of any army in the world and it was led by a cadre of officers who, although prone to regard the rank and file as a bunch of thieves and drunkards, had nonetheless earned the trust and respect of their men so that they fought like heroes in every action and often against formidable odds. Riding with Wellington that day were men of caliber, fiery Tom Picton, who was to die at Waterloo two years later; Sir Thomas Graham, whose beautiful wife provided Gainsborough with one of his classic subjects; Sir Rowland Hill, hero of many a desperate encounter in the rocky valleys of the Sierras; George, Earl of Dalhousie; Sir Lowry Cole; Vandeleur and many other men of wealth and breeding. The social gulf between senior officers and men was all but unbridgeable and, when one compares it with the camaraderie that existed between Marshal Ney and his NCOs and privates, it is astonishing that the British Peninsular army displayed such steadfastness under fire. In the course of five years' campaigning in Spain and Portugal the British soldier had also learned to respect his adversaries. Towards the end of the war one finds instances of the same spirit of tolerance between friend and foe as emerged on the Western Front, and, later, between Montgomery's Eighth Army and Rommel's Afrika Corps. The British did not think much of French marksmanship (a French recruit's shooting course at this time generally consisted of three shots at point blank range) but whenever he was in action against them the British infantryman never failed to take into account French ingenuity, dash, overall toughness and courage. There was reciprocal hatred in the Peninsula between French and Spanish that resulted in innumerable atrocities on both sides, but there was no bitterness between the main protagonists who treated one another as battle-hardened professionals.

The conflict at Vitoria was short, sharp and decisive. The French, 58,000 strong, were not yet augmented by General

Clausel's brigand hunting column and Wellington gave his opponent no opportunity to concentrate. At dawn on June 21st the attack went in from the west, Rowland Hill advancing on the French left over the Madrid highway, a movement that drew off the French reserves in that direction. Later the main attack developed in the center and right of the enemy against the French held bridges over the river Zadora and across their one negotiable escape route, the main highway to Bilbao and the French frontier.

Tom Picton, fighting on the British left in an unsoldiery frock coat and top hat, dashed in with his usual vigor and familiar spate of oaths, crossing the river almost unsupported and hammering his way into the enemy's center. By afternoon Spanish guerillas had cut the main road and the direct line with France while Graham had moved forward against the French left center, valiantly defended by the veteran commander, General Reille. For a time, as long as there was hope, the French fought tenaciously, falling back on positions in front of the town, but the dash and determination of the British brigades and their well-trained Portuguese caçadores soon swept resistance aside. By five in the afternoon the fighting retreat was beginning to develop into a rout as the defeated columns made for the only retreat open to them, the narrow road to Pamplona.

What followed that evening sealed the fate of French hopes in Spain. Seeing the battle lost every man looked to his own safety, from King Joseph down to the humblest private. Combatants and baggage train became confused and soon there was no hope of saving treasure, guns or stores. Indeed, the only factor that saved the French from annihilation was the presence in their rear of more loot than the Allies had seen in the entire war. Troopers and infantrymen, risking their lives for a pittance that was usually months in arrears, were unlikely to lose such a splendid opportunity of enriching themselves, and looting on a large scale enabled the French to rally to some extent and fall back in the direction of the Pyrenees. Military trophies taken that day included 151 brass cannon, 415 caissons of ammunition, nearly two million cartridges, over 40,000 lbs. of gunpowder, 56 forage wagons and 44 forges. The pursuers, however, paid closer attention to other kinds of loot, sacks of dollars including a huge consignment of gold that had just arrived to pay the troops, caskets of jewels, art treasures pilfered from Spanish castles and convents, and all manner of personal effects in portmanteaux and knapsacks flung away by the fugitives.

Describing his adventures that evening with the gaiety of a skylarking schoolboy Johnny Kincaid tells of his descent upon a carriage caught between fires, with the coachman underneath the equipage praying and a gouty old passenger inside surrounded by wines and provisions. "Never did victors make a more legal or useful capture," says Kincaid, "for it was now six in the evening and it had evidently been the old gentleman's fault if he had not already dined, whereas it was our misfortune that we had not tasted anything since three o'clock in the morning. One of our men knocked the neck off a bottle and handed it to me to take a drink. I nodded to the old fellow's health and drank it off without the smallest scruple of conscience. It was excellent claret and if he still lives to tell the story I fear he will not give us the credit of having belonged to such a civil department as his appeared to be."

The French losses in personnel were only 8,000 but their morale was shattered by the defeat. The Allies lost more than 5,000 of whom 1,400 were British but they also suffered a loss in morale on account of the breakdown of discipline in the presence of so much loot. "We started," wrote Wellington, "with the army in the highest order but the battle, as usual, totally annihilated all order and discipline. The soldiers have got among them about a million in money and the night of the battle, instead of being passed in getting rest and food for the pursuit of the following day, was passed by the soldiers looking for plunder."

Notwithstanding a temporary dispersal of troops—"We lost more men in the pursuit than the enemy," grumbled Wellington —the French cause in Spain was lost and by the end of the month they were all behind their own frontier. General Clausel, one of the best generals Napoleon had in Spain (he had saved a beaten army at Salamanca, in 1812), managed to struggle across the frontier with 12,000 of his men. The rest, poor devils, were left exhausted on the road to be dealt with by guerillas who never encumbered themselves with prisoners. Within a fortnight of Vitoria all that remained of Joseph's kingdom were three beseiged fortresses and Suchet's forces in the provinces of Aragon and Catalonia that had been annexed to France the year before. "Your glorious conduct is beyond all praise," wrote the Prince Regent to Wellington. "I feel I have nothing to say but to devoutly offer my prayer of gratitude to Providence that it has blessed my country and myself with such a general."

III

Moving restlessly between Mainz, Dresden and Prague that summer Napoleon also found time to write to his lieutenants, but thankful prayers to Providence did not feature in the correspondence. A defeat on this scale could not have come at a worse time and his anger with brother Joseph and Marshal Jourdan knew no bounds. "If the King of Spain comes to Paris," he wrote to the Minister of Police, "arrest him—he must be under no illusion on this point. . . . Our misfortunes in Spain, as you will have seen from the English papers, are all the more serious because they are absurd . . . they are no dishonour to the army. The army in Spain had no general and a supernumerary king. Ultimately, I admit, I am myself to blame. If I had sent the Duke of Dalmatia (Soult) to Valladolid to take over the command there . . . this would never have happened."

To the Minister of War he wrote, "Express my displeasure to Marshal Jourdan, suspend him from his functions, and give him orders to retire to his country house where he will remain suspended, and without pay, until he has accounted to me for the campaign." Both Joseph and Marshal Jourdan bore the Imperial displeasure with equanimity. The one had never wanted to be king of Spain and the other, whose military service went back to the War of Independence in the United States where he had fought as a private, had never wanted to be recalled from retirement. He had not even wanted to stand and fight at Vitoria and when king and marshal were pounding up the road to Pamplona, with the English Light Dragoons in hot pursuit, Jourdan is said to have remarked to his chief: "Well Sir, you've had your battle and it appears to have been a lost one."

Notwithstanding the profound effect news of Vitoria had

upon negotiations for peace, Spain was still a sideshow. The future of Europe would not be decided in the Pyrenean passes but between the Oder and the Elbe. By late July it was becoming clear to the most optimistic of the belligerents that nothing would be resolved by talk and that more battles, bloodier even than Lutzen and Bautzen, lay ahead.

Pulled back behind the agreed neutral zone that stretched from the mouth of the Elbe down to the Bohemian frontier, Captain Barrès of the 47th was engaged in a cattle roundup for the divisional commissariat. His diary entries, relating to his success in these endeavors, give some indication of what the war was costing local landowners and farmers. Operating from Neudorf under orders of Generals Joubert and Compans, Barrès collected four hundred cows and bullocks, three thousand sheep, and a number of goats and horses, all of which were driven into the army compounds. "If I had wanted to make money I could have done so without difficulty," he says. "The landowning barons offered me gold if I would leave them the half of what I took from them." He did, however, return the livestock soldiers had taken from wretched peasants who came to beg for them but when a wounded Italian general tried to block his requisitioning on behalf of a chateau owner, Barrès asked for counter orders in writing. The general dared not commit himself to paper and the Captain went off with the stock.

Although there was no fighting or marching to be done Barrès had more than enough to occupy him through June and July. He spent most of his time superintending repairs to the boots, the tattered clothing and the broken leather equipment of "his children" and was concerned at the increasing number of self-mutilations that occurred among the conscripts, whose thirst for glory had been assuaged at Lutzen and Bautzen and who were now longing for home and civilian status. The impetus of their unexpected victories had been enough to keep them going through the early summer but the boredom and discomfort of bivouac life, and the near certainty that in the autumn they would be called upon to face fearful odds in the field, had accounted for what remained of their martial ardor. Their morale, however, was at least as high as that of the professional soldiers, particularly among the senior officers of the Grand Army. Through the long weeks of negotiations a gloom settled on the French camp, as though the shadow of ultimate defeat was already creeping over the victors of so many campaigns. Berthier, the Chief of Staff who had never left Napoleon's side since 1796, was urging his master to compromise, to make almost any concessions in order to obtain a general peace and his persuasions were seconded by scarred old warriors like Oudinot and even Ney, not to mention a stream of supplications that arrived at Imperial Headquarters from the politicians in Paris. Napoleon, while understanding the necessity for peace, was impatient with these pleas. Looking back on his situation years later he explained his feelings, saying that while his advisers could see nothing but the general outlines of his dilemma, he alone could study all its implications. A patched up peace, of the kind that had followed some of his earlier triumphs in the field, would in his view be disastrous to France, for it would give the powers leisure to perfect their plans and enlist even greater forces for a resumption of the offensive in a year. To his mind, heavy as were the odds against him at the moment, it seemed better to force a decision now when there was a lack of mutual trust and considerable uncertainty among his enemies and Austria was uncommitted. Another victory in the field and this uncertainty would be certain to lead to a dissolution of the Coalition, after which he could make concessions with dignity and bargain from a position of strength. This was his general line of thinking during the last few weeks of the extended truce.

As to the misgivings of the men in the ranks he was kept in partial ignorance of the general ebb in enthusiasm among veterans and conscripts. Barrès declares that Surgeon-General Larrey lied when he reported to Headquarters that self-inflicted wounds were rare among the lower ranks. "There were," he declares, "more than twenty in my battalion and perhaps more than 15,000 in the whole army." Another problem facing men like Barrès was an outcrop of skin complaints among the men, many of whom were devoured with vermin. Others, unaccustomed to living under these hard conditions, were in need of hospital treatment for minor illnesses. The weak constitution of many of these nineteen-year-old lads would prove a decisive factor in an autumn plagued by persistent rains.

From the top level, however, great efforts were made to keep the morale of the army as high as possible. Napoleon's birthday, August 15th, had always been celebrated in camp with feasts and firework displays. This year, in view of the approaching end of the truce, it was put forward to August 10th, and orders went out that all marshals and generals commanding corps were to entertain their officers, for which they were granted six francs a head, as well as the daily double ration of food. A bonus of twenty sous was also paid out of the Imperial purse to each NCO and soldier in the ranks.

Barrès, serving with Marmont's Sixth Corps, took part in a spectacular review of 27,000 troops with 82 guns, after which the officers' dinner was given in the local Protestant church. Three roebuck were roasted whole on a huge iron trestle and lovers of very high venison "were able to regale themselves for they stank out the banqueting hall." After dinner games were played. "It was a good day, to be followed by many bad," records the captain.

One of Napoleon's weaknesses at this time was his lack of accurate information of what was going on in the Allied camps. Detailed knowledge of the Prussian and Russian morale would have given him more confidence than he in fact possessed for there were dissensions among the staffs and a good deal of despondency regarding the future. In an attempt to secure useful intelligence Napoleon wrote to Berthier from Dresden, instructing him to select four wounded officers with a knowledge of German, who were to be sent to Toplitz and Carlsbad "to take the waters, keep their ears open and report everything that occurred at those spas."

His output of correspondence during this lull was enormous. Besides coping with routine military matters, and dashing off letters concerning the movements of his brother Joseph and other doubters in France, he dictated detailed instructions concerning a vast and complicated network of State and personal affairs. He wrote to Cambacérès, Arch-Chancellor of the Empire, complaining that the Empress Marie Louise was cheapening the function of thanksgiving services at Nôtre Dame by attending one in honor of his victory at Bautzen. "It requires uncommon tact to deal with people like the Parisiens," he remarked shrewdly. He wrote again the same day to his wife, expressing his profound displeasure that she had received the Arch-Chancellor while in bed, pointing out that "this was a very improper act for any woman under the age of thirty!" The next day he was demanding that a troupe of actors be sent to Dresden for the entertainment of the army but warned Cambacères, "If we can't get good actors the whole idea had better be dropped." And from Mainz, in late July, where he traveled to spend a few days with the Empress, he wrote a testy letter to his sister Elisa, Duchess of Tuscany, expressing his annoyance at some local opposition to the appointment of a parish priest by the Bishop of Florence. "Take the most vigorous measures to put down this religious resistance. Send all persons guilty of it to the island of Elba." There is an ironic note in this last instruction. Within ten months he was himself to be a prisoner on Elba.

What continues to astonish students of Napoleon is this ability, on his part, to dart from the general to the particular at a speed that bewildered his staff, confounded his enemies, and reduced his secretaries to nervous wrecks. He would emerge from a conference called to debate the highest matters of policy —the future of Poland, or the constitution of a confederation of minor kingdoms—and plunge at once into a sea of personal trivia, the health of old comrades, the future of orphaned children, the appointment of a minor official in a small town, a slanderous rumor aimed at someone he respected, a police report concerning a couple of gamblers. He seemed to know precisely what was happening everywhere in his dominions (and often outside them) at any one time and to carry in his memory details that a trained secretary would have been obliged to reduce to memoranda sheets before they were buried in the day's business. In the midst of discussions with diplomats like Metternich and Nesselrode, who was acting for Russia, he could spare time to write expressing his genuine sorrow at the fate of General Junot, one of his oldest friends, who had gone mad as a result of a wound in the head and was reported to be eating grass on his estate in Illyria.[1] He gave instructions that Junot should be taken home to his wife and family and expressed his regret that he had bullied him for his failure to push an attack home at Smolensk the previous summer, realizing too late that Junot's mental illness had been the cause of his bad generalship on that occasion.

During his flying visit to Mainz at the end of July, Napoleon made an excursion purely for pleasure up the Rhine and was entertained on this occasion by the Prince of Nassau. One of his ministers, Beugnot, describes how, while passing the castle of Biberich on the right bank, the Emperor leaned far out over the bulwarks of the boat in order to get a good view. Beugnot happened to be watching, accompanied by Jean-Bon-Saint-Andrè, an old and cynical revolutionary who had hobnobbed with men like Marat, Robespierre and Danton. Jean-Bon observed aloud, "What a strange posture! The fate of the world depends on a kick or no kick!" a remark that terrified the minister who implored his companion to keep quiet. "Don't worry," chuckled the old terrorist, "determined men are rare!"

I V

By the end of July Napoleon and his suite were back in Saxony and still negotiations dragged on. Recruitment on both sides proceeded at a far brisker pace and by now Napoleon had a paper strength of some 400,000 men. The man standing at the point of balance, however, his father-in-law Francis of Austria, had 200,000 in camp in Bohemia waiting to fall on the right flank of the Grand Army as soon as they were engaged with the Russians in the center and the Prussians on their left. There was another looming danger. Jean-Baptiste Bernadotte, now Crown Prince of Sweden but once a French sergeant-major and a man who owed his present position to French valor, had at last made up his mind to accept a British bribe and enter the field against his old comrades. His Swedish army was not numerous by Continental standards but it was well-trained and likely to prove efficient under expert leadership. Bernadotte was largely responsible for tempting another Frenchman into the ranks of the Allies. At his invitation General Moreau, victor of Hohenlinden

and once a contender for the highest position in post-revolu-
tionary France, had returned from American exile to add his
counsel to the men who were determined to destroy Napoleon.
The two were soon joined by a third renegade, none other than
General Jomini, the Swiss military theorist whose presence at
Bautzen had resulted in Ney's failure to crush the Allied right
wing. The return of Moreau, who had been living in America
for some years, did not have much more than a moral effect upon
loyal Frenchmen but the defection of Jomini, privy to the present condition of the Grand Army and the temper of its chieftains, was a more serious matter. Jomini might be a mercenary
and a deserter but he was an intelligent soldier and the Allies
could use a man of his experience. On the advice of these three
traitors a new plan of action was formulated by the joint staffs
of the Coalition. The Allies decided that Napoleon himself
should never be opposed in the field by any one of his enemies
but that every effort should be made to engage detached corps
commanded by one or other of the marshals. In the presence
of the Emperor each of them would retreat and defeat the Grand
Army in detail by concentrating superior numbers against men
who lacked Napoleon's ability to snatch success from failure.
Once adopted (and it meant a swallowing of pride all round),
the plan proved a great success.

In a final and desperate attempt to detach Austria, Napoleon
again offered Metternich Warsaw, Illyria and Danzig. He was
still playing for time, awaiting, among other developments, the
arrival of Eugène with his new army of 50,000 Italians but the
Viceroy was having tremendous difficulties in equipping his recruits. Day after day he wrestled with problems that ought
not to have concerned a man in his position. He was short of
forage, short of horses, hopelessly short of clothing. Even the
provision of infantry shakos was a major difficulty and he had
to ransack Milan, Verona, Venice and finally Turin before his
men could cover their heads. There were rumors of a Croatian
uprising in Illyria. The Italian banks closed their doors to him.
It was common talk that Austria would attack. But here was a
man who found the cynicism of men like Bernadotte, Moreau
and Jomini hard to understand. His loyalty was unshakeable.
As long as Eugène was present in Italy there was nothing to be

feared in that quarter and the same applied in Hamburg in the north, where Davout now had the city in a grip that he would not relax despite successive French disasters in the autumn and winter.

With war now a certainty, and Austria finally committed, the Allies organized their forces into three armies. There was the Army of Bohemia, led by the experienced Austrian soldier, Schwartzenberg, the Army of Silesia, led by the veteran Blucher, and the Army of the North, led by Bernadotte. Down in the southwest Marshal Soult was struggling with all his might, and a great deal of tactical skill, to prevent the British-Spanish-Portuguese allies from breaking through the Pyrenean passes into the plain of Languedoc. And in the center, spread out like a great fan, was the Grand Army, its detachments reaching from the vicinity of Berlin to camps south of Dresden. All Europe waited for the first cannon shot and on August 10th the armistice was finally denounced by Prussia and Russia, to be followed, two days later, by a declaration of war by Austria. The event was signaled by a discharge of fireworks that soared into the night sky along the Silesian border, telling the jubilant Allies that Austria had at last declared herself, that Napoleon now faced the combined strength of seven nations amounting, in Germany alone, to a total of a half-million men and 1,380 guns.

Told that peace negotiations had finally broken down Marshal Oudinot, always one of the most outspoken of Napoleon's paladins, said, "In other words it's war! In other words, a bad thing!" He was at once sent from the room, but when they told him he had offended the Emperor he laughed. "He'll soon forget that," he said, "he needs me!" He did need him; in the ten months' fighting ahead, when the Allies were to surge over the Elbe, the Saale, the Rhine and up to the gates of Paris itself, he was to need every Frenchman who could bear arms.

7

THERE ARE SOME things a genius cannot learn. Men of astonishing brilliance have been known to walk the streets all day with untied shoelaces, not because they are careless or absentminded but because their fingers have never mastered the secret of tying a two loop knot. With Napoleon, who could do almost anything, it was the art of horsemanship. He was in the saddle all his youth and most of his adult life, and yet he never acquired the art of balance, of using his knees and calves to advantage, of gathering reins and giving a trained mount confidence in its rider. Time and again he lost his seat and sometimes sustained heavy falls. If there was a deep rut or a rabbit hole in his path he was sure to approach it in such a way that his horse balked or stumbled, and as often as not down he came with his face in the mud. A plowboy, enlisted as a hussar or dragoon, would learn more horsemanship in a week at riding school than Napoleon learned in a lifetime of campaigning. The new campaign that was opening would require rapid movement on his part and perhaps, by the late summer of 1813, he had come to terms with his curious deficiency. He was not often seen on horseback but usually traveled by coach.

It was not a common coach, of the kind then used by ordinary passengers. Neither was it a light equipage, of the kind that one would have thought suitable for cross country journeys across a vast, rectangular battleground, intersected by many rivers. It was a huge, lumbering vehicle, painted green, seating

Garlic and Destiny

two, and specially sprung. It was pulled by six enormous Limousin horses, usually at a fast trot or a canter. It had, in addition to a numerous escort, two coachmen and the Mameluke Roustan on the box. It was fitted with an array of locked compartments, five huge lanterns, a supply of spare candles, a miniature armory, and a shakedown bed. It was at once a mobile headquarters and a small traveling hotel. Its very presence and passage through Saxon towns and villages created havoc and uproar, like the passage of a typhoon, and its approach could be heard a half-mile distant giving the nimble footed ample time to get out of the way. Between August and October, 1813, the coach transformed itself into a demoniac legend of the kind one associates with ghost stories, and General Odelaben, who accompanied its headlong progress to and fro between the Silesian frontier and Leipzig that autumn, was fascinated by it and by its manner of progression so that it became, for him and others, a symbol of Napoleon's personality and destiny.

Duty aides-de-camp, equerries, orderly officers, and outriders surrounded it wherever it went and this throng was invariably attended by twenty-four mounted chasseurs of the Guard. Four chasseurs only preceded it in spaced pairs. "The rest of us," says Odelaben, "were always in danger of breaking our necks or legs." At a word of command from the Emperor the entire cavalcade would go scurrying over the country at breakneck pace, everyone jostling and bumping for room to ride in the narrow roads and sometimes the pace would not even moderate when darkness fell. Attendance upon the Emperor involved far more risk than befell those present on the battlefield. Then, at another sharp command, the whole unwieldy procession would halt, and whenever this happened a set procedure that became a ritual would be observed.

The quartette of chasseurs ahead would form a square, having first fixed bayonets to their carbines and presented arms. Then the square would be enlarged by the rearward party and everybody would stand about in this posture while Napoleon obeyed a call of nature, or took a look through his spyglass at the enemy, using Caulaincourt's shoulder as a rest. Whenever the party bivouacked an enormous fire was lit so that the blaze pinpointed the Emperor's position. Then a table would be set and everyone except Berthier, Chief of Staff, or a commanding officer whose observations were required at the moment, would keep their distance, the square resolving itself into a semicircle. Awaiting an attack or maneuver Napoleon would prowl restlessly about the fire, taking snuff, kicking a pebble, or feeding the blaze with chunks of wood that invited a kick. "He was incapable of doing nothing," adds Odelaben.

Perhaps, of all those who followed the Emperor on these endless excursions, the maximum sympathy should go to Berthier, the only man to share the inside of the coach with his master. The journeys often went on all night and Napoleon's seat could be extended into a bed in which he slept as soundly as a child. But Berthier's seat was not so arranged. He was obliged to sit upright, no matter how far they were going but possibly sympathy with the Chief of Staff is misplaced. Alexandre Berthier had been bumping about Europe and the Near East alongside Napoleon for seventeen years and if the exercise sometimes exhausted him he did not show it. At any hour of the day or night his turnout was impeccable. And if asked the strength and position of any division in the Grand Army he could tell, without reference to the parade states that were kept locked in the coach. Napoleon, and even Napoleon's traveling carriage, has passed into legend but history has yet to do justice to his Sancho Panza.

Both sides had shamelessly exploited the fifty day truce in order to strengthen their forces but Napoleon seems to have been the more energetic. By now, billeted along the left bank of the Elbe, he could call on something approaching 400,000 men of whom at least 40,000 were cavalry. He had also assembled over 1,200 guns and these figures do not take into account the men he had garrisoning fortresses in Poland and Prussia.

Notwithstanding this the potential of the forces opposed to him was enormous. Under arms, in the three armies of the Allies, were nearly 200,000 Russians, about 150,000 Prussians, and 40,000 Swedes, including a strong Congreve rocket battery, a comparatively new weapon in the field, operated by a British contingent. In Bohemia, ready for action, were 120,000 Austrians but the real strength of the Allies lay in their immense reserves. If things went badly for them they could call upon another half-million recruits, whereas France was drained almost dry and very little could be expected from it in the way of replacements. The three sovereigns, Czar Alexander, Frederick William of Prussia and Francis of Austria, were with Schwartzenberg's army in the south and in the fighting ahead this general was to find their presence inhibiting. On the Inn and the Izonzo, in Italy, Eugène's new army was watching a strong Austrian force detailed to challenge any move he might make.

As usual Napoleon decided upon an offensive and once more his gambler's instinct inclined him to strike at the Allied armies before they made any attempt to concentrate. His success would depend upon the long-established superiority of the French in mobility and seizure of the initiative.

His main plan of attack was to maintain defensive operations in the south while developing an offensive from the north based on Hamburg, now in the grip of his most reliable lieutenant, Marshal Davout. In and around Dresden he concentrated the corps of Vandamme, Victor, Ney, Lauriston, Marmont, Macdonald and St. Cyr, together with the Guard and four Corps of Cavalry. The northern attack, led by Oudinot, was to thrust at Berlin and look for support from Davout, issuing from Hamburg. To perform this task Oudinot was given the corps of Bertrand, Reynier, and one Cavalry corps. Napoleon's principal object in this holding operation in the south, and vigorous attack in the north, was to draw the Russians and Prussians off from the Allied center and isolate them from Austria. If Oudinot won a victory in the Berlin area the Imperial main army could then invade Austria and knock that country out of the war in a week.

Blucher broke the terms of the truce by attacking Ney's forces before it had expired, and having learned that a strong force of Russians had already detached itself from Blucher's army at Silesia in the center, Napoleon modified his original plan to some extent and decided to attack "that debauched old Prussian dragoon" before Austria could seriously threaten his right flank, in the Dresden area. To this end he advanced eastward very rapidly, having made what provision he could to defend Dresden, a vitally important base for the campaign he had in mind.

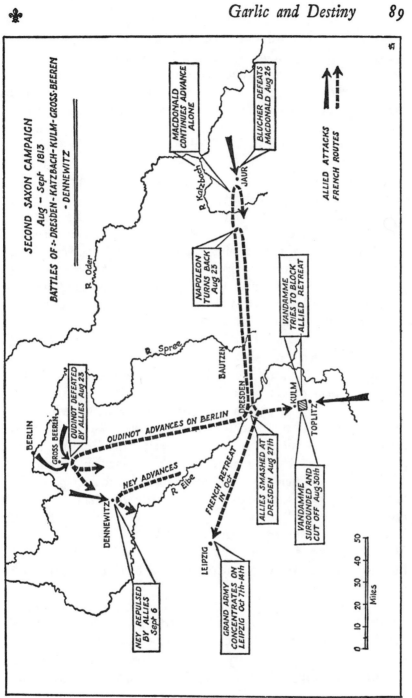

SECOND SAXON CAMPAIGN
Aug – Sept 1813
BATTLES OF :- DRESDEN - KATZBACH - KULM - GROSS-BEEREN
- DENNEWITZ

ALLIED ATTACKS
FRENCH ROUTES

MACDONALD CONTINUES ADVANCE ALONE

BLUCHER DEFEATS MACDONALD Aug 26

R. Oder

R. Katzbach

JAUR

NAPOLEON TURNS BACK Aug 25

VANDAMME TRIES TO BLOCK ALLIED RETREAT

R. Spree

BAUTZEN

OUDINOT DEFEATED BY ALLIES Aug 23

BERLIN

GROSS BEEREN

OUDINOT ADVANCES ON BERLIN

DRESDEN

KULM

TOPLITZ

NEY ADVANCES

R. Elbe

DENNEWITZ

ALLIES SMASHED AT DRESDEN Aug 27th

FRENCH RETREAT IN Oct

VANDAMME SURROUNDED AND CUT OFF Aug 30th

NEY REPULSED BY ALLIES Sept 6

LEIPZIG

GRAND ARMY CONCENTRATES ON LEIPZIG Oct 7th-14th

0 10 20 30 40 50
Miles

He moved forward over the old battlefield of Bautzen to Gorlitz with tremendous speed but even so he did not move fast enough. When he reached Gorlitz he had confirmation that the detached 40,000 Russians were on their way back to join the Army of Bohemia and this could only mean that a major attack on Dresden was imminent. He adapted to the changed situation with his customary flexibility, resolving on a swerve to the south aimed at Zittau in the hope of catching the advancing Austro-Russian army in the flank, but on learning that Blucher was advancing to meet him he changed his mind again and pushed on another forty miles east as far as Lowenberg. The prospects of outnumbering and destroying Blucher seemed excellent and there is no doubt but that the old warrior would have received a terrible drubbing had it not been for his strict adherence to the plan worked out at Allied headquarters —namely, to withdraw when alone in the presence of Napoleon. As soon as the Emperor's presence was reported the Army of Silesia turned and pulled back as fast as it could in the general direction of Jauer.

Then despatches arrived that compelled the French to change the entire plan of campaign in the center. The Austrians had not been fighting Napoleon for twenty years without learning the value of rapid movement against a selected objective. Courier after courier galloped into the Imperial camp from the hard-pressed St. Cyr, holding Dresden with a civilian population of 60,000 and a field force of only 30,000. Advancing on the city in tremendous strength was the entire Austrian army, reinforced by 40,000 Russians.

There was only one thing to be done. Command of the Blucher-hunting force was handed over to Macdonald while the main Grand Army executed an about-face and rushed back to defend Dresden.

It was then very early on the morning of August 25th, only ten days after the campaign had opened, and within three hours the Guard and supporting cavalry were heading towards the southern suburbs of the city, to be followed at top speed by Marmont and Victor, both aiming for Stolpen, about twelve miles east of the city.

"The army," says an officer who was present, "advanced like

a torrent. At 10 A.M. on the 25th the Guard were already in Dresden, having covered the almost incredible distance of 120 miles in four days, and this in full fighting kit."

In these days of motorized infantry, parachute drops, and almost one hundred per cent mechanization, such a feat would be considered commonplace but with nothing faster than a horse to pull their field pieces, and the necessity of relying on their feet to get them over roads that would not qualify as second class motor roads today, this march of the Guard deserves to stand as one of the most impressive in military annals. And yet, in the Grand Army, it was unremarkable. The foot soldiers of that era, and long before that time, performed marches that their descendants would find beyond human endurance. Harold, hurrying to London from Stamford Bridge, Yorkshire, to meet William the Norman covered 190 miles in six days. Davout's corps marched seventy miles in forty-four hours between Pressburg and Austerlitz in midwinter.

Behind the Guard, straggling into Dresden, came Marmont and Victor, who arrived as darkness fell and the appearance of their columns meant that the city was saved. Seeing Latour-Maubourg's cuirassiers thunder into the town the civilian population greeted them with cries of "Vive l'Empereur!" and excitement mounted when Napoleon himself appeared and began marshaling his forces for a thunderbolt attack on the Allies in the region of Pirna, south of the city walls.

II

There seems to be some doubt regarding the Allies' intention when they arrived within striking distance of Dresden. They had come there under the impression that the city was weakly defended, and their original plan had been to strike at Leipzig, about a hundred miles to the northwest and astride the main French line of communications. Napoleon's rapid advance eastward, however, had upset this plan and made the Austrians nervous of invasion, so that they shortened their blow and advanced against the more easterly of the French bases and one which, if lost, would have a shattering moral effect upon the still hesitant minor princes of Germany. What they did not bargain for was Napoleon's return in strength after so brief an interval, and at a council of war on the 25th it was decided, again in accordance with the general plan, to withdraw. That they did not, and the great battle of Dresden was lost to them, was due either to lack of control over their vanguard or to Napoleon's initiative. However it was, early in the afternoon of August 26th, the Allies attacked in six columns, prefacing their advance with a tremendous bombardment.

From the windows of his palace the king of Saxony watched a shower of balls and shells fall on his capital's streets, squares and ornamental gardens and there were many casualties among the civilian population. Under different circumstances an ordeal such as this would have resulted in a speedy surrender of the city. All the time it went on, however, French strength was building up, and having reassured the royal party by his presence Napoleon hurried off to the suburb of Pilnitz to direct a defense that was soon to develop into an irresistable advance. Reconnoitering here he came under direct fire and an Imperial page (one of the "bare necessities") was killed in his presence.

By late afternoon fighting became general and an Allied attack having been repulsed by tremendous fire at close range, Napoleon passed over to the offensive. Marshal Mortier, with the Young Guard, went in from the right, mainly against Russians, St. Cyr threw the Prussians out of the central suburbs, and Ney attacked from the Pirna and Plauen gates. Then the heavy cavalry drove the disorganized Allies out on to the plain and soon it was no longer a question of whether the Allies would take Dresden but whether they would rally sufficiently on the following day to prevent total collapse. Fighting all but ceased with the fall of darkness, although a corps of Austrians, fortified by an ample issue of brandy, made a desperate counterattack on the Plauen gate but were repulsed by General Dumoustier.

The appearance of French Cavalry on the level ground beyond the suburb of Fredrichstadt, had been decisive in the first day's fighting. Ney's infantry and the Guard had forced the enemy into the open but it was the cavalry that prevented all hope of an Allied counterattack and although nobody realized it at the time they were witnessing, in that furious advance, the penultimate charge of the greatest cavalryman of all time, Joachim

Murat, who had begun as an innkeeper's son in Cahors, Gascony, and ended his career as king in Naples. For years now Murat's thundering charges had set the seal on Napoleonic victories but those of Dresden were about the last of them, not only as far as he personally was concerned, but for all the veteran cuirassiers, chasseurs, dragoons, lancers and hussars in his squadrons. Dresden was to prove Murat's last triumph.

His presence there at all was due to a misunderstanding. His plotting with the Austrians down in Naples had made steady progress during the summer and had it not been for the unfortunate incident of the uncoded despatch, he might now have been fighting Eugène in Italy, or adding his advice to that of traitors like Moreau, Bernadotte and Jomini. As it was, tossed between the scorn of his wife Caroline and the threats of his brother-in-law, he had trailed into Dresden and smelled battle, a whiff that put everything else out of his mind until the excitement of action was over and he could reflect upon what was likely to happen to his crown if final victory eluded the Emperor. He did his work well that day and the next but it would have been better for his reputation as a soldier if an Allied ball had struck him and he had died in action like Bessières and Duroc.

At eleven o'clock that night Napoleon made a round of the bivouacs before returning to the palace. There would, he knew, be even sharper work tomorrow for the enemy, although heavily repulsed, was still in position on higher ground south of the city but the army's morale was high, much higher than it had been during the fifty day truce. The conscripts, no doubt, were exhausted by forced marches and combat but the men of Egypt, Austerlitz and Wagram, scented victory, and the man who had proved that he could accomplish anything was among them, a tired, hunched little figure with a pale, brooding face, who presently left them to sit closeted with Berthier over his war charts and parade states, "the Emperor's bible" as they were known among the staff. Perhaps he shared their confidence, or perhaps he was too exhausted to care. The next day—the day of his last great victory in a chain of fifty triumphs on the field—he was to fall sick from a stomach disorder, or the effects of a drenching, or both. This minor indisposition was to cost him and them a campaign, possibly the war.

III

Fighting was resumed at six A.M. the next morning and there was never a doubt concerning the issue.

Napoleon's design was to pin down the enemy's center and drive in both wings while Vandamme, whose corps was in position higher up the Elbe in the vicinity of Tetschen, moved across to cut off the Allies' retreat into the rugged defiles of the Bohemian mountains where there were no roads and few tracks.

Luck was with him that day. In the enemy's line was a space left for General Klenau's Austrians, expected to arrive at any moment and the gap extended between the enemy's left and center. At least a dozen of the Allied senior commanders present had been fighting Napoleon for years and in their ranks were three men who had learned their trade in the French army. In spite of this Schwartzenberg and the sovereigns committed the unbelievable folly of leaving a wide breach in their defenses in order to accommodate reinforcements that might or might not arrive. Napoleon exploited their error to the full. Sending Murat, Victor and Latour-Maubourg far out on the right he told them to fall on the Allies' left wing with all the cavalry at their disposal as soon as the center and right were fully engaged. Meantime he opened a terrible cannonade and sent orders to Ney and Mortier to move in from the left.

It was a classic battle from the French viewpoint, worthy to take its place among the setpieces of 1800, 1805, 1807 and 1809. At seven A.M. the artillery of the Young Guard began pounding the enemy center, riveting Schwartzenberg's attention to the point where he expected the attack and thus keeping the fatal gap open. Torrential rain began to fall but the pounding continued. Artillery commanders in the Guard complained that their fire was doing no damage because the target was too high for the elevation of the guns but the order came, "Keep firing!" and one ball at least found a target. A gunner observed, at a range of about five hundred yards, a small group of mounted officers and laid his piece at the party. The first casualty was General Moreau, who, a moment before, had been discussing the situation with the Czar. The ball plowed through his horse and mangled both his legs, inflicting what was clearly a fatal wound. A subsequent discharge killed another talented French emigré, General Sainte-Priest, also serving with the Russians. It was rumored that the Czar had paid two million roubles to tempt Moreau from his American exile and fight against his countrymen. If this is so the investment was a bad one. Captain Barrès, coming up too late to take part in the battle, heard about Moreau's death the following day. "A punishment from Heaven!" he observed, piously, and made the requisite note in his diary, adding with satisfaction that his own company's losses that day were two wounded.

The great Republican General, once the idol of France and a serious rival of General Bonaparte, was carried from the field on a litter made of Cossack lances and both legs were amputated in a cottage, Moreau smoking a cigar and, according to a witness, not uttering a groan. Twice removed owing to advances of the French, his final resting place was a baker's house in a Bohemian village. In a letter dictated to his wife he said, "That rascal Bonaparte is always fortunate." He died two days later and his embalmed body was conveyed to St. Petersburg where it was buried with military honors.

In the meantime the cavalry attack on the French right was developing according to plan. At eleven A.M., with rain still falling in sheets, Murat and Victor swept down on the Allied left and rode into the gap still awaiting the arrival of the laggard Klenau. Observers training their glasses on this part of the field saw the flicker of French sabers as the gorgeously attired Murat led his squadrons into the heart of the enemy's wing, and out on the French left things were going equally well, Ney, Marmont, Mortier, St. Cyr and the cavalryman Nansouty, driving the Allies' right back upon their center. By three in the afternoon the Coalition troops were in headlong flight and Napoleon, reflecting that Vandamme's corps was advancing across their line of retreat, was justified in regarding the battle a potential Wagram. He had confronted a superior army and driven it from the field in a day and a half's fighting, and this success had been achieved by men who had gone into action at the end of a hundred miles of forced marching. But Napoleon, in this instance, was wrong. The campaign of Saxony was not like any previous campaign he had fought. Its scale was too vast and its contestants too scattered and numerous to be beaten in any single battle, however complete that victory might seem. Apart from that, during the second day's fighting at Dresden, he was a sick man and when he returned to the Saxon king's palace that night he was obliged to leave pursuit to others who lacked his unique sense of urgency. Peeling off his dripping grey coat he threw himself down to sleep, the first rest he had had in thirty-six hours. The opportunity to knock Austria out of the war at a blow was lost through factors outside his personal control.

IV

The listlessness that characterized Napoleon's behavior that night and on the subsequent day, when triumph was within his grasp, has been the subject of dispute for a century and a half. It is difficult to see why. Not even a military genius can make clear-cut decisions when he is attacked by diarrhea, brought on by garlic taken in some mutton stew and aggravated by a day spent in the saddle under drenching rain. "He looked," says his valet Constant, who received him on his return, "as if he had been dragged from the river." Count Daru, his companion on the road from Moscow, encountered him on the way back to Dresden and Napoleon told him briefly that he had been obliged to give up direction of the pursuit, having been assailed with violent stomach pains. He was better the following day but he was still not himself. Even a touch of garlic has a place in the history of nations and the major opportunity was lost, as it almost always was when Napoleon had to leave major strategical decisions to his marshals, even the best of them like Masséna and Davout. In this case responsibility rested on the impulsive General Vandamme.

Napoleon's sudden illness is only one factor in a chain of misfortunes that robbed him of a decision between Dresden and the defiles of Bohemia. There were others and more important ones, notably complete failure on the part of the two men commanding his two other armies in action that week—Marshal Macdonald, facing the Prussian Blucher across the river Katzbach on the Silesian frontier, and Marshal Oudinot, charged with bringing the Allied army of the north to battle outside Berlin. Both ran into serious trouble and both were ignominiously defeated. The repercussions of those defeats, plus the subsequent folly of Vandamme, robbed France of all the fruits of the Dresden triumph.

Oudinot's defeat was the least disastrous of the French reverses. Hoping to enhance his reputation by capturing Berlin, overwhelming and perhaps capturing Bernadotte, and preventing Swedes and Prussians in the north advancing to the Elbe, Oudinot (never at any time more than a promoted grenadier, despite his reputation for bravery in the field) marched rapidly north and was approaching his objective by August 20th, five days after the resumption of hostilities. He had with him, in addition to his own troops, the Fourth Corps under Bertrand, and the Seventh, under Reynier, both capable soldiers. In all he led a body of sixty-four thousand men. Their quality, however, was inferior. Only half of them were French and the other half was composed of Italians and Saxons, the latter of questionable loyalty. The country over which he was advancing was broken up by marshes, watercourses and forests, so that concentration proved difficult. Awaiting him, Bernadotte had a mixed force of Swedes, Russians and Prussians that Madame Oudinot, in her memoirs, puts as high as ninety thousand. This figure is probably an exaggeration.

The French stormed the little town of Treblin on the 21st and continued their advance, much to Bernadotte's concern for his own inclination was to retreat across the Spree and abandon the Prussian capital. The Prussian commander, Von Bulow, would not countenance this and determined to stand and fight at the village of Gross-Beeren, less than thirty kilometers south of Berlin.

Oudinot ordered his advance in three columns, with Bertrand on the right, Reynier in the center and himself on the left, but Bertrand's corps was held up by the enemy and its commander showed too much caution, whereas Reynier, having stormed his objectives, was too rash and advanced without waiting for Oudinot so that he soon found himself attacked by the main body of Bernadotte's army. Thrown back he lost 2,000 prisoners and would have been annihilated had not Oudinot converted the attack into a fighting retreat and retired on Wittenburg, on the Elbe. Bad weather prevented pursuit, and, viewed all round, Oudinot was lucky to get off with comparatively little loss. The attempt on Berlin, however, had been foiled. What was worse the morale of the Prussians and Swedes had been given a tremendous boost at a time when the Allies were much in need of encouragement.

They were getting more than they had hoped for in another quarter of the immense battlefield, this time east of the river Katzbach, on the road to Jauer, the direction in which Blucher had retired when facing the main strength of the Grand Army on August 22nd. It was here, aided by poor judgment on the part of Marshal Macdonald and very heavy rainfall, that Blucher won the most resounding Allied victory up to that time, a triumph that made Bernadotte's victory outside Berlin trifling when reckoned in terms of prisoners, captured guns and damage to French morale.

It will be recalled that Napoleon handed over his command to Macdonald when he had been obliged to turn and hurry to St. Cyr's assistance at Dresden. Macdonald, son of a Scots clansman who had taken service with France after the defeat of the Young Pretender in 1746, was a competent and very honorable man but a singularly unlucky general. Colonel Marbot, who fought under him and has left us a detailed account of the drubbing the French received on the Katzbach, says that Macdonald's ideas were always sound and practical but inflexibility robbed him of the ability to make them work on the battlefield. A study of what occurred when Macdonald was left to cope with Blucher while the Emperor won the battle of Dresden confirms Marbot's judgment.

No sooner had he learned that Napoleon and the bulk of his army were on their way back to Dresden than Blucher halted his retreat and began to probe westward again, confident that he could now engage the French on more than equal terms.

Macdonald, massed on the left bank of the river with 75,000 men, should have remained where he was and awaited attack. The ground, cut up into wooded hillocks, was favorable to infantry and of Macdonald's total force only 6,000 were mounted, a corps commanded by General Sébastiani opposed to three times that number of cavalry in Blucher's Army of Silesia.

The bridges over the Katzbach were few and the fords narrow, so that any attack on the part of the Prussians could have been repulsed with heavy loss, the French being amply protected by the stream. On August 26th, however, Macdonald made up his mind to advance and being a precise man gave his orders in such detail that it was early afternoon before the French cavalry were across and approaching the plateau of Jauer. Marbot, colonel of the 23rd Chausseurs and riding with Exelman's division, was surprised to find no opposition on the far bank and at once suspected a trap. Apparently Marshal Macdonald did not, for he pressed on, notwithstanding heavy skies that promised rain and would increase his difficulties in the event of a hasty retreat.

In his memoirs Macdonald declares that Napoleon had ordered him to advance on Breslau, pointing out the necessity of a diversion. This is probably true but Napoleon also expected a subordinate commander leading 75,000 men to use his common sense. By putting a rising river at his back in the face of superior cavalry Macdonald was taking a terrible risk.

Colonel Marbot's fears of an ambush were soon justified. Blucher had laid a trap and Macdonald walked straight into it. The narrow road leading up to the plateau proved so slippery that horses and men floundered and guns sank axle-deep in mud. Three French cavalry regiments had reached the summit—they had to dismount to do it—when they were set upon by Prussian Uhlans and a sharp fight ensued of which, for the moment, the French had the advantage. Marbot, whose Chasseurs were mixed up in this melée, tells how an unhorsed Prussian colonel trotted at his stirrup leather for fifteen minutes, crying, "You are my guardian angel!" The angel found him a horse and sent him to the rear as a prisoner and the incident was to have a pleasing sequel later in the campaign.

The plateau was now erupting with Prussians, both horse and foot, who had been concealed in clumps of woodland, and as the engagement became general the threatened rain began to fall, so that the muskets of the infantry were useless. A curious situation developed at a point where the French chasseurs, having dispersed the Uhlans, confronted an unbroken Prussian square. The horsemen could not reach the infantry and the infantry could not fire at the cavalry. Both groups stood in pouring rain and glared at one another but not for long. As more French appeared on the plateau, and lancers opened up the square for the sabers of the chasseurs, Sébastiani's horsemen were charged by twenty thousand Prussian cavalry, and horse and foot were pushed off the plateau, the Prussians bringing up guns to complete the rout.

Descent down to the river level under cannon fire was a terrifying ordeal for a mounted man and Marbot says that he owed his life to his clever Turkish horse, who minced along the edge of the precipice "like a cat on a roof." To the dismay of the beaten army the level of the river had risen very considerably during the battle and was now lapping the few bridges, whereas the fords were all but unpassable. As many men were drowned as died under the hail of grapeshot poured on them from the plateau, or the sabers and lances of Prussian cavalry that had found an easier descent and ridden along the bank to break up the mob of fugitives.

Not for years had a Napoleonic army been so utterly demoralized, for even during the long trek across the snow from Moscow the honor of the eagles had been safe with Ney and his starving, frostbitten rearguard who had defied all the Cossacks of the Czar but here was seen the fatal weakness of the 1813 levies. The young conscripts of Lutzen and Bautzen had learned very quickly that glory is an expensive luxury for untrained men. Marbot's regiment, a splendidly disciplined body, recrossed the river with the loss of two troopers but had it not been for the presence, on the far bank, of General Saint-Germain's fresh division of cavalry that mounted a sharp counter-attack, French losses would have been more severe than was the case. They were heavy enough to daunt Macdonald—thirteen thousand killed or drowned, twenty thousand prisoners, and fifty guns, including all but one of Sébastiani's pieces.

Concerning the single surviving gun Macdonald tells a story that indicates how Napoleon viewed this disaster. Fearing to lose his last gun Sébastiani sent it along with the baggage train and it was captured during the pursuit, pressed by Blucher for five days. "The artillery is for the protection of the troops and not to be defended by baggage wagons!" roared the Emperor, within the hearing of the general's men. Sébastiani was so humiliated by this public rebuke that he wanted to blow out his brains. It required all Macdonald's tact and patience to calm him.

Macdonald's behavior after the battle illustrates the type of man he was. A lesser man would have blamed the weather and terrain, or the Imperial command to push on at all costs and attack Breslau, but that was not Macdonald's way. He called all officers of colonel and above together, told them that every man in the army had done his duty and himself accepted full responsibility for the disaster. "The loss of the battle was due to one man only, myself!" he said, and Marbot, who heard the frank admission adds, "This noble confession disarmed criticism and each man did his utmost to contribute to the safety of the army during the retreat to the Elbe."

Reorganizing at Pilnitz a few days later Marbot learned that not all Prussians shared Blucher's hatred of the French. He received a letter of thanks from Herr Von Blankensee, the colonel whose life he had saved during the cavalry melée on the Jauer plateau and who now returned to him a lieutenant and ten troopers from the 23rd Chasseurs, men who had been wounded and taken prisoner after Von Blankensee had been rescued by his own troops. The gesture, unthinkable in terms of modern war, shows that chivalrous conduct in the field lived on into the nineteenth century but it was becoming rare under the pressures of Continental strife, as is illustrated by Vandamme's reception by the Czar, after the Frenchman had been captured, together with most of his men, in the Allied withdrawal from Dresden. For it was Vandamme, the man whom Napoleon once designated as potential commander of the invasion of the Underworld, who was personally responsible for the third disaster that struck the French army in the week of its great victory at Dresden on August 26th.

V

The garlic, the weather, pressure of affairs or possibly over-confidence on Napoleon's part, had resulted in a situation in which Vandamme became the key figure in the pursuit of the beaten Coalition, on August 30th.

Northern Bohemia, a place of wooded mountain slopes and deep, rock-strewn defiles, was no place for a man of Vandamme's temperament to maneuver troops. Initially he was well placed across the Allied line of retreat but a prudent general would have played a waiting game until the corps of Marmont and St. Cyr, with Murat's victorious cavalry in support, could move up to help him block the columns of Austrians, Russians and Prussians streaming back from Dresden. Dropping down on to the plain of Kulm, about sixty miles south of the city and only fifteen from the Elbe, he found himself vigorously attacked by the Russian Guard in superior numbers and retreated into a de-file leading northeast to Peterswalde, the direction from which he had approached after crossing the Elbe a few days earlier. At the outlet of the gorge, however, he ran headlong into a Prussian corps led by Kleist and each column, under the impres-sion that it was trapped, flew at one another in the hope of breaking a way out of the trap.

For a time the battle was indecisive but the advantage lay with the Prussians for the Russian Guards were soon pressing on the rear of Vandamme's column and the French were neatly boxed between thousands of Dresden fugitives driving forward to Toplitz where they had a pile-up of stores, and the Russian General, Ostermann, who believed that he was fighting to save the Czar from capture. Vandamme fought on as long as he could but in the end he was obliged to surrender, along with Generals Haxo, Guyon and seven thousand troops. Five thou-sand others were casualties.

General Corbincau saved what remained of the corps by an action typical of the spirit that had won so many battles for France since the days of Sambre-et-Meuse. Heading a furious cavalry charge up the hill towards Peterswalde he stormed the guns, sabered the gunners, and opened a passage through which survivors could fall back on the vanguard of the Grand Army, coming up too late to avert the disaster.

The action had an effect out of all proportion to the numbers engaged or the casualties inflicted upon Vandamme's troops. On the morning of August 30th the Coalition army had been little more than a beaten mob, falling back in disorder upon its Bohemian bases. Its rank and file were dispirited and its leaders in despair. By evening the same day, with seven thousand prisoners including Vandamme, it could re-enter Toplitz as a victorious army home from what could now pass as a successful raid on Napoleon's headquarters. Some of the humiliation inflicted upon the sovereigns at Dresden showed itself in spleen at the expense of the prisoners. Vandamme, brought before the Czar, was taunted for his brigandage in Germany. He answered with a sneer, "At least I have not been accused of killing my own father," referring to current belief that Czar Alexander had played a role in the assassination of Czar Paul, his predecessor.

Captain Barrès, whose regiment had been part of the rearward force of the French pursuit, was marginally involved in this debacle and was himself lucky to escape death or capture. He received a Cossack lance thrust in his right shoulder and in the sporadic fighting in the forests and gorges north of Toplitz, he lost eight more of his men. His company were fighting a frantic rearguard action again all day on the 31st. "My weapons were so encrusted that bullets would not enter the barrel," he records. Almost one-third of his battalion were lost in this day-long fight and the survivors escaped by lighting great bivouac fires and withdrawing into even wilder country under cover of darkness. It was not until the morning of September 1st that Barrès learned of Vandamme's capture and realized why his people had been so violently attacked. On the following day his diary records, "For six days we had been without food. I ate nothing but the strawberries and bilberries that abounded in the woods. At last the canteen-woman of the company, in whose cart I had some provisions, rejoined us. The wretched woman had abandoned us when she saw us entering such a wild country." In the circumstances, and encumbered with a loaded wagon, one can scarcely criticize her caution. Bad roads and no lack of nerve had probably halted her, for most records of the period establish that the courage of the regimental cantinières equaled that of Napoleon's soldiers. Often enough they were serving drinks and tending wounded under fire.

Napoleon, still pivoted on Dresden, received the news of Macdonald's defeat at the Katzbach at 8:30 P.M. on August 28th. Before morning news came of Oudinot's reverse at Gross-Beeren and his retreat to the Elbe. At two o'clock on the morning of the 31st the Emperor was roused and told what had happened to Vandamme in the Bohemian forests. Baron Fain, compiler of the "Manuscript of 1813," suggests that he accepted news of this string of disasters philosophically, toying with a pair of dividers and quietly repeating the lines of a poem by Corneille that seemed to him applicable:—

J'ai servi, commandé, vaincu quarante années;
Du monde entre mes mains j'ai vu les destinées;
Et j'ai toujours connu qu'en chaque événement
Le destin des états dépendait d'un moment.

Destiny had another buffet for him that week, surely the unluckiest of his career. For many years it had been the custom in the Imperial army that the aide-de-camp bringing good news was promoted on the spot. This was the way the marshals regulated the seniority of the young men on the staffs but there were few promotions of this kind in the late summer and autumn of 1813. Within a week of the tidings of Gross-Beeren, Katzbach and Kulm, news came of a fourth disaster, this time involving Ney, who had replaced the defeated Oudinot in the north. Despite his reverses Napoleon had still not abandoned his plan of taking Berlin, designed to draw the bulk of Allied strength away from Austria and isolate a power he felt sure he could detach, given a little luck and one more determined effort.

About forty miles due south of Berlin lies the town of Baruth and Ney received orders to march on it, with the general idea of preventing the Allies in the north advancing on the Elbe and to keep them separated from Blucher who was still menacing Macdonald in the river country east of Dresden, and also from Schwartzenberg, who was striving to restore order to his battalions at Toplitz, in Bohemia. Once again it was an excellent strategical conception but it depended for its success on the part Napoleon himself promised to play in it, namely, to join Ney in his thrust and assemble the main body of the Grand Army at Luckau, south of Baruth, by September 6th.

Ney rushed off on his errand with his usual impetuosity but Napoleon was unable to give him the support he had promised. News reached Dresden that the enfeebled army of Macdonald was having great difficulty in holding its own against Blucher and on September 3rd the Emperor took the road to Bautzen for the third time since May, in order to go to the Scotsman's assistance.

It was the same game of catch-as-catch-can all over again. The moment Blucher realized Napoleon was in personal command he drew back and his refusal to stand and fight, says Odeleben, put Napoleon in a furious temper. By September 6th St. Cyr, left in Dresden, was appealing for help once more, rumors having spread that Ney was in difficulties and that Schwartzenberg was making ready to make a second attempt upon the Saxon capital. Back he went, cursing the men who would throw their whole weight against any combination of his lieutenants but would not stand and fight him in any one theater of the war. They were already calling him "The Bautzen Messenger" and surely it must have been clear to him by now that no one man, and no single army, however ardent and venturesome, could contain four strong adversaries, grouped into three units and each capable of offensive or defensive action. He was like a superb duelist in an arena sown with obstacles. His blade and his skill were more than equal to any two of his adversaries but there was always a third working round towards his rear, passing right or left outside his range and moving over terrain that favored the stealthy and the cautious. He could not pin down the alert Blucher. He could not eliminate Bernadotte and his aggressive partner, Von Bulow. To storm into Bohemia and bring Schwartzenberg's army to battle was beyond his resources. All that he could do was mask his base of operations, prevent the Allies from uniting in overwhelming strength, and hope that Ney would send him cheering news from the north. Reconnaissance raids and skirmishes, big and little, continued east and south of Dresden and in one of them Blucher's son was made prisoner. The capture was small consolation for the loss of Vandamme and most of his men.

On September 8th a dispatch arrived from Ney but it contained news that made everyone at Headquarters staff aware that territory east of the Elbe would soon be untenable and that a major battle, if indeed one could be forced upon the Allies, would have to be fought much further west, in the neighborhood of Leipzig and also that Dresden would have to be abandoned. For Michel Ney, storming Berlinwards at the head of Oudinot's command, had met the Allied Army of the North at Dennewitz, some twenty-five miles northeast of the Elbe, and had been all but annihilated, losing 22,000 men (13,000 of them prisoners), forty of his guns, and four hundred wagon loads of stores. And along with this intelligence came news that confirmed the pessimists in their belief that the whole of Germany was as good as lost, for Ney's Saxons, until then the most loyal German auxiliaries in the Grand Army, had fled or deserted in the face of the enemy.

Ney's offensive had been botched, partly by his own delay but more certainly by Allied strength, their returning confidence and Prussian courage. Bertrand, attacking Bernadotte's right wing was held and Ney, three hours late coming up, found himself opposed by Bulow and the victors of Gross-Beeren, and was unable to make headway against them. Then, without warning, the Saxons gave way, streaming from the field or passing straight over to the enemy, so that Prussian cavalry rode into the gap and sent the French reeling back on Torgau. The fugitive army was split into two halves by the ferocity of the attack and retired, as best it could, in opposite directions.

Bernadotte could claim no credit for this victory. By the time he came up with his Swedes the work was done and he could move in safety upon the Elbe, a long if somewhat leisurely step towards the throne he hoped was awaiting him in Paris. Bernadotte on the Elbe, Blucher ready to harry Macdonald's weakened army into Dresden, Schwartzenberg already feeling with his left for Leipzig. "My game of chess," Napoleon said to Marmont, "is becoming confused." It was desperately confused and high time to concentrate nearer France. In another fortnight it might be too late and the Allies would trap what remained of the Grand Army in hostile territory two hundred miles east of its sources of ammunition, remounts, and the trickle of recruits assembling on the Rhine and the Saale.

Oudinot, restored to favor as he had prophesied, was left to cover the rear with part of the Young Guard. The main body marched westward through thin autumn rain to unite with Ney's shattered regiments moving down from the north. The rendevous was Leipzig, a name that would soon dominate every other in the two campaigns of Saxony.

8

THE SENIOR COMMANDERS of the Grand Army who
had ridden into Saxony with Napoleon in April had not hoped
for much. There was not one among them who would not
have settled for a compromised peace that left them their
honors, their rank, their not inconsiderable incomes, and a
chance of repose in the company of wives and family after
twenty years' campaigning. Now that they were moving back
they would have accepted even less, the sacrifice of Italy and
even a dignified withdrawal behind France's natural frontiers
so long as they could keep the Lowlands. They saw little hope
of this, knowing their chief too well and understanding that
the armies of the Czar, Frederick William, and Francis of Austria, were beginning to acquire a taste for triumph. From the
standpoint of the marshals there would seem to be nothing
ahead but more lost fields, further withdrawals, and perhaps, at
the end of it all, a re-establishment of the old nobility in France
that would involve them all in their master's ruin. In spite
of this they remained loyal, all but Murat. Some of them would
stay loyal for a long time but only one for as long as he lived.

They were already reduced in numbers. Bessières and Duroc
were dead. Vandamme, together with Generals Guyon and
Haxo, were on their way to Siberia. Jomini was fighting with
the Allies. General Kirchener lay buried at Bautzen. General
Sibuet's body had been washed down the Katzbach. Others were
nursing severe wounds.

Battle of the Nations

The loyalty of the junior officers was not in question, not even after four defeats in thirteen days. Men like Colonel Marbot of the Chasseurs, and Captain Barrès of the Infantry of the Line, were professionals through and through. Wounds, casualties and costly battles were the small change of their lives and had been since they were youths. They soldiered on, conscientiously and uncomplaining, taking the good with the bad, obeying orders, and leaving the big decisions to their seniors. Shaving before a mirror hung on a branch outside his bivouac one morning Colonel Marbot felt a tap on the shoulder and looked round into the grey eyes of the Emperor, making a reconnaissance with a single aide-de-camp. He asked Marbot to take command of his escort and Marbot, wiping the lather from his face, saddled up and followed him about all day. "Nor had I any fault to find with him in the matter of his kindness to me," he records, recalling the incident years later. Captain Barrès and his company, fighting their way down the Elbe that September, confined their grumbling to the poor quality of the cavalry that they had to protect. At one point, where the Cossacks swarmed on the rearguard, Barrès hid his company in a churchyard and opened a pointblank fire on the Russian horsemen as they chased a body of French dragoons down the road. "What a raking they got and how swiftly they disappeared," he remembers with relish. Men like this would hold together in the face of disaster, sustained by experience and regimental pride.

It was otherwise with the conscripts, the boys whose unexpected steadiness had won the battles of Lutzen, Bautzen and Dresden. One real victory, four disasters and endless marches across a country stripped bare by marching columns, had accounted for 150,000 of them in five weeks. Another 50,000 lay in hospitals. The rest, pitifully undernourished, fell out on the line of march and died under hedges, or surrendered and went to swell the increasing numbers of Frenchmen in captivity. Their plight during this second half of the campaign is accurately described by the authors of the documentary novels, *The Story of a Conscript of 1813* and *Waterloo*. Severely wounded at Lutzen their hero, Joseph Bertha, had spent four months in the hospital and rejoined his unit during the concentration on Leipzig in September. His original squad, composed of local men, had dwindled to three, himself and his comrades Zebedee and Klipfel. Attacked by Prussian hussars on the edge of a wood it was soon reduced to two. Trapped in a muddy trench Bertha was saved from the sabers of the horsemen by a lucky shot but Klipfel was cut to pieces, crying for help. "It is a dreadful thing to hear one of your old friends appealing to you for help and to be unable to render it but there were too many of them, they quite surrounded him," says Zebedee who saw it happen.

"Too many of them." It was true of every wasted corps struggling along the banks of the Elbe in the direction of Leipzig and youngsters like Bertha, fighting and marching all day, and standing guard half the night, had not learned how to husband such food as could be found, how to drive a bargain with peasants, or how to exist on horseflesh soup cooked in a cuirass and seasoned with black powder. The veteran NCOs pitied them but they had as much as they could do to keep themselves fit and active, to close up the columns and prevent further desertions. Orders had gone out after Kulm that one in every ten men found away from their unit was to be shot. Under these circumstances it says a great deal for the discipline of the Grand Army that Napoleon could still field 256,000 men and 784 guns at the end of September.

Behind the Grand Army confidence was ebbing and allies were stealing away one by one. The king of Bavaria wrote before the end of the month, saying that he could not promise to hold his people to the French alliance for more than six weeks. The Kingdom of Wurtemberg proved equally unreliable. On October 1st a few hundred Cossacks under Tchernichef stormed into Cassel, the capital of Westphalia, realm of Napoleon's brother Jerome. As useless in an emergency as his brother Joseph, King Jerome bolted for Coblenz. General Allix, commanding in Cassel, had a stouter heart. He rallied some troops and on October 13th had reoccupied the city and for this he was "granted" an annual pension of 6,000 francs a year. It does not seem to have occurred to the spoiled child of the Bonaparte clan that his reign was over and that Westphalia, a fairytale kingdom created for him a few years before, had no economic or geographical significance and would melt like a piece of confectionery in the current temperature of international affairs.

Still at Dresden, although part of his army had already concentrated further back, Napoleon juggled with various alternatives. The forces of Murat, Victor, Lauriston, the Pole, Poniatowski (soon to become the twenty-fifth marshal and hold the rank for thirty-six hours), and the best of the French cavalry, were just able to prevent Schwartzenberg's army from marching west. Bernadotte and his allies were temporarily checked on the lower Elbe but with the whole of Western Germany erupting some gigantic stroke was needed to stave off disaster. For a day or so the Emperor thought he had such a plan and its scope and boldness dazzled some of his lieutenants. It was a plan to reverse the situation, to shift all available forces *outside* the Allied ring and ravage the territory of the advancing sovereigns so that they would be compelled to retrace their steps and give battle. To do this he would have to withdraw his garrisons in the north and re-establish his lines on the Oder instead of the Elbe, already crossed by sections of the enemy. It was a daring plan, having the stamp of earlier Napoleonic campaigns, but in the end it proved impractical. News came in early October that Bavaria had broken away, that Wurtemberg had followed suit, that both former allies were already threatening the French frontier and also that the Czar had received a reinforcement of sixty thousand men, including Bashkirs and Tartars, who fought with bows and arrows and rode into battle in sheepskin uniforms. It was too late for such grandiose strategy and there was no real alternative but to fall back on Leipzig, concentrate there, and hope for the best. In the meantime Bernadotte's Army of the North had crossed the Elbe at Rosslau, below Wittenberg, and Blucher, with his battle-hardened Army of Silesia, had decided to march north and join him. Schwartzenberg, with 180,000 men in Bohemia, was edging westward in an effort to outflank the Grand Army. Saxony would have to be sacrificed and the only real problem to be settled now was should Dresden, its capital, be garrisoned or evacuated?

It was not an easy decision to make and reviewing it Napoleon changed his mind twice. In the end, probably as a political gesture, he left St. Cyr, one of his best defensive marshals, in the city with some 20,000 men. It was, as it turned out, another wrong decision. Saxony deserted him like all the other German states and the garrison of Dresden might have made all the difference at Leipzig later in the month. With 150,000 men the Emperor drew off towards the west. By October 8th he was at Wurzen, unaware that Blucher was on the point of joining his forces with those of Bernadotte. Six days later he entered Leipzig where Murat's forces, retreating before Schwartzenberg's army, joined him. The steel ring, now all but enclosing him, continued to contract day by day.

Macdonald was not a brilliant strategist but he was one of the few men around Napoleon who was never afraid to give him realistic advice. As long ago as January, when the marshal had had to fight his way back to the Baltic coast after half his army had deserted to the Russians, he had urged a calling-in of all the eastern garrisons and consolidation much further west. Now he offered similar counsel. "Retreat behind the Saale and defend the frontier," he told the Emperor. "We can hold the enemy there, but only by abandoning Germany." This excellent advice was ignored, partly because Napoleon was still reluctant to admit local defeat and look to the safety of his own realm but also because the Allies were already too close upon his heels to make disengagement possible.

As late as October 15th, the day before the opening of the most gigantic single battle of the Napoleonic wars, Murat was having to fight his way towards the Leipzig rendezvous and to the north Blucher was also closing in on the city. There was no prospect of getting off without a fight and in his heart Napoleon realized this and preferred to put a bold front on what was rapidly becoming a desperate situation. He still believed that he could best any Allied army separately and the results of spectacular victories in the past had conditioned him, psychologically, to a gambler's winner-take-all philosophy. Even now, however, it is doubtful if he really understood that he was not fighting governments but nations, as in Spain, and that a single victory would settle nothing for long.

It is easy enough, with the benefit of historical hindsight, to condemn his decision to stand at Dresden, and later at Leipzig, but in middle age most men's actions are governed by the experience gained in their youth. Napoleon had overturned every obstacle in his way for half a lifetime and it was very difficult for him to adjust to failure. After all, he had survived the Russian adventure and even in the summer campaign he, personally, had beaten the enemy every time he met him face to face. It was only his lieutenants who had been routed and it must have seemed to him, surveying the broad plain south of Leipzig on that October evening, that he had a good fighting chance of destroying Schwartzenberg and then turning north to cross the Parthe and overwhelm Blucher and the Swedish army in Blucher's rear.

He had with him now 157,000 men and against him, north and south, were ranged about 197,000, with another 100,000 reserves within call. The quality of the enemy's commanders did not impress him—Schwartzenberg and Bernadotte, deserters both; Czar Alexander, who had sat on the ground and wept after Austerlitz; Frederick William and Blucher, who had been driven right across Prussia after Jena and had surrendered every man and every gun; and the Austrian, General Meerveldt, who had twice been a prisoner-of-war and was to be captured again the following day. Abruptly he summoned the marshals and drew up a plan of battle.

II

The city of Leipzig, then with a population of 40,000, is situated on a plain girdled by three main waterways, the Parthe, the Pleisse, and the Elster, and numerous minor streams and dykes all connected to these rivers. Outside, along the right bank of the Elster and particularly to the south, east of the Pleisse, were many villages, linked by a network of roads. Between October 16th–18th each village was to become the scene of some of the bloodiest hand-to-hand encounters of the century.

To appreciate the ebb and flow of the three-day battle it is necessary to study the map. The names of the villages are not easily remembered by those unfamiliar with German but

there are certain keypoints in the three main areas of battle
that are mentioned again and again in all accounts of the engagement. Northwest of the city, along the river Elster, is
Mockern, where Marmont commanded, with orders to hold off
the Prussians. West of the city is Lindenau, where the main
road to Weissenfels and the west crossed the Elster on a single
bridge, the sole escape route of the French should they be defeated. To the south, just east of the Pleisse and running in a
broad semi-circle as far as the Parthe, were the fifteen to twenty
villages or hamlets used as rallying points by both sides—Connewitz, Dolitz, Probstheida, Zuckelhausen, Holzhausen, and
Molkau; and outside this inner ring, Markkleeberg, Wachau,
Liebertwolkwitz and Klein Possna. The main battlefield, excluding the areas around Mockern, in the north, and Lindenau,
in the west, extends for approximately two miles to the southeast and its outer circumference is about twice this distance.
There were several wooded patches but only one eminence, the
Kolmberg, or "Swedish Redoubt," rising midway between the
villages of Wachau and Liebertwolkwitz. This, on the night
before the battle, was the scene of a trivial incident that might
have won the campaign for France and secured the future of
Napoleon's dynasty.

At dusk on the 15th three white rockets soared from Schwartzenberg's lines, to be answered by three red ones from Blucher's
bivouacs, north of the Parthe. The Allies were signaling to one
another and making sure of one another's position. Macdonald,
not wanting the Swedish Redoubt to be occupied by the enemy,
sent Marbot's 23rd Chausseurs to watch it. Sitting there under
the stars on a clear night Marbot noticed a group of officers
ascend the high ground and heard them discoursing in French.
Hoping to capture some members of the enemy staff he sent
two squadrons left and right of the hill but unluckily a
trooper, dropping his sword and not wishing the reconnaissance team to escape, fired his carbine, killing a Prussian major. The group immediately fled and Marbot, unable to pursue
them because an enemy escort was approaching, lost the prize
of a lifetime. The group included the czar of Russia, the king
of Prussia and some of their closest advisers. It was the kind

of bad luck that dogged the Grand Army all the way from Moscow to Waterloo.

At nine o'clock the next morning, the battle opened on all three fronts. Blucher and the deserter, General Yorck, attacked Marmont at Mockern; the Austrian, General Gyulai, stormed into Lindenau with 19,000 men and on the main field, moving against Victor, Oudinot, Lauriston, Macdonald and Mortier in and around Wachau and Liebertwolkwitz; General Schwartzenberg's army attacked in four columns, with General Meerveldt thrusting over the Pleisse at Poniatowski, stationed in Connewitz. The cannonade was like nothing ever heard in the past, "one long continuous sound" says a combatant in the area where General Drouot was hammering the Allied center with a battery of one hundred and fifty guns.

Schwartzenberg's aim on this first day of battle was to work round the French right resting on the Pleisse but the ground here was swampy and he made little progress against the determined Poniatowski, clinging to a string of three villages on the right bank. Napoleon's intention was to smash through the enemy center at Guldengossa and roll up his right. As soon as the initial attacks of the Allies had been repulsed he was in a position to do this, for Schwartzenberg had committed too many men to his encircling movement against Poniatowski and the attack was still bogged down in the water meadows.

At two P.M. the French moved forward with irresistable impetus. Victor carried Wachau and Markkleeburg and swept on beyond Guldengossa, with Oudinot and the Guard in close support. Further left, Macdonald and Mortier, supported by Sébastiani's cavalry, overthrew everything in their path. An hour later Murat's cavalry charged through their lines to launch what began to look like the pursuit of a beaten army and away to the north the bells of Leipzig began to peal for an Imperial victory. It was premature applause. The Allies were shaken but they were far from beaten.

For once the Czar intervened to some purpose. Countermanding Schwartzenberg's orders he stopped the flow of reinforcements to his left wing and ordered a mass counterattack using all the reserves at his disposal, including thirteen squadrons of

Russian cuirassiers and their Cossack supports. This torrent of fresh Allied horsemen thundered down upon Murat's badly blown ten thousand, pushing them back over the ground they had won. Victor, to avoid being flanked, was obliged to fall back to Wachau, and Lauriston and Oudinot gave ground in the center but Macdonald clung desperately to the ruins of Leibertwolkwitz. At the same time, in concert with this furious cavalry attack, the Austrian General Meerveldt at last made good his crossing of the Pleisse on the French right flank, taking Connewitz from Poniatowski and storming the neighboring village of Dolitz but he had to fight every inch of the way and was almost annihilated. A counterattack by the Chausseurs of the Old Guard under General Curial not only hurled the Austrians back across the river but captured their General.

In the meantime two other battles, each of which would have qualified as a major clash under ordinary circumstances, were being fought west and north of the Elster, the one for the possession of the suburb of Lindenau, the other for Marmont's positions in Mockern and adjacent villages.

Both were vitally important to the French. If Bertrand was beaten at Lindenau the enemy would cut the bridge and the one escape route to France; if Marmont collapsed Blucher's Prussians would pour into the city and take the embattled main army in the rear. Bertrand acquitted himself well. For a time, and after seven hours' desperate fighting, the Austrian Gyulai carried and held Lindenau, but Bertrand threw him out again with the bayonet and thereafter refused to yield an inch of ground, thus securing the vital bridge over the Elster.

In the northern sector things did not go so well. Outnumbered, and furiously attacked by Yorck's corps, Marmont had to give ground but he did so slowly, retiring in good order on the suburbs of Halle and Gohlis. Ney was in command of the northern sector of the Grand Army and his dispatch of one of Souham's divisions, that would have been invaluable to Marmont, to a threatened sector in the battle around Wachau, was an error of judgment. Souham's men spent the day marching from one part of the field to another and did not fire a shot. With their help Marmont could have held Mockern.[1]

As autumn dusk stole over the fields firing began to die away and gradually all fighting ceased, both armies occupying practically the same ground as the night before. The Prussians were in Mockern but Schwartzenberg's Army of Bohemia, after having suffered very heavy casualties, had gained hardly a yard. Dazed by the din of battle the men of both sides lit their fires and spoiled one another's rest by sporadic alarms. Bertrand clung to the Lindenau bridge, looking over his shoulder at the prospect of a retreat. Napoleon, hoping to encourage the Poles who had fought so valiantly along the banks of the Pleisse, conferred a marshal's baton on their leader, Prince Poniatowski.[2] Elsewhere on that vast field men bandaged their own and their comrades' flesh wounds or, like the cavalry leader Latour-Maubourg, submitted to an amputation without anesthetic.

Out on the extreme left of the Grand Army Captain Barrès, of the 47th, spent an anxious night after an exceptionally bewildering day. Fighting on the left of Macdonald's Corps in the area of Holzhausen he had attacked a wood defended by Croats but as he advanced he was checked by cries of "Don't fire, we are French!" He gave the order to cease firing and at once became the target for a fusilade of musket shots, whereupon, ordering the charge, he burst into the wood and discovered a party of Croats with some French prisoners, one of whom called out, "To me, Barrès!" It was a captain of his own battalion who had been used by the Croats as a decoy. Those of the enemy who could run disappeared at once and emerging from dense cover, Barrès found no enemy in sight. To his left and center there was nothing but a pastoral landscape. To his right, he says, "it sounded as if all hell was loose." He raided the village of Klein-Possna for rations and bivouacked at a crossroads. He had no idea where he was and nobody could tell him where he could find his unit. All day he had fought a soldier's battle, acting entirely on his own initiative and had lost eight men wounded. "We were melting away day by day," he records. The next morning a cavalry general, Reiset, rode by and invited Barrès and his forty survivors to accompany them back to the main body but Barrès, with many years' battle experience behind him, politely declined the offer.

"Thank you, general," he said, "but if the battle should reopen while I am in the plain I should be pounded to bits among so many horses." Reiset, amused at the remark, agreed and rode away. It was hours later that Barrès found his battalion in Holthausen and they were agreeably surprised to see him, supposing him to have been killed or taken prisoner, together with all his men.

Marbot, fighting under Macdonald and Lauriston, also had an eventful day. Having moved up to occupy University Wood at Gross Possna, on the left of the battle line, his chasseurs were attacked by a mass of Russian and Austrian cavalry. They counterattacked under Sébastiani and drove the enemy off. Marbot lost a number of troopers in this clash and his senior major was wounded in the breast by a Cossack lance, ". . . in consequence of having omitted to adopt the customary protection of his rolled-up cloak," comments the colonel, a stickler for text book regulations.

Notwithstanding the fact that they had held their ground, however, the French rank and file were dispirited that night. The more intelligent among them were disconcerted by Headquarters' apparent lack of preparation for a retreat, particularly in the matter of bridges over the various waterways between the field and the road to Weissenfels leading to the French frontier. The lower ranks were beginning to wonder if there would ever be an end to all this marching and fighting against an enemy who seemed to outnumber them in every contest. The authors Erkmann and Chatrian echo the despondency of these men in a passage where their hero, Joseph Bertha, watches the movement of the Imperial Staff at Leipzig, its path cleared by mounted Grenadiers of the Guards, ". . . men like giants, with huge boots and tall bearskins that reached their shoulders, leaving only their eyes, noses and moustaches visible . . . everybody was rejoiced to call out, 'These fellows are on our side and they are terrible fighters.'" Then came the Emperor's staff, between 150 and 250 generals, marshals and officers, "mounted on thoroughbred horses and so covered with gold lace and decorations that one could hardly see the colour of their uniforms; some of them tall and thin, with haughty features, and others short and thick, with ruddy faces; others younger, sitting upright on their horses like statues, with flashing eyes and noses like eagles' beaks. It was magnificent and yet fearful. What struck me most among all these officers who had made Europe tremble for the past twenty years, was the appearance of Napoleon himself, in his old hat and grey overcoat. I think I see him still, as he passed me with his large firm set jaw and his massive head sunk in his shoulders. Everybody cried 'Vive l'Empereur!' but he said not a word; he noticed us no more than the fine rain drizzling through the air."

It is an authentic picture. Down through the decades of the nineteenth century hundreds of thousands of men who had witnessed that somber, striking spectacle were to recall it in their old age, when France was ruled by nonentities and glory was unfashionable. It was memories such as this that nurtured the Napoleonic legend and won, in the final instance, a more enduring victory than the autocrats won at Leipzig.

In the meantime, before the fighting began again, he was willing to compromise, to discover if anything at all could be salvaged from the wreck of his spring plans. He sent for the Austrian prisoner, General Meerveldt, and returned to that astonished gentleman his sword, surrendered the same afternoon at Dolitz, telling him to return to the Allied camp with fresh terms pending an armistice. He offered renunciation of Poland and Illyria, the independence of Holland, the Hanse towns, Spain (already lost) and a united Italy. Meerveldt rode off, congratulating himself on his luck, but no answer came to Napoleon, not even a courtesy reply. The Allies were resolved to fight on until the last Frenchman had recrossed the Rhine.

All day on the 17th there was an undeclared truce. The only firing, and that was halfhearted, came from the northwestern suburbs, where Marmont outfaced Blucher. In the meantime Bernadotte came up with his Swedes, and the Russian General Bennigsen joined the Allies with a considerable reinforcement, the two contingents adding something like 100,000 to the depleted ranks of the Coalition. The augmentation to French forces was limited to that of Reynier's Corps, perhaps ten

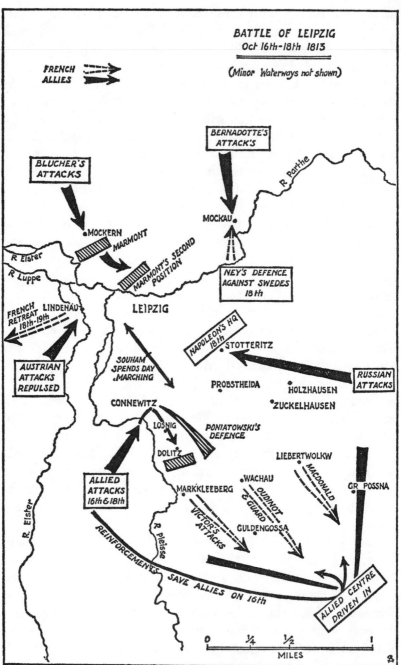

BATTLE OF LEIPZIG
Oct 16th–18th 1813

(Minor Waterways not shown)

FRENCH
ALLIES

BERNADOTTE'S
ATTACK'S

BLUCHER'S
ATTACKS

R. Parthe

MOCKAU

•MOCKERN

MARMONT

MARMONT'S SECOND
POSITION

NEY'S DEFENCE
AGAINST SWEDES
18th

R. Elster

R. Luppe

FRENCH LINDENAU
RETREAT
18th-19th

LEIPZIG

NAPOLEON'S HQ
18th

STOTTERITZ

SOUHAM
SPENDS DAY
•MARCHING

AUSTRIAN
ATTACKS
REPULSED

PROBSTHEIDA

HOLZHAUSEN

RUSSIAN
ATTACKS

•ZUCKELHAUSEN

CONNEWITZ

LOSNIG

PONIATOWSKI'S
DEFENCE

DOLITZ

LIEBERTWOLKW

•WACHAU

MACDONALD

R. Elster

ALLIED
ATTACKS
16th & 18th

MARKKLEEBERG

OUDINOT
& GUARD

GR. POSSNA

R. Pleisse

VICTOR'S
ATTACKS

GULDENGOSSA

REINFORCEMENTS SAVE ALLIES ON 16th

ALLIED CENTRE
DRIVEN IN

0   ¼   ½   1

MILES

thousand men. At midnight on the 17th, no reply having come from the sovereigns, Napoleon drew in his outposts and gave orders for a renewal of the battle.

III

Retreat was in his mind. It could hardly have been otherwise for the French now lay in an arc around the closely invested city, with only one road open to the west and even that menaced. The right wing, under Murat, was anchored to the villages of Connewitz and Dolitz on the Pleisse. The center, held by reliable men like Macdonald and Oudinot, was at Probstheida occupying a salient. The left, commanded by Ney, reached northward to Gohlis, where Marmont was stationed to repel the Prussians. Napoleon, having spent most of the night on rounds that took him as far east as Reudnitz to confer with Ney, and as far west as Lindenau to confer with Bertrand, fixed his headquarters at Stotteritz, a short way behind the dangerously angled center at Probstheida. Cannon began firing at 8 A.M. and orders went to Bertrand to start moving out on the Weissenfels road but at all costs to hold the Elster bridge open.

Once more the fighting centered on three points but now they were less widely separated than on the 16th. The remarkable feature of this bloody day is the successful defense of almost every sector of the arc, notwithstanding dwindling ammunition stocks, cannon and small arms rendered useless by repeated firing, vast inferiority of numbers, treachery within the French ranks, and the fury of the Allied attacks, particularly on the center where the Coalition troops fought with great determination in the face of daunting losses.

In the Lindenau area Bertrand easily beat off the attacks of Gyulai and began to execute a successful withdrawal, and during the morning and early afternoon Ney and Marmont kept the Prussians and Swedes at bay in the area of the Parthe, but the fighting in the center, between the river Pleisse and the French pivot at Probstheida, reached a new pitch of ferocity. Ten times Schwartzenberg assaulted Connewitz, Probstheida and the ground in between, and ten times he was flung back, by the Poles in Connewitz, by Victor's and Lauriston's infantry in the center. Here the combatants became so interlocked that the battle lost all cohesion and resolved itself into a hundred desperate bayonet fights but by mid afternoon the Russian, Barclay de Tolly, commanding the Allies in this sector, was obliged to go over to the defensive and Schwartzenberg had been stopped dead by Poniatowski at Connewitz.

Progress of a sort was being made on the right of the Allied line, however, for Bennigsen, whose troops were relatively fresh, took Holzhausen and advanced almost to Stotteritz where Napoleon was posted with the Guard. A counterattack by the veterans checked the Allied thrust and the pressure along the battlefront to the extreme left of the French, where Ney was fighting desperately to prevent Bernadotte and Blucher breaking through to enfilade the entire French line.

In mid afternoon came a new crisis on the French left. Thousands of Saxons, mostly from Reynier's corps and opposing Bernadotte, suddenly deserted to the enemy, taking with them forty pieces of cannon. The defection was so swift and unexpected that French cavalry, supposing the Saxons to be advancing to the attack, gave them a cheer. The loss was more than could be withstood by the hardpressed left wing and Ney contracted his line at once, ordering all Saxons who had not deserted to the rear. A defiant Saxon sergeant, who had intended to desert, shouted "To Paris, to Paris!" as he passed through the lines. A French sergeant, maddened by this exhibition of treachery, shouted back "To Dresden!" and shot him dead. The mass desertion was probably premeditated and had been arranged with Bernadotte in advance, for the crown prince of Sweden had led a Saxon corps into battle at Wagram, in 1809, when they had panicked and fled.[3]

Pressure in this quarter now increased in direct relation to French difficulties but there was no collapse, not even when Bernadotte, using a concentration of guns and the new Congreve rockets[4] operated by a British team, took the village of Paunsdorf. Napoleon at once retook it with the Young Guard but finding it untenable retired with Ney to a line based on Schonefeld, Sellerhausen and Stuntz.

According to Lord Londonderry, one of the few British present at Leipzig, the Congreve rockets produced a powerful effect upon the infantry "paralysing a solid square which, after our fire, delivered themselves up as if panic struck." Unluckily for the rocketeers their commander, Captain Brogue of the Royal Artillery, received a mortal wound soon after this success and command of the team, still largely experimental, devolved upon Lieutenant Strangeways.[5]

Taking part in the murderous infighting around Probstheida that day Marbot was assailed by a horde of enemies that would have been familiar to Gauls of the fifth century defending the West against Attila, but which astounded the colonel of the 23rd Chasseurs. Having dealt successfully with a furious assault by Klenau's Austrian and Doctoroff's Russian cavalry, his regiment was set upon by massed squadrons of Cossacks and Bashkirs, the latter discharging thousands of arrows. "The losses these caused were slight," he records, "for the Bashkirs are totally undrilled and have no more notion of any formation than a flock of sheep. Thus they cannot shoot horizontally without hitting their own comrades and are obliged to fire their arrows parabolically into the air, with more or less elevation according to the distance at which they judge the enemy to be. As this method does not allow of accurate aiming nine-tenths of the arrows are lost, while the few that hit are pretty well spent and only fall with the force of their own weight . . . However, as they were coming up in myriads, and the more of these wasps one killed the more came on, the vast number of arrows with which they filled the air were bound sooner or later to inflict some severe wounds."

One of Marbot's NCOs was pierced from breast to back. The poor devil seized both ends, broke it and pulled out both halves but died within minutes. Marbot himself was struck without even being conscious of the wound. Raising his sword he found its upward progress unexpectedly checked and looking down saw a four-foot arrow sticking in his right thigh. The regimental doctor extracted it and the wound was trifling but Marbot regretted losing this curious souvenir in the subsequent retreat.

Captain Barrès, fighting on the left wing that day, was one of many flung into the line to make good the desertion of the Saxons that he actually witnessed. At Schonefeld he came face to face with the Swedes and fought under Marmont and General Compans, whose troops had been all but wiped out. The reinforcement at once came under terrific fire. "Officers and soldiers fell like ears of corn before the reaper's sickle," he says. Cannon balls, sometimes taking the column full on, swept away as many as thirty men, and the officers could do little but dart about closing the ranks and preventing the battalion wheeling round on itself. Marmont was wounded and then Compans before Ney came up to encourage the defenders of Schonefeld but soon Ney was hit and at last the battered French fell back on the city, halting on the right bank of the Parthe. "It was dismal, painful, cruel!" Barrès recalls when he came to write down what he remembered of this most terrible of all Napoleonic battles. "The grief of having lost a great and bloody battle, the frightful prospect of a morrow that might perhaps be still more wretched, the guns raging at every point of our unhappy lines, the defection of our cowardly allies, and lastly the privations of every kind that had for days been crushing us." He had lost, in this single day's fighting, the majority of his officers and more than half his men. Not twenty remained of the two hundred who had answered the roll at the commencement of the campaign. The army corps, he adds, existed only in name. More than two-thirds of its generals had been killed or wounded.[6]

For the third night in succession the contending armies bivouacked on the field among the broken bodies of so many of their comrades. Dusk fell, watch fires began to twinkle and the moon came up. Somebody brought a wooden chair for the Emperor and he sat dozing in the open, later learning that Ney, wounded in the shoulder, had left the battlefield and that many other friends were dead or being driven as casualties along the Weissenfels road, where Bertrand and a section of the army had already retreated. A long stream of wagons was passing over the stone bridge and arrangements were being made to mine it so that its destruction would give the French time to withdraw as soon as the enemy broke into the city. For this was now inevitable. Another day's fighting on the scale would mean the destruction of the Grand Army. There seemed, however, no urgency in Napoleon's mind. Presently he got up and went into the town, taking up his quarters at an inn bearing a signboard painted with the arms of the royal house of Prussia.

Detailed orders concerning the retreat were issued through Berthier and Maret. Blucher, learning that the French vanguard was already on its way to Weissenfels, dispatched Yorck's corps in pursuit on the other side of the Elster.

Outside, beyond the city walls, three villages were seen to be burning and one of Leipzig's suburbs was already ablaze. There had been talk of firing the whole city to give general cover for the retreat but Napoleon recoiled from vandalism on such a scale. Instead he sent an officer with a flag of truce, proposing that measures be taken by both sides to prevent Leipzig's population being subjected to the ordeal of storm. No reply was received. After their savage mauling the Allies were in no mood to negotiate. The people of Leipzig would have to take their chance.

At two o'clock in the morning on the 19th orders reached the exhausted defenders of Probstheida, Connewitz and Stotteritz to break camp and pull back. Leaving their fires burning they moved into the city, carrying their wounded to add to the 23,000 inside Leipzig's hospitals. Macdonald and Poniatowski, charged with the heavy responsibility of holding the city until the last moment, had with them Reynier's remnant, Lauriston's survivors and the wrecks of their own corps, in all about 30,000 men. Gathering outside the city and preparing to advance on all points were nearly 300,000 Russians, Prussians, Saxons, Austrians and Swedes.

Word was sent to St. Cyr in Dresden to escape if he could but there was small hope of this. Between St. Cyr and the remnant of the Grand Army was a Europe in arms.

At first light the Allies began to assault the suburbs and Napoleon took leave of Frederick Augustus, the old king of Saxony, loyal even in this extremity. "Make the best terms you can," he advised him, "you have done all that a man can do." With the roar of battle mounting outside the gates of Halle, Grimma and St. Peter, Napoleon wandered off into the town, jostled by men who failed to recognize him, dazed by the uproar and by lack of sleep. General Chateau, meeting him near the bridge, took him for a burgher and was on the point of asking for directions when he recognized the roughly clad man as he who, not long ago, had been fawned upon by kings for territory, honors and revenues. Napoleon showed no sign of outrage but whistled the air "Malbrook s'en va-t'en guerre." He was in the mental vacuum that accompanies extreme physical and nervous exhaustion. At eleven A.M. he crossed the bridge and halted at a mill in Lindenau and here, in the midst of all the uproar surrounding him, he fell asleep.

He was awakened at two P.M. by an explosion that dwarfed the rumble of the Allied guns battering away at the suburbs where Macdonald and Poniatowski were still holding their positions. The bridge had been blown, with thirty thousand Frenchmen on the wrong side, and the Allies closing in from every quarter.

I V

The destruction of the Lindenau bridge before more than two-thirds of the survivors of the three-day battle had crossed is one of those imponderables that abound in military history. There will never be a definitive answer. The general consensus of opinion seems to be that the explosive charges were left in the care of a junior NCO after his superior, unable to decide what proportion of the Grand Army had crossed, had gone to seek out Colonel Montfort, the engineer selected to take charge of the operation. The junior officer, and probably Montfort also, were then swept forward by the press of the fugitives, and were unable to return against this tide so that the corporal, alone with his fearful responsibilities, had to make his own decision. His action was probably dictated by infiltration along the river banks of Saxon riflemen, already established inside the town and anxious to demonstrate their sympathy with the Prussians in defiance of the wishes of their king. In the circumstances it is not surprising that the unfortunate corporal should assume that the city was already lost and only a mob of stragglers and wounded and disarmed prisoners remained on the right bank. Marbot, who had

crossed early in the morning and was now well on the road to
Weissenfels, blames Berthier, Chief of Staff, not for the destruction of the bridge over which he had no immediate control,
but for his failure to provide alternative crossings during the
day-long lull on the 17th. "The entire army assumed this
had been done," Marbot says, "but when the order to retreat
was given on the night of the 18th there was not a beam or
a plank across a single brook."

By then columns of Austrians, Russians, Prussians and Swedes
had made their way into the suburbs and all that remained of
Napoleon's German allies, roving bands of Saxons, Wurtem-
bergers, Bavarians and Hessians, began to direct their fire on
the French. But even in these dire circumstances the rearguard
did not disintegrate but continued to retreat step by step, firing from behind garden walls, from boulevard trees and the
windows of houses until they were pushed right back to the
immediate vicinity of the river.

With the bridge gone and enemy sharpshooters closing in
on all sides, their position was hopeless but Macdonald and
Poniatowski, backed by Generals Reynier, Lauriston and several others, showed the kind of courage Ney had shown on the
road from Smolensk to Kovno the year before. When there was
no longer any hope of maintaining organized resistance Macdonald
and Poniatowski cut their way through to some marshy fields
alongside the Pleisse so that there were now two river obstacles
between them and the main body. Here they became separated and each made his individual attempt to escape. Reynier,
followed by other senior officers, was trapped and surrendered
but Macdonald preferred death to the indignity of capture. "I
was dragged along," he says, "by the crowds and crossed the
two arms of the Elster, the first on a little bridge, holding on
to the handrail for my feet did not touch the ground, the
other on a horse lent me by the quartermaster. I found myself
in an open field still surrounded by a crowd. I wandered about
but it still followed me, convinced that I must know a way
out though I could find none marked on the map. There was
still the main arm of the river to cross."

At this point Lauriston, who had been with him, disappeared,
to join other senior officers who had been taken prisoner but

the Scotsman pushed on, meeting some aides-de-camp of Poniatowski who told him they thought the new marshal was dead. One of his own aides rushed up at this juncture and told him that a colonel of the Engineers had constructed some kind of bridge ahead that might offer a chance of escape and had, in fact, already been used by Marshals Augereau and Marmont who had crossed on horseback. They went there at once, still followed by stragglers who saw hope in the presence of a marshal of France. No one could cross the improvised bridge on horseback now. It had originally consisted of two felled trees linked by doors, shutters and planks but the trunks of the trees were not anchored to the bank and had slipped apart so that the flooring had floated away. It was Macdonald's sole chance and he took it without hesitation. Dismounting he put a foot on each trunk and began to edge across. His cloak bellied out in the wind and fearing it would cause him to lose his balance, or serve some equally desperate man as a handhold, he loosened the fastenings and got rid of it. He was three-fourths of the way over when others, following him closely, caused the trunks to shake and he fell into the shoulder-high water and tried to wade ashore. He failed for the opposite bank was so slippery that he could not climb it, and enemy skirmishers now began firing at him from the further shore until they were driven off by a party of French who dragged the marshal on to firm ground. Here he met Marmont who lent him a horse but had no dry clothes to offer. He did, however, give the exhausted Macdonald some money to reward a soldier who, having been entrusted with the marshal's pocketbook, had stripped and swum across. In some such way Macdonald's father, the clansman, had survived the ruin of the Jacobite cause at Culloden.

Pontiatowski was less fortunate. Wounded in the left arm he plunged into the Pleisse and got across although he lost his horse in the process. He found another and still closely pursued plunged into the Elster. Neither horse nor rider reached the other side. Five days later the prince's body was found by a fisherman in a riverside garden. It was still clad in gala uniform, with diamond-studded epaulettes and in the pockets of the tunic were valuable snuff-boxes and trinkets.

They were eagerly purchased by Poles who had been taken prisoner. Pontiatowski had held the rank of marshal of the French Empire for a little over forty-eight hours.

Two-thirds of the army had escaped. The Emperor and the remaining marshals were temporarily safe. A clutch of generals, senior officers, thirty thousand men, and all the wounded were made prisoner. What of those who did manage to cross the bridge with their exhausted conscripts of which Joseph Bertha is the prototype?

Barrès, like Marbot, was exceptionally lucky. He was on the far side of the bridge when it erupted. In the attack on the suburb of Halle he lost touch with every member of his unit. Finding himself alone and on the point of capture he slipped through the gate of a garden and made his way to the boulevard where he eased himself into a stream of fugitives and was literally swept across the bridge a few moments before the explosion. He was so near that he was showered with debris. Pushing on in the company of a grenadier captain, who had also lost all his men, Barrès caught up with the Emperor who was doing all that could be done to rally the fugitives. Signposts containing the numerals of army corps were set up beside the road, directing the men where to rally. It was Barrès' final glimpse of Napoleon.

At Markrundstadt, on the road to Lutzen, he caught up with survivors of his battalion who had crossed the bridge ahead of him and managed to buy a stray horse from an infantryman. Judging by the contents of the portmanteau on its back the animal was the property of a military commissary for, in addition to papers, there was some clothing which Barrès at once distributed among officers who had lost everything in the rout. In case of an enquiry he kept the papers, stuffing them in the holsters. Then he bivouacked and at first light set out on the road to Weissenfels on the Saale, passing the spring battlefield of Lutzen. "Times were indeed altered," he comments. Then comes a passage in his diary illustrating the spirit of comradeship that existed in the rank and file in the Napoleonic armies. A corporal of his company, badly wounded in the foot, begged the loan of the horse to carry him home to France but the rightful owner had turned up and claimed not only the horse but the portmanteau. "Having abandoned him you have lost all right to possess him," said Barrès, and gave the animal to the wounded corporal, condemning himself to make the long journey on foot.

Marbot, well clear of the river when the bridge was blown up, assumed the army was safe from pursuit when he heard the explosion while halted at Markrundstadt, three leagues west of Leipzig. He took the opportunity to call the roll and was appalled to learn that of the seven hundred troopers who had answered their names on the 16th, the day the battle opened, 149 were missing of which sixty, including two captains, three lieutenants, and eleven NCOs were known to be dead. As soon as it was realized what had in fact occurred at Lindenau, Napoleon ordered Sébastiani's cavalry to gallop back and do everything possible to rescue survivors. Marbot's chasseurs led the relief column, Marbot himself commanding the brigade. As soon as they came in sight of the broken bridge the chasseurs could see what was happening. The marooned French were being hunted from street to street and butchered by Prussians, troops from Baden and Swedes. Soon they came up with 2,000 naked men, most of them wounded, who had escaped by swimming. Among these was Macdonald, likewise practically naked. Marbot lent him some clothes and a led horse and then pushed on to the head of the bridge. Here he witnessed further scenes of butchery among the disarmed French who had managed to cross but were now being cut down by a body of about five hundred Germans who had bridged the broken arches with planks. Sheathing his sword lest he should "actually find pleasure in killing some of these scoundrels with my own hand," Marbot ordered the charge and accompanied by the 24th Chasseurs his regiment galloped into the water meadows and surrounded the pursuers. "The effect of the charge," he says "was terrible. The bandits, taken by surprise, offered only a feeble resistance and there was very great slaughter, no quarter being given." Having seen the slaughter of unarmed men the French cavalry were not disposed to spare the venturesome Germans, particularly the former allies among them, and when, unable to recross the bridge, some of them took refuge in an inn, Marbot dismounted his troopers, ringed the rear of the premises and set fire to the stables. A Saxon officer came out to offer surrender but Marbot, ordinarily a very chivalrous soldier, refused to treat with him. Caught between the flames of the burning building and the carbine volleys of the chasseurs outside the Germans died to the last man. Then, shepherding the two thousand French fugitives before them, the chasseurs remounted and rode back to Markrundstadt. It is probable that Marshal Macdonald owed his life to Marbot's sally but the Scotsman was so enraged by the lack of provision for a retreat that for a time he refused to report to Napoleon. He had heard his men crying for help from the far bank and had been unable to do anything to save them. The incident made such a profound impression on him that his disenchantment with the Emperor dates from that hour.

He was only one of many. All the marshals and senior officers of the Grand Army were disgusted with staff bungling that had occasioned such a disaster and the former street urchin Augereau was only voicing a general opinion when he asked, furiously, "Does the bugger know what he's doing?" At Erfurt, a few stages further on, King Murat slipped away and headed for Naples, fully determined to make what terms he could with the victorious Allies.

For the rest of the men left behind in Leipzig there was a choice of surrender or dying where they stood and not always that choice. Something like 13,000 of the trapped garrison were shot or bayoneted out of hand. Joseph Bertha, hero of *A Conscript of 1813,* was one of the trapped and in describing his trials Erckmann and Chatrian must have followed their source material very closely, for Bertha's graphic description of the rout can be verified from factual accounts in every particular. He was caught up in the desperate hand-to-hand fighting on the town ramparts and was rescued by a charge of the Polish lancers described as "the best soldiers I ever saw." Having witnessed their one escape route blocked by the premature explosion most of Bertha's comrades went berserk and rushed at the enemy but the conscript, who had been a convalescent at Leipzig after Lutzen, told his officer of a ford higher up the Elster and the remnants of the company got across but were in no condition for the march back to France, in spite of being refitted at Erfurt three days later. Typhus broke out and the men who had survived all the horrors and exertions of the campaign died beside the road by the hundreds. "The sky was grey, and the rain poured down," says Bertha, describing this stage of the retreat, "while the autumnal wind seemed to freeze us. How could poor conscripts, so young that they had no moustache, and so emaciated that you could almost see through their ribs as through a lantern, how, I ask, could poor creatures like this endure such misery?"

On the other side there was rejoicing and mutual congratulations. The Allied leaders converged on the great square at Leipzig, the emperors of Russia and Austria, the king of Prussia, Blucher, Schwartzenberg and Crown Prince Bernadotte, not yet fully alive to the magnitude of their victory. They had reason to suspend judgment. It had taken them four days, at odds of about three to one and, ultimately, ten to one, to batter their way into a single city and even then their principal prey had escaped, with more than half his remaining strength. In the period between October 16th and 19th they had lost 54,000 killed and wounded to the French loss in the field of under 40,000. About 23,000 French wounded had been taken but only 20,000 prisoners. Their haul in booty was more impressive. They had captured most of the French ammunition train but their own loss in material must have been immense, for Baron Fain reports that on the 18th alone the French fired 95,000 rounds of artillery and upwards of 200,000 in the battle as a whole.

The flaw in the Allied victory was strategical. A capable commander would have sent troops ahead to trap the entire Grand Army by encircling it further west and making certain that the road to Lutzen, Weissenfels, Erfurt and Mainz was cut in advance. In this way they might have captured the Emperor and all his marshals and ended a war that was to continue for another seven months. The few Germans who had remained loyal to France received short shrift from the vic- king of Saxony was packed off to Berlin under a acks and was to remain a prisoner until Napo- ffense was that he had not betrayed a friend

The Coalition's most important dividend at Leipzig was a moral one. For the first time in his career Napoleon, in personal command of an army, had been decisively defeated in a pitched battle. This in itself was in the nature of a phenomenon. But the victory at Leipzig did not justify the subsequent raising of a huge and rather vulgar memorial. For the third time in six months the net had been cast and twice the *secutor* had won the contest on points. On the final occasion he had been savagely mauled but he had escaped and was very much in being, as the Coalition was to discover when its troops reached and crossed the Rhine in the new year.

9

"WE ARRIVED ON the banks of the Rhine as we had left the banks of the Elster, in a state of complete dissolution. We had covered our track with the relics of the army. At every step we took we left behind us corpses of men and carcasses of horses, guns, baggage, the tatters of our one-time glory." In these dolorous terms Captain Barrès records his unit's arrival at Mainz, on November 2nd, fourteen days after the evacuation of Leipzig.

Taking this passage from its context implies that the route from the Elster to the Rhine was a repetition of the retreat from Moscow and that the Grand Army was now ruined as a fighting machine but this was very far from being the case. In a way the withdrawal to the Rhine was a remarkable achievement and the Bavarian army, that did its best to complete the work of the Allies, bore witness to the ability of the French to extricate themselves from appalling situations. Ten thousand Bavarians fell in an attempt to bar the passage of the fugitives at Hanau.

It was as though Napoleon's ingenuity increased in direct proportion to his adversities and this, indeed, was to become demonstrably clear to his enemies during the next few months. As a young man, with the ragged, half-mutinous army of Italy, he had astonished the world. Later, in his heyday, directing a highly trained and brilliantly maneuvered instrument, he had proved invincible. Now, with a shrinking, ill-equipped, half-demoralized force, he was to achieve miracles.

The Tatters of One-Time Glory

The distance from the Elster at Leipzig to the Rhine at Mainz is over two hundred miles. Rivers had to be crossed, forests traversed and a close watch kept not only on militant former allies in the rear but on the parallel-marching corps of Yorck in the north and the pursuing Allied armies in the east. The odds were now at least six to one and the Allies were spurred by the tremendous moral advantage they had just gained at Leipzig. But Napoleon refused to be hurried. News that they were burning him in effigy in London, that Eugène was on the defensive in Italy, that Murat was defecting in Naples and that Wellington and his Spanish and Portuguese allies were masters of all Spain, concerned him but in no way impressed him with the hopelessness of his situation. Methodically he addressed himself to the daunting task of re-forming the military mob that had streamed across the Lindenau bridge, halting three days at Erfurt, where there were plentiful supplies of guns and uniforms. Then he moved leisurely on Frankfurt, fending off Yorck's forces in the north and closing up his columns for a breakthrough on the River Kinzig, a tributary of the Rhine, where the Bavarian General Wrede, commanding upwards of 60,000 men, aimed at blocking the main road back to France.

There were those in his ranks who doubted if disengagement could be achieved and King Murat was the least hopeful of them. At Erfurt, on October 23rd, he said his final farewells to the Grand Army and its chief, pleading the necessity of his presence in Naples. He gave Macdonald what the Scotsman interpreted as a broad hint concerning his state of mind when that marshal told him he had been asked by Napoleon to find a defensive position. "Make sure it's a weak one!" was Murat's advice. Napoleon had no illusions concerning Murat's real intentions but he did not arrest or even accuse him. Instead he embraced the man who was on the point of betraying him, sensing perhaps that they were never to meet again. They had been together a long time and had shared a thousand adventures, beginning the night of the famous "Whiff of Grapeshot" in republican Paris, in 1795, when Captain Murat had ridden across the city to bring the guns from the artillery park at Les Sablons. They were not merely comrades-in-arms but brothers-in-law. It made no difference now. Murat's only chance of keeping the crown won by French blood and sweat was to betray his comrades to the Austrians and this, with the active support of Caroline Bonaparte, he had resolved to do. The spectacular charges he had led at Dresden, and in front of Probstheida outside Leipzig, were his final appearances as a Grand Army captain. Ahead of him were a few months of pottering, an ignominious failure, months of profitless intrigue, and a brave but inglorious death in front of a firing squad. In a sense he had already crossed from the world of public affairs into legend.

The others remained loyal, at least outwardly so. Augereau, still muttering abuse and accusations of gross incompetence against Headquarters, followed the retreat. So did Marmont, challenging Imperial decisions in a way he would never have dared to do a year before and perhaps recalling a time in his youth when young Bonaparte, shoddily dressed and unemployed, had been glad to share a meal with him at his parents' home. Macdonald was there but sulking over the incident of the blown bridge and Victor, who had once been a mutinous drummer boy in the Royal Army, was beginning to wonder whether a restored Bourbon would confirm him in his hard-won title, the Duke of Belluno. The old grenadier Oudinot was the most useful and least complaining of the veterans. On the banks of the Unstrutt he had a brush with Yorck's Prussians and beat them away from the line of march. He was the last man to cross the river and at night, in bivouac, he heard Cossacks howling "To Paris, to Paris!" in the darkness beyond the camp. The barbarians bothered him less than his health. He had been twice severely wounded in the Russian campaign and it occurred to him that he had used the last of his nine lives escaping from that wilderness with an unextracted Russian bullet in his body. His fears were justified. At a later stage of the retreat he contracted typhus and had to leave the army and make the hazardous journey home by carriage, arriving on his doorstep delirious and shouting orders to imaginary troops.

The rest of them plodded on through rain and mud. On October 27th, the first snow of the winter fell and Captain Barrès, of the 47th, took refuge in a church where his servant came to tell him that some rascal had stolen their cooking pot and there would be no breakfast. Colonel Marbot, as usual, was attentive to duty. Riding ahead with the survivors of the 23rd Chasseurs he came into collision with the Austrian corps that had failed to drive Bertrand from the Lindenau bridge approaches on October 18th. The French won the day and Count Gyulai, the Austrian commander, was taken prisoner but the capture did not give Marbot much satisfaction. His mind kept returning to the 100,000 Frenchmen left behind in a dozen German fortresses for whom there was now no prospect but that of surrender.

Before leaving Erfurt, Colonel Montfort of the Engineers, together with his unlucky corporal who had blown the bridge, were brought before their superiors and asked to explain an act that had severed the escape route of 30,000 of their comrades. The results of this court martial are not known with any certainty, except that Montfort admitted enough to exonerate Napoleon from the charge that he, personally, had given orders for the demolition in order to secure his own escape.

News reached the column confirming the loss of the last German ally. King Jerome's kingdom of Westphalia had finally collapsed and the playboy of the Bonaparte family was already on his way home. On October 27th, before news of Leipzig was generally known, the *Moniteur Westphalian* appeared for the last time, announcing, "Imperious circumstances of the moment oblige His Majesty to leave his realm." It went on to express a pious hope that "His Majesty's faithful subjects will continue to conduct themselves with the same devotion and the same calm for which they have always been distinguished." The Westphalians were not touched by this flattering appeal. Less than a fortnight later they were dragging the coach of the Elector of Hesse through the streets of Cassel in triumph but by that time King Jerome had crossed the Rhine at Coblenz. In Jerome, however, the pretentions of royalty died a lingering death. Although occupying an ordinary house instead of a palace his Westphalian Guards continued to stand about in their gold laced uniforms while his chamberlains, lacking an anteroom, gathered in a group on the stairs. An eyewitness describes the scene as "a tragedy being played by a troupe of provincial actors."[1]

Napoleon, reorganizing at Erfurt until the 23rd, was at last coming to grips with military realities. Summoning the loyal rump of his Bavarian troops he explained the predicament of their sovereign and gave them leave to go, at the same time writing to the king to explain that, in the circumstances, he would have been entitled to regard them as prisoners of war. At St. Helena he recalled the German desertions without bitterness. "I never had cause to complain, individually, of the princes, our allies," he said. "The good King of Saxony remained faithful to the last. The King of Bavaria avowed to me that he was no longer his own master. The generosity of the King of Wurtemberg was particularly remarkable. The Prince of Baden yielded only to force and at the very last extremity. All gave me due notice of the storm that was gathering in order that I might adopt the necessary precautions." He excused the rulers but not the ruled, a strange judgment in a man who had so many opportunities to measure the loyalty of the former hussars and ex-grenadiers he had ennobled against that of the NCOs and privates who remained steadfast to the end. Perhaps, in judging the German satraps who had held high office under the Empire he came to realize that Pan-Germanism was inevitable, and that the pressures of patriots like Baron Stein were too strong to be resisted. Fifty-seven years after the last Frenchman had been driven back across the Rhine a Prussian-dominated Germany became a reality. The present generation of Europeans has had two opportunities to see what that meant to Europe in terms of misery. The westward surge of modern Germany began in the spring of 1813. It was to result in three tidal waves in the span of one man's life—between 1870 and 1945—and be halted only at a cost of millions of lives and a new partition of Germany at the end of World War II. Reflecting on the Russian campaign towards the end of his St. Helena exile Napoleon justified it on the grounds of halting the march of the Russians beyond a point where the global balance of power would be upset. The Western world would concede him this point today. Might it not also concede that the campaign of 1813 made possible the sack of Louvain in 1914 and the gas chambers of Dachau in the years 1939–45?

After the loyal Bavarians had departed Napoleon summoned the Poles and offered to release them from their allegiance. They elected to fight on. There was nothing else they could do. It was obvious that their homeland would now be partitioned between Russia, Austria and Prussia, and that the Czar would demand the largest slice. Poniatowski could have held high command in the Russian army if he had been less of a patriot. He had preferred to throw in his lot with the man who was always promising that he would re-establish the ancient kingdom but never did and lived to regret his unfulfilled promises. With the Czar and his allies approaching the eastern bank of the Rhine there was no future for a Polish soldier in Poland. One and all they remained with the Grand Army and most of them died in its final battles.

II

Hanau, the last pitched battle of the campaign, has been likened to the battle fought at Krasnoi, west of Smolensk, in November, 1812. There are obvious similarities. Both resulted in unexpected French victories and both secured the escape of a beaten army. Apart from this both grand assaults were commanded by Napoleon in person, a circumstance that increased the aggressive valor of his men.

Marbot, leading the light cavalry of Exelmans with a brigade composed of the 23rd and 24th Chasseurs, had doubts concerning the wisdom of the order of march. The way led through dense forests surrounding the defile of Geluhausen cut by the river Kinzig, and to his mind the cavalry should have been held back and replaced by a cloud of skirmishers. No orders of this kind were issued and the light cavalryman advanced into the elbow of the valley until he ran headlong into Ott's hussars, the vanguard of the Bavarian-Austrian army, poised at Hanau. He identified the troopers at once by their handsome theatrical uniforms. "You might have thought they came from a ballroom or a theater," he writes, comparing their ultra-smart turnout with that of his own squadrons whose uniforms were stained with smoke, dust and the bivouac mud of two campaigns. Smart or not they were unable to withstand the charge of the French chasseurs. Without the loss of a trooper Marbot put them all to flight and in the pursuit the Austrians lost more than two hundred killed and wounded. "We took," records Marbot, "a number of excellent horses and gold-laced jackets."

Emerging from the defile the chasseurs expected to meet battalions of massed infantry but luckily for them the enemy had made the same mistake as the French. Only more cavalry were stationed there and were swept away with the retreating hussars. French infantry came up at the double and made dispositions for a general attack. A mood of desperation hung over the Imperial camp. Either the enemy must be defeated and dispersed or no survivor of Leipzig would recross the Rhine.

On the following morning, October 30th, it was seen that General Wrede had made the same error as that made by Macdonald at the Katzbach, posting the greater part of his men with their backs to the river and their first line on the edge of the forest. Trees screened the weakness of the French, a force of no more than 6,000 bayonets at this point, supported by Sébastiani's cavalry.

Marbot described the battle as a kind of hunting expedition, fought from tree to tree and clearing to clearing, but once the enemy had been flushed from the forest the French were brought up short by the enemy's main line of battle, 40,000 strong and covered by a battery of eighty guns. In the Bavarian rear was a single bridge, the bridge of Lamboi, and had Napoleon been in a position to have deployed his full strength the battle would have been over in an hour and Wrede's forces destroyed or captured to a man. It was not to be, however, for the corps of Mortier, Marmont and Bertrand, together with most of the guns, had been delayed by the defile where the light cavalry had met Ott's hussars the previous day, but Wrede missed his opportunity of launching a counterattack that must have driven the French back into the forest. Instead Napoleon, showing the form of Lodi and Arcola, brought up the artillery of the Guard under its commander, General Drouot[2] and as soon as the artilleryman had placed fifteen pieces in position he opened a hot fire and gradually extended his line as each additional gun was unlimbered. Battery smoke continued to mask the weakness of the French front but when a momentary puff of wind revealed to the Bavarians the bearskins of the Guard there was a noticeable wavering in their ranks. No Continental infantry cared to face the Imperial Guard, not even when the French were on the run. In an effort to check the recoil, Wrede ordered all his available cavalry to charge the guns and in a moment the French artillerymen were isolated in a torrent of horsemen.

It must have seemed to Wrede at that moment that the battle was won and that to him would go the honor of capturing Napoleon or at least throwing him back on to the bayonets of the victors of Leipzig. The situation was saved by one man and that man was General Drouot of the Guard.

There were a number of eccentrics in the Grand Army. Murat had ridden into battle in pink pantaloons, waving a golden wand. Lannes had "salved his conscience" at Napoleon's coronation by swearing throughout the service. Cafarelli went to war with a wooden leg. Berthier worshipped at an altar raised in honor of his mistress, the beautiful Madame Visconti. Drouot was another type. A deeply religious man he was often to be seen reading his pocket Bible during a lull in a bombardment and would have been more at home in Cromwell's ranks than among the hardbitten professionals of the Grand Army. He saved the day at Hanau. Overwhelmed by the charge of enemy cavalry he drew his sword, rallied the gunners and defied all attempts to capture or dismantle his pieces. His resistance gave Napoleon time to mount a counterattack. In a confused mass every mounted man in the French center charged into the melée, an irresistable column of Mamelukes, grenadiers à cheval, lancers, dragoons and chasseurs, who cut their way through the cavalry surrounding Drouot's batteries and then galloped on to break Wrede's infantry squares. Soon the entire Bavarian army was stampeding for the single bridge leading to Hanau.

The prompt and courageous action of a local miller saved most of the fugitives. This man, emerging from his house into a hail of shot, closed the floodgates of his millstream on the banks of the Kinzig and enabled those who could not re-cross the bridge to cross by the dam. He was subsequently rewarded by the king of Bavaria, who allocated to him and his family a substantial pension. Notwithstanding this the French followed the enemy as far as the town and the rival pickets were so close to one another during the night that the watch-word had to be changed seven times.

The Bavarians were badly beaten but they were not de-stroyed. On the following day Marmont had to storm the town, which he did without much loss and the capture of 4,000 pris-oners. Napoleon, bivouacked in the forest, sent for the chief magistrate and stormed at him for his friendly reception of his own countrymen. "I can't command you to love the French," he said, "but I should have thought it was your pol-icy to hold more to France than to Russia." The prefect, poor devil, had certainly not anticipated this sequel to Wrede's ar-rival in his town with fifty thousand men, boasting that he would capture the Emperor and prevent the Grand Army's re-turn to France. Pleading that, over a period of seven years, the citizens of Hanau had been kind hosts to the French, he asked for mercy.

Augereau, who had governed the district for a time, con-firmed the mayor's claim. "Very well," growled the Emperor, "I'll now leave you to the Cossacks," and set out for Frankfurt.

Hanau might have been Captain Barrès's last battle. He was warming himself by a fire soon after the main action when a cannon ball killed a naval artillery commandant close by, rico-cheted, and passed between Barrès and his companion, showering them with red hot embers and the remains of some potatoes they were cooking. Barrès was singularly unfortunate in the matter of rations on this march. A thief had deprived him of his break-fast and a cannon ball his dinner but when a bugler who had been absent without leave for three days brought him a propitiatory gift of a fowl, he was obliged to share it with his major, General Joubert, General Lagrange and two other senior officers. "Six of us, all famished, round a poor fowl which would not have sufficed to appease the devouring hunger of a single one of us." The captain's spirits were at a low ebb during the long march back to the Rhine. An incident in a village east of Hanau had depressed him. Here he had witnessed the suicide of a wounded conscript who flung himself out of a window and in spite of everything Barrès could say to the contrary the wretched house-holder was seized, accused of pushing him out, and executed on the spot. Professionals like Barrès hated to see the men of the Grand Army degenerate into a pack of brigands under the scourge of their unending misfortunes. That a man who had seen so much carnage could be so shocked by this incident as to re-call it years later is proof that the junior officers of Napoleon retained their martial pride and sense of discipline to the end.

Hanau was almost Marbot's last day as well. His life was again saved by his Turkish horse, Azolan, that had carried him down the precipitous road from the Katzbach plateau, in Au-gust. During the great cavalry charge on the 30th he and his trumpeter were boxed in by falling trees beside a burning pow-der wagon. By a series of convulsive leaps Azolan carried his rider clear of the explosion but the young trumpeter was blown to pieces. Only that morning the young man had amused Marshal Macdonald by quoting the *Eclogues* of Vergil under fire. The Scotsman remarked, "There's a little chap whose memory isn't disturbed by his surroundings!"

There were those for whom the effort needed to break through another circle of enemies was beyond their strength. Joseph Bertha, prototype of the conscripts of 1813, was such a one. Worn out with marching and fighting on an empty stomach, drenched by the rains and burning with fever, Bertha lay down beside the road to die. He was saved and carried home to France by an artilleryman whom he recognized es-corting one of the last wagons at the tail of the army. His deliverance was not typical. All the way from Leipzig to Mainz the boys who had stood up to the terrible cannonades of Lutzen, Bautzen, Dresden and Leipzig lined the route, sick, typhus ridden, dying of untended wounds, of hunger, of exhaustion and exposure. A few were picked up by the ad-vancing Allies and subsequently recovered in hospitals but not one in ten lived to return to their homes when the prisoners were exchanged the following spring.

Barrès and his men struggled into Frankfurt on the first day of November and bivouacked in mud up to their knees, with rain drumming on their emaciated bodies. At Mainz, however, he had a heartening encounter with the corporal to whom he had loaned his horse on the banks of the Elster and the man, now recovered, returned the animal. After footslogging two hundred miles through mud the horse must have been a godsend.

Marshal Macdonald, holding Hanau in the rear with a hopelessly inadequate garrison, saw a prospect of being overwhelmed when the commandant of his engineers, having just climbed the church steeple, reported the mounting of another attack by fresh masses of the enemy. Macdonald left his breakfast to reorganize resistance but at that moment General Bertrand appeared with orders to relieve him. Bertrand asked Macdonald how many troops he should take into the town as a garrison. "All you have will not be enough," replied Macdonald and mounting his horse took the road to Frankfurt.

At Mainz, in conference with the Emperor, he had an opportunity to speak his mind about the dire necessity for peace and the folly of rejecting the terms offered during the Armistice. Napoleon countered by saying that acceptance on his part would have only resulted in the Allies demanding more concessions. He asked Macdonald what personal losses he had incurred during the campaign and when the marshal told him he did not possess so much as a clean shirt Napoleon promised compensation. The instinct of a Scotsman, however, recognized the Emperor's comment concerning his dwindling financial reserves as a hint that recompense would be small. "In fact he only sent me a draft on Paris for 30,000 francs (£1,200 in England or $6,000 in the United States) and I had great difficulty in getting it cashed," complains Macdonald in his memoirs.

Another veteran was not yet ready to concede defeat. Hurried from the battlefield of Hanau in a raging fever Marshal Oudinot hovered between life and death for five days, watched over by his devoted wife, who had shared many of his trials and hazards in Russia the previous year. As soon as the marshal's fever left him another took its place. He was impatient to be back in the field at the head of his corps and his wife knew him too well to protest. Helping him to take his first steps across the sickroom floor she saw him pause in front of a cheval glass and exclaim, "There's an ugly beggar for you!" By the third week in December, seven weeks after he had left the field of Hanau, he was on the road, ready to defend France against an invasion that he knew to be imminent. There were not many malingerers among the captains of the Grand Army.

III

Nobody could rise to an occasion as swiftly and dramatically as Napoleon Bonaparte. One has the impression that, when the world was falling about his ears, he derived some secret satisfaction from the process of reasserting his authority and summoning fresh reserves of nervous energy. Time and again he had demonstrated this ability to fly in the face of disadvantageous circumstances. It had been this way on the banks of the Danube, in 1809, and again at Smolensk, two hundred miles east of Moscow. It was as though his inner convictions were never shaken by failure and that once he applied himself to alter them in his favor the shadows over his Empire were not merely lifted but transformed into the glow of success. During the trek from the Elster to the Rhine he had been moody and thoughtful but now, inside his own frontiers, he became once again the human dynamo of administrative expertise that had distinguished him after his sleigh ride from Russia in December, 1812.

His tremendous spurt of energy was heralded by the usual orgy of dictation. Letters of exhortation, crisply worded instructions, and any number of storming complaints set couriers galloping in all directions. In an attempt to blow life into the dying embers of French patriotism he sent sixteen captured standards to the Ministry of War, with instructions to parade them through the streets of the capital and afterwards present them to the Empress Marie Louise. "The forty flags I captured at Dresden were unluckily left behind in that town," he writes. He does not add what else had been left behind, one of the finest soldiers in Europe and a garrison of 30,000 men. Neither did Napoleon warn General Clarke, Minister of War, of the possible embarrassment of Marie Louise on receiving trophies captured in combat with her father. Possibly he relied on the complaisance of a Habsburg whose emotional responses had been atrophied by protocol and inbreeding.

Marmont and Macdonald were dispatched north and south along the banks of the Rhine, sharing between them the 70,000 scarecrows they had led back to France. Then, estimates having been made of the civil forces that might be raised against an invasion, Napoleon attended to domestic matters. He dashed off one letter to his mother, Madame Mère, concerning the eccentric behavior of her son Louis, once king of Holland, and another to Cambacères, the Imperial Chancellor, concerning brother Jerome, formerly king of Westphalia.

Both brothers had come limping home to France, the one hoping he would be restored to his kingdom in the Netherlands, the other to indulge in what was, for Jerome, a mild spending spree including the purchase of a chateau to compensate him for the loss of his palace at Cassel. Napoleon, who was always extremely well-informed on the antics of his family, read the minds of both brothers and expressed himself very forcibly. Louis' aspirations, he declared to his mother, caused him great embarrassment. Holland was French and would remain French. "If Louis still has that bee in his bonnet I appeal to you to spare me the pain of having to arrest him as a rebel. Get him to leave Paris. Let him go and live quietly and unostentatiously in some out-of-the-way place in Italy." Word had reached him that Louis had been libeling him in every Court in Europe and although by no means a vindictive man (certainly not as regards his shiftless brothers and sisters) he found it hard to forgive disloyalty on the part of a man who, as a child, had shared his barrack lodgings and subsisted on his lieutenant's pay.[3]

His letter concerning Jerome, the youngest of the family, was even more explosive. To the Imperial Chancellor he wrote concerning Jerome's new purchase, "Have the sale annulled . . . I am shocked that when all private citizens are sacrificing themselves for the defence of their country, a king who is losing his throne should be so tactless as to choose such a moment to buy property as if he were only thinking of his private interests." It is curious that Napoleon, the great psychologist, should have been surprised by his younger brother in this instance. Jerome, throughout his entire dissipated life, never gave a single thought

to anything except his own interests. Concerning his closest kin
Napoleon could deceive himself to a point of fatuity. Notwithstanding this he could be excused loss of temper concerning
the behavior of his family at this crisis in his fortunes. Europe
was poised to invade from the north, the east, and the southwest. Two great armies had been all but destroyed in a little
over a year. Every alliance save the one with a few rootless
Poles was in ruins. And what contributions were the family
making to the Imperial cause? Joseph, bundled out of Spain, was
suggesting he should now abdicate, as though his abdication
was not an accomplished fact. Lucien, who had quarreled with
his brother years ago and had been captured by the British on
his way to America, was living the life of a dilettante squire
in a comfortable house in Worcestershire. Louis, having done
all the harm he could to Napoleon's reputation, was soliciting
the throne of a country on the point of being overrun by the
Allies. Jerome, trailing his troupe of theatrical guardsmen,
was buying himself a new chateau. Finally, down in Naples,
Caroline, youngest of the girls, had already joined the ranks of
his enemies and nagged her husband into turning traitor. Looking back on their behavior, collectively and individually, one
cannot but feel Napoleon would have been justified in instructing his Chief of Police to arrest the entire brood and lock them
away in Vincennes, the state prison.

Having, as it were, disposed of family matters, Napoleon
climbed into his famous green coach and set off for Paris, arriving there on November 9th. By then the Allies had reached
Frankfurt where they made preparations for a prolonged stay.
They did not share Napoleon's sense of urgency. Russians,
Prussians, Austrians, Swedes, Bavarians, Saxons and men from
Wurtemberg and Baden—their field army had now been swollen
to about a half-million men, with a formidable train of artillery,
their own and what they had captured at Leipzig. It was the
most powerful army that had ever approached the Rhine and
news arriving day by day from their rear was as reassuring
as their numerical strength. St. Cyr surrendered Dresden on
November 11th and Rapp, an Alsatian general and hero of a
thousand fights, surrendered Danzig on December 2nd, the
anniversary of Napoleon's coronation and of Austerlitz. Both

capitulations were attended by acts of bad faith by the Allies. St. Cyr, whose men were on starvation rations, surrendered on condition that he and his troops would be allowed free passage to France but after ascertaining that Dresden could not support an Allied garrison for a day, and having made a careful note of its defenses, the sovereigns offered the marshal a cynical choice of going back into the city or into captivity in Austria. The same thing occurred at Danzig, where Rapp commanded 15,000 men, half French, half German. Under the terms of surrender Rapp was to be given the honors of war but ultimately he too was offered a choice of returning to his positions or being sent to Russia to await exchange. Without provisions he had no alternative but to take the road to captivity. The thoughts of those among his garrison who had escaped across the Niemen the previous winter can be imagined. Stettin surrendered on November 30th, Modlin on December 1st, and Torgau on December 26th. Magdeburg and Hamburg held on, the latter city in the iron grip of Davout.

The abandonment of these garrisons after Leipzig has been cited as an example of callousness or crass stupidity on the part of Napoleon but, quite apart from his critical situation at that time, it was neither. In part, at least, it was due to another stroke of bad luck.

On leaving Leipzig Napoleon had despatched a messenger to St. Cyr, instructing him to march out while there was still time, descend the Elbe, gather in the garrisons of Torgau, Wittenberg, Magdeburg and Hamburg, and menace the enemy's rear and communications. Had this been achieved St. Cyr could have assembled an army of 150,000 and the plan was by no means impracticable and would have delayed, if not canceled, Allied preparations for an invasion of France in 1814. But the dice rarely fell advantageously for Napoleon in the year 1813. His Leipzig dispatch rider was captured so that St. Cyr never received his orders. Protesting against the baseness of his treatment the inscrutable former actor, who had also been an art student, a drawing master, and an engineer, marched his disarmed corps into Bohemia. For him, as for General Rapp, the war was over.

Imperial prospects were equally adverse in two other spheres, northern Italy and northeastern Spain. In Italy the situation of Prince Eugène was growing more critical every day. As soon as Austria had joined the Coalition in late August, General Hiller, with sixty thousand men, had crossed the Tyrol resolved to recover Lombardy and Venice. With forty thousand newly recruited men Eugène had to retreat but his position would not have been so menacing had he been able to trust Caroline Murat, still tirelessly intriguing in Naples far to the south of the Viceroy's line of battle. Eugène fell back over the Tagliamento to the Adige and his new enemies included his father-in-law, the king of Bavaria. The king, hoping to detach Eugène from Napoleon, sent a special messenger[4] through the lines with a letter offering very advantageous terms, but Eugène, unlike Murat, was a man of honor. At a village near Verona he met the envoy and showed him every courtesy but when he read the letter the messenger had brought from Frankfurt he said, quietly, "It grieves me very much to have to say 'no' to the King, my father-in-law, but he demands the impossible." Then, having given instructions for the visitor to be fed, he went in and wrote his reply: "I am deeply touched that you should have thought of me, and so kindly, but it is quite impossible for me to depart by an inch from the line of conduct I have laid down for myself. I would much rather sacrifice my future happiness and that of my family than break the solemn vows which I have taken." To us, at this distance in time, the answer might seem sententious but it was not considered so at the time. It was, in fact, a simple expression of how Eugène de Beauharnais saw his duty as a soldier. In rejecting the offer he automatically rejected an offer of the crown of Italy. It would have made no difference to him if they had offered him Napoleon's throne. It is not true that every man has his price; most have, but not all.

There were compensations of a kind. Eugène kept his self-respect and the respect and affection of his wife, who had already been approached by her father. Pregnant, and once again separated from her husband by the exigencies of war, she wrote to her brother, the crown prince, declaring that her loyalty was to Eugène and the French Empire. Her dynastic marriage to Eugène had since developed into a love match. "To save Bavaria and my family I offered myself as a sacrifice and

I shall never regret it," she wrote, bitterly, "but what has been my reward? To be forced to beg for mercy on my children. God gave me an angel for a husband. That is my sole happiness."

Eugène had been suspicious of Murat's behavior ever since the king of Naples had abandoned his post at the head of the survivors of the Moscow campaign a year before, but it was difficult for a man of his temperament to comprehend treachery on the scale contemplated by Murat and Caroline now that the Empire was seen to be breaking up. Until the very last moment (and notwithstanding the hints given him by the king of Bavaria's envoy) Eugène still half-hoped that Murat and his Neapolitans would march to his aid and Napoleon must have cherished the same hope for he drew up plans for the union of the two Italian armies and sent his chief of police, Fouché, to Naples to assess the real situation. It was a fruitless journey on Fouché's part. News reached France that the Neapolitan army had marched into Rome and Ancona and was now heading for Upper Italy. An English naval force took Trieste. The Illyrians and Tyrolese were in revolt. And even Lombardy was wobbling. Threatened from the flank by Hiller and his father-in-law, and from the rear by his old comrade-in-arms, Eugène fell back on the Mincio. There would be no juncture of French troops and no descent upon Austria when Habsburg armies were far away on the Rhine. From now on it would be the utmost Eugène could do to hold on for as long as possible and act as circumstances might dictate.

One small piece of cheering news did come from the south. French officers and soldiers retained in Murat's service rejected his overtures to keep them as soon as his intentions were known, "proving," says the historian Bussey, "that good faith and patriotism had not yet become entirely obsolete among the soldiers of Napoleon." As the position became desperate Eugène issued his own proclamation. "My motto," it said, "is 'Honor and Fidelity.' Take it for your own. Then, with the Grace of God, we shall triumph over our enemies." Learning that the Viceroy could not be detached the Austrian Chancellor Metternich, the chief manipulator of all these threads of intrigue, is said to have remarked: "There is a man of lofty character." It is surprising that Metternich could recognize integrity when he encountered it.

IV

Away to the southwest, where the Bidassoa separates France and Spain at the northern end of the Pyrenees, all would have been lost long ago had it not been for Napoleon's prompt action in sending Soult to take supreme command after news of the battle of Vitoria, in June.

Down here Soult was fighting the campaign of his life, and one that was to earn him the grudging respect of Wellington, the admiration of Wellington's troops and, ultimately, the plaudits of the London crowd when he rode in Victoria's coronation procession twenty-five years later. After the rout at Vitoria the invasion of southwestern France by the British, Portuguese and Spanish was a foregone conclusion. There were those in both camps who expected it to begin within a matter of days but they underestimated Wellington's difficulties and French powers of recovery. A long time was to pass, and much blood spilled, before British grenadiers, and the green-jacketed riflemen of the Light Division, laid siege to French towns.

Wellington's problems stemmed from the completeness of his victory. For years now he had been based at Lisbon for his supplies and reinforcements but now he was obliged to shift his bases to ports in northern Spain. With command of the sea this should have been a relatively simple maneuver but it was far from being so, for America was now France's ally (its sole ally discounting the Poles), and American privateers were so active in Atlantic waters that no supply ship could leave the coast of Portugal without escorts. Added to this were the problems of two Spanish fortresses that still held out, San Sebastian, on the coast, and Pamplona, about fifty miles inland. Both were heavily garrisoned and could menace lines of communication if the British moved beyond the Pyrenees, whereas Wellington had only one siege train and was obliged to tackle them one at a time.

He chose San Sebastian as the most rewarding prize and here Graham, one of his most capable lieutenants, sat down with the 1st and 5th Divisions, a Portuguese brigade, and 15,000 Spaniards. To his right Hill held the river line and passes and beyond Hill, in the famous pass of Roncevalles, was Sir Lowry Cole, with the 4th Division and other Spanish allies. Wellington established his Headquarters on the left-center of the line at Lesaca. To his right-rear there was the menace of Marshal Suchet, still firmly established in Catalonia, but the country between swarmed with guerillas and it was unlikely that Suchet would be able to move up and unite with Soult in a combined attempt to relieve San Sebastian and Pamplona. The latter strongpoint was besieged by Spaniards, who sat down and waited for the French garrison to starve.

On arrival at Bayonne Soult set to work in a way that demonstrated he had learned his trade under Napoleon. Of all the marshals he was the most familiar with Spain, having spent five years in the Peninsula, and his defensive tactics had been perfected under the eye of Masséna, whose grip on Zurich and Genoa in 1799 and 1800 had saved northern Italy and made possible Napoleon's victory at Marengo under the Alps.

San Sebastian, supplied from the sea, was in no immediate danger of falling, so Soult decided first to relieve Pamplona and advance against the Allied right. He had at his disposal 72,000 infantry and 7,000 cavalry but the latter were of very little use in this kind of country.

On July 25th, when Graham was on the point of storming San Sebastian, Soult struck far to the British right, D'Erlon attacking Hill who was defending the Maya pass. Twenty miles to the southeast the French brought immensely superior forces to bear on the troops of Byng, defending the defiles of Altobiscar and Linduz. The line held during the day but by late afternoon a dense fog came down and Sir Lowry Cole, fearful of being outflanked, drew back, leaving the passes open.

For the French prospects looked good and Soult sent off a jubilant dispatch. The element of surprise had been lost, however, and Wellington, having at first believed that Soult's real intention was to relieve San Sebastian and not Pamplona, was already aware of his error and was hurriedly moving reserves along the battle line to the southeast. The eternal problem of the war in Spain—the impossibility of feeding an army in this barren, inhospitable country—continued to plague the French. It was essential to capture the stores of the force that had been besieging Pamplona in order to keep in the field. The advance continued but General Reille got lost in a fog on a mountain goat track and was obliged to descend to the main road and join Clausel.

In the meantime British resistance around Pamplona was hardening and troops were cheered by the appearance of Tommy Picton's tall hat. On the afternoon of the 28th the French appeared, 20,000 of them, to force a defensive ridge held by 11,000 but British reinforcements were rippling down from the north all the time and soon Soult had to deplete his storming force to hold them in check. That day and the next the French were fought to a standstill. On the 30th, without a day's rations in reserve, they abandoned all hope of relieving the starving garrison of Pamplona. The appearance on the ridge of Wellington, mounted on his thoroughbred, had put new heart into the defenders. Having lost nearly 4,000 to the Allies' 2,600, Soult realized that his original project was impossible and made the mistake of switching to an attempt to raise the siege of San Sebastian instead.

For a man of his ability and experience it was an act of supreme folly, for it meant marching along the entire British front within artillery range and under the direct eye of a soldier who would be extremely unlikely to miss an opportunity of catching an adversary at such a disadvantage. Neither did he. Striking hard at the French rearguard he almost destroyed it. With a total loss of 13,000 Soult struggled back over the frontier to plan new strategy and perhaps, like Wellington, to see what would emerge from the extended truce in Saxony. For the time being, separated by the Bidassoa, the two veteran armies watched one another. The blockade of Pamplona was resumed and renewed preparations made for the storming of San Sebastian.

Johnny Kincaid, of the Light Division, took no active part in the battle but was among those who chased the French through the passes during the pursuit. Comparing his diary, *Random Shots of a Rifleman*, with Marbot's account of the fighting at the Lindenau bridge after Leipzig, one cannot but note the difference between the tempo of the war in Saxony and the war in Spain. Throughout the past five years atrocities were common between Frenchman and Spaniard but the long duel between the veterans of Soult and Wellington was conducted on a relatively civilized level. Sometimes it qualified as a kind of lethal sport, both sides taking and giving hard knocks without rancor or brutality. Thus Kincaid writes of this particular pursuit, "The sight of a Frenchman always acted like a cordial on the spirits of the rifleman and the fatigues of the day were forgotten as our three battalions extended among the brushwood and went down to knock the dust out of their hairy knapsacks.[5] . . . Foes as they were it was impossible not to feel a degree of pity for their situation, pressed by an enemy in their rear, an inaccessible mountain on their right, and a river on their left, lined by an invisible foe, from whom there was no escape but the desperate one of running the gauntlet. However, as every ―――― has his day, and this was ours, we must stand excused for making the most of it."

After hounding the French all day Kincaid and his fellow officers returned to quarters and found their tables spread and a good dinner awaiting them, one of the bonuses of fighting a war backed by unchallenged sea communications. "This was one of the most gentleman-like day's fighting that I ever experienced," he concludes, "although we had to lament the vacant seats of one or two of our messmates."

And yet Soult was by no means ready to concede defeat, or even to remain on the defensive, hoping that news of another Austerlitz would come from Germany and cause the British and their allies to hesitate before crossing the frontier and moving up the road to Bayonne. To him, and him alone, had been entrusted the key to the back door of France and he meant to hold it come what might. All things considered he acquitted himself brilliantly in the complicated struggle that was to continue in the southwest until Cossacks were riding into Paris and the dominion of Napoleon had been reduced to the sovereignty of Elba.

On August 31st he made his final attempt to relieve San Sebastian, throwing 45,000 men across the Bidassoa under Reille, who struck at the Spaniards, and the brilliant Clausel, who fought a diversionary action against three Allied brigades. Surprisingly the Spaniards not only held their ground but counterattacked and Reille's men were driven off, leaving over 2,000 casualties. At this juncture, with Clausel drawing back as well, a heavy rainstorm flooded the shallow river fords to a depth of six feet and four French brigades under Vandermaesen had no means of retreat save by a single bridge at Vera, covered by two weak companies of riflemen, about a hundred men in all. The result was a minor epic. Fighting desperately the French eventually broke through but British marksmanship cost them casualties totaling nearly five hundred, including their commander. Sixty-one of the riflemen fell in this action but they and their surviving comrades had accounted for more than four Frenchmen apiece. Then, as a century later at Mons and Ypres, British target practice was superior to that of any army in the world.[6]

In his attempt to relieve General Rey, shut up in San Sebastian, Soult had lost another 3,800 men. Thereafter he went over to the defensive, constructing a long chain of strongpoints reaching southward from the sea. He had, it would seem, learned a valuable lesson from Wellington's strategic withdrawal to the lines of Torres Vedras in the years when the French were the aggressors.

On the very morning of Soult's audacious but fruitless attempt to relieve the town, San Sebastian was stormed. The first attempt, in July, had cost the assaulting columns 570 casualties. The successful attack was even bloodier. In the end it was only achieved by Graham firing siege guns over the heads of the storming parties as they climbed the breach and even then part of Rey's stubborn garrison escaped into the castle. Counting their appalling cost, nearly 2,500 dead or desperately wounded, the British and Portuguese erupted and the night developed into an orgy of drunken looting of the type that had sullied the British capture of Badajoz in 1812. Officers attempting to stop the troops looting, burning and raping were threatened and in two cases fired upon, one fatally. "This storm," writes Napier, "seemed to be the signal from hell for the perpetration of villainy which would have shamed the most ferocious barbarians of antiquity." Rey held out in the castle until September 8th when he surrendered and was accorded the honors of war. "A third-class fortress town, in bad condition when first invested, resisted a besieging army possessing an enormous battery-train for sixty-three days," adds Napier, in one of his many tributes to the valor of French soldiers in the Peninsula.

News of the end of the Dresden armistice, and the enlistment of the Austrians against Napoleon, reached Wellington on September 3rd but he still entertained misgivings concerning an invasion of France. Marshal Suchet, in the right rear, was still maintaining himself successfully in Catalonia constituting a permanent menace, but there was another and more important reason why Wellington held back and it had nothing to do with Soult's formidable defenses beyond the river. Throughout the whole of the campaigns in the Peninsula the Spanish government had made no provision for feeding its troops. For the most part they existed on what they could forage, or buy from the British. Kincaid relates an instance of a Spanish officer approaching him and offering to relieve his company of three days' rations they were carrying in exchange for a receipt. "We refused," he says, "telling him that the trouble of carrying was a pleasure." Wellington had no doubts as to what would happen when thousands of starving Spaniards were loosed upon enemy territory. Their excesses would provoke a general rising, a patriotic war that would add a great deal to his difficulties. Badajoz and San Sebastian had shown what British and Portuguese could do when they were in an ugly temper but he was confident that he could exercise some kind of restraint on men he had led all the way from Lisbon. He had no such confidence regarding the Spaniards. Apart from this consideration his hesitation to march into France is understandable. He had seen several Continental coalitions against Napoleon dissolve almost overnight and during the summer truce he began to entertain doubts concerning the durability of the latest consortium. If the sovereigns of Europe were able to strike an advantageous bargain with Napoleon they would be unlikely to consider its effect upon the British, hundreds of miles away from the center of operations in Saxony, and if they did come to terms then Napoleon would be free to turn and march against him in overwhelming strength. News of what was happening in Germany traveled slowly. On the resumption of hostilities there he learned, from the French, of Napoleon's shattering victory over the Allies at Dresden. Nobody told him about French reverses at the Katzbach, at Kulm, and at Dennewitz.

Resolved, however, that the war would continue he made up

his mind in the first days of autumn. On the morning of October 7th, with Pamplona still holding out in his rear, he launched a seaward attack against Soult's fortified posts and was himself surprised by its immediate success. Enthusiasm was ebbing in the French camp. Memories of the hammerings they had received at the hands of the British at Vitoria, outside Pamplona and, more recently, during their final attempt to relieve San Sebastian, were eroding their morale. "They stood to their ramparts well enough," says a British soldier, engaged in this attack, "but at the last moment they bolted." "They met us like lions," says another, "but in the end it was like hares."

By the evening the battle was over and all Wellington's objectives were gained, at surprisingly little cost to the victors. Soult fell back on the Nivelle and from their new positions the British could now look down on the neat, highly cultivated southwestern corner of France. The veterans among them were elated and understandably so. It had been a five-year tramp, dating back to the August day in 1808 when the Duke (then Sir Arthur Wellesley) had beaten General Junot at Vimiero but there had been periods since then when the expulsion of the French legions from Portugal, to say nothing of Spain, had seemed an impossibility by an army as small as Wellington's. Even now the old habit of caution, of moving step by step, of awaiting the moment when the odds were wholly in his favor that had characterized every phase of the war, persisted in the mind of the Duke. Victories did not dazzle him. Only when he learned the result of the battle of Leipzig did he issue orders for the final heave that was to uproot Soult and drive him all the way back to Toulouse.

On October 31st Pamplona fell. On November 10th, eight days after the wreck of the Grand Army had recrossed the Rhine, the British and their allies marched on Soult's new positions, overextended along the Nivelle with the right hinged on the picturesque seaport of St. Jean-de-Luz. It was the same story over again. By nightfall the French were driven from their strongpoints and were retreating on a broad front from Bayonne to Cambo, on the river Nive. Their casualties were 4,350, of whom 1,200 were prisoners. The cost to the Allies was 3,000, five-sixths of them British. The backdoor had not been opened.

It had been battered down and the war in the Peninsula was virtually over.

Exploring the positions they captured that November day British soldiers looked curiously at the neatly constructed huts the French had built for themselves, so unlike the temporary shakedowns the men of the Light Brigade used on the line of march. Encampments were laid out in streets and squares and some of them were named. One, prophetically, was called "Rue de Paris."

10

IT PROMISED TO be another hard winter. Before Christmas snow was falling on eastern France and in the streets of Paris, where it turned into slush under the hooves of couriers scurrying to and fro with proclamations and call-up papers. Another sound replaced the familiar clatter of horse traffic. It was one that awakened nostalgic memories in the hearts of Parisiens, reminding the middle aged that they had come full circle in twenty years. Hand organs, whirring at the command of Imperial agents, were playing a song that had summoned France to arms long ago, Roguet de Lisle's *Marseillaise*.

The war chant of the Revolution had been out of vogue since the day a young Napoleon, home from his Egyptian adventure, had taken personal control of the state, bundling elected representatives through the window of the Orangery at the point of the bayonet. It had been heard, no doubt, in many a private parlor and certainly in the cellars at clandestine gatherings of Jacobins, but Napoleon, the apostle of order, had no ear for music of this kind. Now, with France certain to become Europe's battleground, de Lisle's anthem had propaganda value. The tune that had been heard ad nauseum in the faubourgs in '92 and '93 evoked a period when young men armed themselves with a pike at a street corner forge and marched off to the frontiers in sabots and blouses, proud to die in defense of the Republic, one and indivisible. Now, after two decades of unimaginable glory followed by eighteen months of catastrophe,

Music in the Snow

they were being called upon to do so again against far greater
odds than in '93. Some of them, but not a majority, responded.
It was cold weather for hiding out in barns and woods and hay-
stacks but this was preferable, at least to the practical, to trudging northeast through the rain and sleet to meet a Prussian bullet
or a Cossack lance. More often than not, when the dreaded
summons arrived for Jean and Joseph, they were not to be
found and nothing was served by waiting for them to return
to field or workshop. All over France plows were driven by
womenfolk, and the men at the work benches were too old and
bent to shoulder a musket. Provosts with lists authorizing them
to assemble a hundred men were lucky if they returned to their
depots with ten, for the roll of the side drum no longer spoke
of glory. To the conscripts of the year 1815, and to those who,
by heaven knows what artifice, had evaded successive conscriptions as far back as 1804, it had a more sinister connotation.
It recalled the rattle of clods on the lid of a coffin.

In the presence of an assembly of marshals and generals shortly
before leaving Mainz for Paris in November, Napoleon had
irritated Marmont and Macdonald by his irrational optimism.
When they questioned the validity of his plans he reproached
them for lack of zeal. "What I need," he declared, tapping General Drouot of the Guard upon the chest, "is a hundred men like
this!" Drouot had not read his Bible without learning how to
distinguish between praise and flattery. "What you need, Sire,"
he replied, "is one hundred thousand!"

It was true. Seventy thousand survivors of Leipzig could not
defend the long eastern frontier against five hundred thousand
and what use were veterans, isolated in faraway Catalonia, or
conscripts pinned down in Bayonne by Wellington, or seasoned
troops existing on siege rations in beleaguered fortress towns
like Hamburg? From some national reservoir another army
would have to be produced and during the eleven weeks the
Emperor spent in St. Cloud and the Tuileries, between early
November, 1813, and January 25, 1814, he addressed himself to
the task of raising one.

It was an undertaking that was both more difficult and less
difficult than the gigantic recruiting drive he had initiated after

his dramatic return from Russia in December, 1812. More difficult because the sources of manpower had been tapped and tapped again; less difficult because it was seen that the autocrats were already on the frontiers and there were still many Frenchmen who believed the gains of the revolution were worth preserving.

The call to arms was heard in strange quarters that winter, sometimes by those who had been deaf to earlier appeals to glory and foreign conquest. Carnot, the infant republic's organizer of victory heard it. So did men of property, who had been enriched by the confiscation of church lands and saw beggary in a return of the Bourbons. Diehard Jacobins came forward and were politely rejected. "If I must fall I will not bequeath France to the Revolution from which I rescued her," said Napoleon, remembering the trail of slime Paris mobs had left across the Tuileries Gardens in August, 1792. But Carnot's offer was accepted. Napoleon could recognize a patriot of integrity and Carnot was such a man. The brain behind the Republic's frontier victories of twenty years before, he had forsworn the Empire and retired from political life to live in poverty and obscurity. "Iron Carnot, far-planning, unconquerable," Carlyle was to write of him thirty years later, "Carnot with his cold, mathematical head and silent stubbornness of will who, in the hour of need shall not be found wanting."

"The offer of an arm sixty years old is, without doubt, but little," Carnot wrote to Napoleon, "but I thought that the example of a soldier, whose patriotic sentiments are known, might have the effect of rallying to your eagles a number of persons hesitating as to the part which they should take and who might possibly think that the only way to serve their country was to abandon it." Carnot was sent off to hold Antwerp against the Prussians and Swedes and acquitted himself well both as patriot and soldier.

Carnot was an exception but there were offers of help from more obscure Frenchmen. The acceptance of one volunteer indicates the desperation of the War Department. A certain Colonel Viriot, victim of one of the most despicable slanders on the national record, was given command of a body of irregular troops and sent to harass the invaders. His enrollment at this hour is interesting because it illustrates how the demands of a national crisis can sometimes right a wrong and outface villainy. For Viriot, a fearless soldier with a spotless record, had been dismissed from the service for daring to defy Fouché, chief of police, and for refusing to perjure himself by sending two innocent victims of a police plot to the guillotine. [1]

In ones and twos and dozens they presented themselves but not enough, not nearly enough for the nation's needs. Five hundred and seventy-five thousand Frenchmen had been called to the colors in 1812 and 1813 and three hundred thousand were now prisoners, or on the point of becoming prisoners. Another one hundred and seventy-five thousand were dead or missing, and only about a hundred thousand available for service. In spite of this and in spite of the attrition of the years between Valmy and Hanau, the population of France under Napoleon had continued to rise by an annual half-million and now, by Imperial and Senatorial decree, he was demanding *nine hundred thousand*. Impossible as it sounds the yield was a mathematical possibility. It was estimated, by men working in Government departments, that a comb-out of exemptions granted between 1804 and 1814 could be made to yield a hundred and sixty thousand. This total could be doubled by anticipating the call-up of 1815. There were nearly two hundred thousand more on the rolls of the National Guard and another paper reserve was available in what was known as the Home Guard. But names on nominal rolls are not always readily convertible into flesh and blood. Figures, especially when used by civil servants, can sometimes be made to prove that two and two add up to two and twenty, and this was the approximate difference between estimate and actuality in December, 1813. The comb-out of exemptions alone produced the anticipated total, or something approaching it; in every other column of the complicated sum the answer was a fraction of what it should have been. The effort to anticipate the 1815 conscription, for instance, was such an obvious failure that it had to be officially abandoned, whereas the drive for recruits to serve in the reserve and home forces resulted in hundreds of thousands of able-bodied men effacing themselves until the provosts had gone their way.

More than a century later, when Nazi Germany was trying

to recruit French labor after the French collapse of 1940, French officials were puzzled by the sudden dearth of young men north and south of the Vichy demarcation line. They should not have been. They could have read their own history books and reminded themselves what had occurred in every department of France between November, 1813, and spring the following year. Every city and town, every village and hamlet had its quota of stowaways, concealed by anxious relatives in attics and outhouses, or living primatively in caves and woodland shacks. They were beyond the reach of patriotic proclamations, a direct result of the terrible 29th Bulletin of 1812 and the disturbing rumors that came out of Saxony the following summer.

The illiterate plowboy, the apprentice existing on a few sous a day, feared the Imperial drillmasters more than the anticipated atrocities of Cossacks and Prussians but a substantial section of the population did in fact respond to the call to arms. In the main, it was the more enlightened section. Both inside and outside France Napoleon was still regarded by the petit bourgeoisie as the champion of a new age in which merit took precedence over hereditary privilege, a brilliant improvisor who had somehow contrived to strike an exact balance between the tyranny of feudalism and the anarchy of mob rule that had tarnished the Revolution. They were the people who rallied to the colors now, men who saw in the advance of the Allies a return to the brutish class distinctions of the eighteenth century. There were many among this group ready to concede that Napoleon had staked the gains of the Revolution on the table of personal aggrandizement but this did not mean they did not prefer his autocracy to that of the Bourbons and their cohorts seeking position. Napoleon, it was true, had involved them in endless wars, some of his own making, but he had also built roads, endowed public institutions, codified and enforced just laws, revived local industries, encouraged and developed modern husbandry, and, more important than any of these things, opened up broad avenues of advancement to those among the bourgeoisie who had ambition and the inclination to save money and work hard. It was because a very substantial number of Frenchmen remembered this that made it necessary for Blucher,

Schwartzenberg and the Czar to fight their way to Paris when their progress, judged on purely military terms, should have been little more than a parade.

The nation, however, had first to be convinced that all reasonable compromises had been explored and this Napoleon set himself to do in the period after his return to Paris. Bourrienne tells us that during this interval the Emperor only slept between the hours of eleven and three in the morning, thus putting in twenty hours of unremitting labor in one sphere or another.

Committees of the Senate and Legislature were appointed to study the terms that had been offered at Prague and to bring out reports but the findings of the latter body (implying that France should accept what Napoleon considered to be humiliating terms) provoked one of the stormiest public speeches of his career after he had forbidden their deliberations to be printed in the press. "We should wash our dirty linen in private," he answered in a fury, "and not drag it out before the world! I am alone the representative of the people. Twice twenty-four millions of French have called me to the throne. Which of you durst undertake such a burden? You have talked of concessions—concessions that even my enemies dared not ask. . . . France needs me more than I need France." There was a great deal more in this strain.

Humiliated as he was by this lack of trust in his ability to extricate France from its dilemma, he was yet privately determined to make "concessions" that would have a political impact. His first was to release the captive Ferdinand, heir apparent of the senile king of Spain, who had quarreled bitterly with his parents shortly before both of them had been lured into captivity in 1808.[2] "My political situation induces me to wish for a final adjustment of the affairs of Spain," he wrote blandly, to the unpleasant young man who had been captive in France for nearly five years, and then proceeded to accuse the English of "exciting anarchy and Jacobinism in Spain" and endeavoring to create a republic there. It is probably the only occasion the Duke of Wellington was charged with fomenting revolution.

The sudden appearance of Ferdinand in Spain would have undoubtedly embarrassed the British at that moment but in the event the Imperial bluff was called. Talleyrand, chief among the many holders of high office in France who were seeking to re-insure themselves against a return of the Bourbons, delayed matters until the Spanish Cortés had rejected Ferdinand and the tangled skein of the Spanish politics could be unraveled at leisure. Napoleon had no more success with his other gesture, an unconditional release of the Pope, also a prisoner in France, whom he directed should be sent back to Rome "in order to burst on the place like a clap of thunder." The explosion His Holiness occasioned there was not heard in the north. He was sedately re-installed by King Murat, now aligned with the Coalition while the old man himself, before leaving Fontainebleau, summoned the French cardinals and encouraged them to snub Napoleon whenever the opportunity presented itself. His lack of co-operation is not hard to understand. Napoleon, it is true, had been the means of re-establishing the Catholic Church in France after the atheistic posturings of the Terrorists, but since then his treatment of Christ's Vicar had been so highhanded that it had outraged the conscience of Catholic Europe. He was now paying the price for the impatience he showed toward all who opposed his personal conception of the reorganization of Western Europe upon modern lines.

In some ways, notwithstanding his unshakeable confidence in himself and his demoniacal energy, he was striking out like a blind Samson goaded to madness by his tormentors. A note of despotism creeps into his correspondence of this period and it is not to his credit as a man who had, time and again, set himself up as the patron of sound judgment and civic virtue. In a letter to the governor of Antwerp concerning the mutinous Dutch, he wrote, "Burn the first village within your reach which puts on the Orange cockade and publish an Order of the Day, to the effect that the first person to be found wearing such a cockade will be shot." A thread of hysteria is apparent in nearly all the letters he dictated before rejoining the army. "You will do this. . . ." "He is to do that. . . ." "This will not be tolerated. . . ." "Swift justice on the evil-disposed will be meted out. . . ." It was as though he now saw himself as the baffled and bedeviled father of a vast, unruly family, whose extravagancies and follies were courting universal ruin and thus qualified them for merciless chastisement. He took no share of the responsibility for the war that was bleeding Europe white. Then or later he did not see himself as the man who could be blamed for any war save that in the Peninsula, where he frankly admitted his error.

II

Even now it was not too late to temporize. The Allies, poised on the Rhine, were by no means the band of brothers subsequent generations came to consider them at this point of crisis in the European story. On the contrary they were a querulous, shifty, meanspirited, bewildered concert of egotists, torn by mutual distrust and having but one thing in common, a rigid belief in absolutism. Beyond that there was hardly any common ground. Britain, with the cold and inscrutable Castlereagh as her spokesman,[3] was concerned, as always, with restoring to Europe a balance of power that would insure her maritime supremacy. To achieve this it was absolutely essential that the Lowlands directly opposite her coasts remained independent. For this, in past centuries, she had fought again and again. She was to do so twice more in the twentieth century.

The Prussians had no real common purpose, not even among one another. Blucher and his lieutenants pursued personal vengeance, the idealist Stein sought German unity, the king any enlargement of his realm so long as its population could be dominated by a Hohenzollern.

The Austrians, guided by Metternich, wanted no more than to confine Napoleon behind what they thought of as his natural boundaries and were quite willing to see him continue to menace British trade in the north so long as he was prepared to let Austria dominate Italy and regain her lost provinces on the Adriatic. What Metternich feared most of all was a Prussia strong enough to challenge Austria's dominant position in Europe.

Russia, physically the most powerful partner in the Coalition, was also indifferent to British maritime interests for she had ambitions of her own in the east and although prepared to see Prussia enlarged at anybody else's expense the prospect of a strong and resurgent Austria made no appeal to her. Among the Russians there were those who, like Blucher, hoped to see

Napoleon repaid in his own coin and Paris occupied after the fashion of Moscow, but they were not a majority. Fanaticism, in the main, was confined to the Prussian ranks. The Czar would have been content to see Bernadotte rule France but such a solution was unthinkable to Francis of Austria. He was not conducting an expensive war in order to unseat his daughter and replace her, as Queen-Empress, by a soapboiler's daughter who had made a lucky match with a Gascon sergeant-major.

As the junior partner in this vast enterprise Bernadotte had little to say in their councils. Already he had infuriated the Czar by promising Marshal Davout and his Hamburg garrison free passage back to France if he would surrender the city. He took this opportunity to move north and menace Norway which he not only coveted but had been promised as part of his Judas money. Two of his best corps were attached to the Prussian General Bulow for a descent upon the Netherlands.

Apart from mutual mistrust of one another there was another aspect of the situation that was beginning to worry the victors of Leipzig. Nationalism was on the march, not only west of the Rhine, where it might conceivably repeat its startling performance of '93 and '94, but also among the underprivileged in Vienna, Berlin and even St. Petersburg. In proclaiming a people's war on their own soil the autocrats of Europe began to suspect that they had started a fire their heirs would be unable to put out after the original incendiaries had been punished and reformed. As one Austrian diplomat noted, almost plaintively, "The war for the emancipation of the States bids fair to become one for the emancipation of the people." This was a daunting prospect to men who had fought their way to the Rhine with no real war aims in mind other than securing their own futures as hereditary officeholders and adding to their patrimony countries like Poland.

Out of this hellish brew of greed, bitterness, jealousy and insecurity, Austria, least belligerent of the partners, secured a temporary advantage. Hoping to bring the war to a conclusion without the cost and the long-term risks of an invasion of France, Metternich persuaded his country's allies to put forward yet another set of proposals. They came to be known as "The Frankfurt Proposals."

They were comparatively simple terms. Austria was to keep sufficient Italian territory to insure her domination of that area. France was to keep Nice and Savoy. Holland and Spain were to be liberated and France to rest within her "natural" rather than her "ancient" boundaries. Napoleon was to maintain an "influence" in Germany, and Great Britain, assured of her maritime rights, was to return the French colonies that had fallen to her during the long war.

Even Metternich, who stood to gain most from these arrangements, could not have believed that they would form a practical basis for a general settlement. Neither Prussia nor Russia favored them, and Castlereagh, on behalf of Britain, must have seen in them the futility of going to the help of Continental powers for any but national motives. And yet they were put forward as a final attempt to seek pacification before a single Allied soldier crossed the Rhine and some weeks were to pass before they were disowned by Russia and Britain, the former because they would have robbed her of her triumph, the latter because peace on these lines would have left France in possession of the Belgian ports and, in the words of Castlereagh, "imposed upon Britain the charge of a perpetual war establishment."

Had Napoleon made prompt acceptance of the Frankfurt Proposals—and he would have been well advised to do so—there is a possibility that Austria might have been detached, Russia turned back in disgust, and Britain and Prussia left to fight on alone against a patriotically united France. Perhaps Napoleon did not take them seriously. He had an excuse for not doing so. On the very day he returned his qualified reply, suggesting the setting up of a new conference at Mannheim, the Allies issued a new proclamation designed for circulation in France. It was aimed specifically at him. "We desire France," declared this latest broadsheet, "to be great, strong and prosperous and are making war, not on France but on that preponderance which Napoleon had too long exercised, to the misfortune of Europe and to France herself."

Stripped of equivocal, politicians' double talk the Frankfurt Proposals were simply an offer, on the part of Austria, to acknowledge the early conquests of Republican France (mainly in Belgium and Savoy) in return for a free hand in Italy and some kind of guarantee against the creation of a strong, unified Prussia. How could they succeed, even supposing that Napoleon was now ready to settle for a much smaller slice of the European cake? Neither the Czar, who had seen his capital burned, the Baron Stein group, who dreamed of a pan-German State, nor Britain, who had fought for twenty years to keep France from dominating the Continent, could derive the least satisfaction from Metternich's offer. A conference was indeed established without an armistice, and deliberated for six unrewarding weeks at Châtillon, but its bargaining counters were battles lost and won and it was soon overtaken by events that eliminated the reason for its assembly.

During this lull between the autumn fighting and the invasion of France, Francis of Austria, perhaps one of the most accomplished hypocrites the House of Habsburg has ever produced, continued to write fondly to his daughter, Marie Louise, about to be installed as Regent in the absence of her husband fighting Austrian troops on French soil. "As regards peace," he wrote in December, 1813, "be assured that I desire it no less than you, than all France and—as I hope also—your husband. In peace alone lies happiness and prosperity. My ideas are moderate. I only wish for what accords with a lasting peace, but in this world wishes are not enough." It is a depressing reflection upon human affairs that in the nineteen sixties, after two world wars ending in the mushroom cloud over Hiroshima, the heads of state all over the world correspond in identical terms.

III

On January 23rd in the Tuileries there occurred almost the last of those glittering confrontations between a man who knew how to extract the last drop of loyalty from a tincture of emotional oratory and careful stage management, and the captives of his spellbinding sway over the Gallic heart. Summoning the officers of the National Guard, some of whom were known royalists and other dedicated republicans, he appeared before them accompanied only by his wife, the Empress, and his son, the three-year-old King of Rome. "I entrust my wife and my son to your courage," he said and the result of this deceptively simple appeal was what might have been expected. Breaking their ranks the officers surged forward with clamorous cries of "Vive l'Empereur!" At four in the morning on the 25th he left for the front. He was never to see Marie Louise or his son again.

Napoleon expected invasion by way of Liége and with an initial force of only 50,000 men his plans to meet it were obliged to be flexible. Macdonald held the lower Rhine at Cologne. Marmont, Napoleon's oldest friend, was stationed on the middle course of the frontier river. Victor commanded in the fortress area on the higher reaches and was expected to strengthen himself with new levies. Bertrand was on the right bank of the river opposite Mainz. Ney, wounded at Leipzig, had reported back for duty and so had Oudinot, who had just risen from his typhus sick bed. Mortier also joined him and Berthier was in his old post as Chief of Staff. Augereau, grumbling that nothing much could be expected of him with boys who did not even know how to load a musket, was at Lyons with 25,000. Soult was still battling for his life east of the Pyrenees, with Wellington and his allies keeping him on the defensive in the Toulouse area.

In the meantime the Allies were already west of the Rhine at two points. There was no question, as Napoleon had hoped, of them awaiting the arrival of spring. They were on the march along some three hundred miles of France's eastern frontier, an immense array that might be checked, pushed back here and there, and even kept from converging upon Paris for a few weeks, but could never be halted in its slow, westward surge. Only one professional soldier in the world would have accepted such a challenge, at odds of at least ten to one, but it was met. For eight weeks, as columns fought and maneuvered in the snow and mud between Arnhem in the north and the Swiss border in the south, Europe held its breath.

Schwartzenberg, with 209,000, was the first in the field. He crossed the river between Basle and Schaffhausen (the goal of many escaping British, French and American P.O.W.s in a later war) on December 20th, violating Swiss neutrality and hoping to turn to the frontier fortresses and the Vosges Mountains. Blucher, with 47,000 men, passed the Rhine between Cologne and Rastadt on the first day of the new year, aiming at Liége and Brussels, the route chosen by Von Kluck's legions in the summer of 1914. The Prussian General Bulow, who had proved such a stubborn opponent in Saxony, invaded further north with 30,000, including some of Bernadotte's Swedes, striking into the Netherlands where the Dutch were already in revolt.

It was a clumsy, old fashioned approach and making full allowance for divided councils and national jealousies proved that the Allied leaders had learned very little from the Napoleonic text book. With a massive preponderance in men and armament they again presented the master strategist with an opportunity to attack and defeat them in detail and within days of his arrival at Châlons he took that opportunity. A week later the Allied columns were presenting Europe with a spectacle that was not without humor, a group of amateur fishermen falling over one another in an attempt to catch the tail of a harpooned whale.

Before looking closely at this absorbing game of catch-as-catch-can it is useful to return to the memoirs of three Frenchmen actually caught up in the struggle. Each of them throw some light on the temper of the times.

Captain Barrès, based at Mainz, was a witness to Blucher's New Year's day advance. At Ogersheim, on the last night of 1813, he met a friend leaving to occupy a redoubt in front of Mannheim, where the river Neckar joins the Rhine. The man commanded three officers and a hundred other ranks; his orders were to "conquer or die," and on no account enter into any negotiation. Towards dawn Barrès heard the Prussian cannonade. It told him that Blucher was on the point of crossing the river and was actually attacking his comrade's post. Hastening to his aid Barrès found the plain covered with Prussian scouts and the redoubt enveloped. There was no hope of relieving it in the face of the enemy's main advance and he retired to Mainz. The little garrison held out for three hours, accounting for seven hundred Prussians. It was a foretaste of what the Allies could expect when they entered France. The fifty-odd French survivors of this fight were treated with consideration, the king of Prussia himself ordering that the officers' swords be returned to them.

On January 2nd, having once again been obliged to abandon

a meal owing to the enemy's rapid advance, Barrès and his men retreated by way of Worms. The pâté de foie gras with which he and his fellow officers were about to celebrate the New Year was hastily divided. "There was no longer any question of eating it en famille," Barrès recalls, smiling at the memory of the commandant shouting ten times over, as he called for his horse, "Don't forget the pâté!" They arrived in Mainz with the Russian cavalry at their heels.

From then on, for Barrès and his comrades, it was siege warfare. The blockade began on January 4th. It did not end until May 4th when the Emperor was on his way into exile.

Colonel Marbot, of the 23rd Chasseurs, saw the new year in at Mons, in a countryside that had witnessed the triumphs of the revolutionary army more than twenty-one years before. It was now disaffected, yearning to return to the old paternal government of Austria. As commandant of the department Marbot had four hundred recruits, some gendarmes, and two hundred dismounted troopers of his own regiment of whom fifty were deemed unreliable because they were Belgians. Every day brought news of fresh enemy advances and the townspeople grew so restive that the mayor warned Marbot, in his own interests, that he would be wise to evacuate. He was talking to the wrong man. For fourteen years Marbot, still only thirty-one years of age and carrying the scars of wounds received in Spain, Russia, Poland, Germany, Austria and Italy, had been conditioned to expect submissive co-operation from civilians. No mayor on earth was going to talk him into leaving a post assigned to him without orders. Instead, he recalls, "I decided to show my teeth," and at once bared them in a manner that caused both mayor and populace to have second thoughts concerning an uprising.

At Marbot's request the mayor assembled all the notables and their peasant supporters in the town square where they might hear the proposition put to the garrison. Having thus concentrated all the potential leaders of the district in one place under the muzzles of French carbines, Marbot made a different proposal. "At three rolls of the drum," he said, "I shall give the order to fire into the crowd and put a torch to the town." To underline his threat he added that his men would shoot anyone attempting to extinguish burning houses. Incipient revolt gave way to instant conciliation. The people of Mons settled down to await the advance of the Prussians.

They arrived more secretively than had been anticipated. A band of three hundred Prussian marauders, dressed as Cossacks in order that the subjects of the Czar should incur the odium their outrages caused among civilians, entered Mons by night in the hope of kidnapping Marbot and depriving the garrison of its leader. Like the mayor they chose the wrong town. Surrounding Marbot's hotel, and furious at not finding him (he was sleeping with his chasseurs at the barracks) they looted the wine, got uproariously drunk, and killed an old soldier of Marbot's regiment who had lost his leg in Russia and was a respected native of the district. The townspeople reacted violently. Warning Marbot of the danger they co-operated with him in laying an ambush and in the fight that followed over two-thirds of the Prussian "Cossacks" were killed. They were so drunk that they were incapable of defending themselves. With three hundred captured horses Marbot was able to remount his squadrons and thereafter lived at peace with the inhabitants until ordered to pull back to Cambrai.

Up in the Arnhem district where, as a young officer with no thoughts of becoming a marshal of France, Macdonald had shared in the republican victories of '94–'95, the son of the clansman again advanced the policy he had urged on his Chief ever since the retreat of 1812, one of concentrating garrison troops in the field and not leaving them to be mopped up in pockets like the garrisons on the Elbe and the Oder. Pressed by overwhelming numbers he evacuated Bois-le-Duc, Wessel, Venloo and Maestricht. "I could only watch the Rhine, not defend it," he says. "On paper I was supposed to be commanding a force of 50,000 to 60,000 men whereas actually I had not more than 3,000."

Three thousand was enough for a man who had escaped across the Elster on a tree trunk. Skillfully he fought his way back to the rendezvous at Châlons to find that this town was on the point of being evacuated, but within hours a cry for help came from the French commander of Vitry, to the southeast. So Macdonald held on, fighting off the same corps of Prussians that had deserted him at the end of the Russian campaign. The Prussian commander came in under a flag of truce, threatening that unless Macdonald vacated Châlons at once he would shell it and set it on fire. "As you please," said Macdonald, indifferently, and the threat was put into execution, French civilians running about in their nightshirts with the thermometer well below zero. Experiences of this kind were common enough to civilians in vast areas of Europe between Moscow and Cádiz but it was a very long time since such indignities had been visited upon the French.

11

To the generation that grew to manhood in the first decade of the twentieth century the place names of the terrain have terrible significance: Mons, Verdun, the Marne, Châlons, Soissons and Château Thierry. Its river barriers, its woods and eminences would have been familiar to earlier generations of warriors. Men had fought here for two thousand years, Roman and Gaul, Frank and Hun, French and English, Armagnac and Burgundian. The bones of hundreds of thousands of them lay under the soil of the great triangle with its apex at Paris, its northerly and southerly extremities at Rheims and Bar-sur-Aube. A whole string of battles were to be fought here in snow covered fields and winding, second class wagon roads, churned to a slough under the hobnailed boots of five armies.

His original plan was in ruins. Pondering his chances at St. Cloud he had conceived a vast strategical gamble that, if carried into effect, would have resembled his thunderflash descent from the Channel coasts to Bohemia in the autumn of 1805. Augereau's augmented reserve, lying at Lyons, was to invade Switzerland and make contact with Eugène's Italians while he, with his main striking force, would interpose between Blucher moving west and Schwartzenberg advancing on Paris from the southeast. But Augereau's sloth (or worse), and Murat's treachery, made nonsense of such a grandiose scheme. The former fencing master at Lyons would not move, and down on the Mincio Eugène was still boxed between Hiller's Austrian-Bavarian army and

The Boots of Resolution

King Murat's Neapolitans. The gap between Blucher and Schwartzenberg presented Napoleon with his sole opportunity and he hurried forward to widen it without a moment's delay.

Oudinot and two divisions of the Young Guard struck at the Prussians at St. Dizier, twenty-five miles to the southeast, driving them back to the gates of Bar-le-Duc. Here the marshal was on familiar ground. Bar-le-Duc was his home town, where he might have been a prosperous brewer had there been no revolution and no Bonaparte. He was denied the pleasure of expelling the Prussians from his own backyard. Napoleon, studying reconnaissance reports and maps, called him back and the army turned south for Brienne on the Aube. Word had come that Blucher himself and the Russian General Alsusieff were already in possession of town and castle.

Oudinot was not alone in recognizing local hedgerows. Napoleon himself was making a sentimental journey. Brienne had housed the Military Academy at which a twelve-year-old Corsican child studied in the last days of the ancient regime; a strange, moody little pensioner, unfamiliar with the French language, puffed up with a pride that his schoolfellows thought comic and insolent. Returning to Brienne near the end of his interminable journeying Napoleon found it bristling with foreign bayonets. "Drive them out!" he told Ney and Ney, happy to be on the offensive again, did so in the grand manner he had stormed the great redoubt at Borodino. The conscripts followed him eagerly. If Napoleon's presence was worth a hundred thousand, "Le Rougeaud's" was worth two divisions. Beside him, as they chased the Russians and Prussians from the town and terraces, was Oudinot and also Victor's son-in-law, General Chateau, whose death in action later in the campaign was to have an important effect on French fortunes.

By the time the short winter afternoon was spent, the enemy retained only the castle and were evacuating even that. Blucher, stunned by the speed and fury of the attack, left a half-eaten dinner and would have been taken prisoner had he not led his horse down a stone stairway minutes before the French columns sealed the exits of the fortress.

Two terrified women emerged from the vaults and were recognized by Oudinot as cousins. They had taken shelter there after fleeing from Bar-le-Duc and the marshal, who had appeared like a prince in a fairy tale, asked them to join the Emperor at supper. It must have been a happy occasion for, apart from the cousins' strange encounter and the speed of the victory, Napoleon himself had just escaped death. In the early evening dusk, riding forward with a small escort, he was suddenly surrounded by a band of Cossacks. Two of them, probably not recognizing their target but intent only upon fighting their way out, charged him with leveled lances. General Gourgaud shot the lancer attacking from behind and General Corbineau killed the other. Under almost identical circumstances he had been rescued from the horsemen of the plains one day's march from Moscow. "I shall die in my bed, like a damned coglione," he had prophesied at the time. Six thousand of Blucher's Prussians died at Brienne but the loss to the French was not much less.

On the next day, January 30th, the Emperor took a closer look at the town, recognizing a tree beside the river where, as a twelve-year-old, he had first read the Italian poet Tasso. He might have reflected that Tasso spent the last seven years of his life in an asylum, dying shortly before he could be crowned Poet Laureate in Rome. From Brienne to a grave on St. Helena was seven years and four months. The writer of fiction would think twice before using the coincidence to end a saga that had carried this man from Brienne and back again in a little over thirty years. Since leaving here, to pursue his studies at the Cadet School in Paris, he had dominated a continent and commanded in fields as far apart as Spain, Russia and the Holy Land; now he was back, leading an army along the banks of a river where he had spent five unhappy years of his lonely childhood. Emil Ludwig, who, of all his biographers has come closest to the poet and dreamer in Napoleon Bonaparte, writes of his period here: "No one tells us that he ever saw the boy laugh." What had he to laugh about? Thinking of himself as an alien in a land of enemies he had no money, wore shabby ill-fitting clothes, was of puny stature, and possessed little more than a rudimentary grasp of the French language. "If you Corsicans are such brave fellows, why did you let yourselves be beaten by our unconquerable troops?" he was asked by one of the young snobs abounding in the school. "We were one to ten," Napoleon replied. Here, after so long a journey, the odds were about the same.

There was no time to measure the dreams of boyhood against the achievements and blunders of middle age. Blucher, swearing like the trooper he never ceased to be, drew off and groped for Schwartzenberg's right wing, finding it at Bar-sur-Aube and getting a welcome reinforcement of twelve thousand to make good his losses if not his pride. Down here, in the path of the Allies, history was lifting the corner of the curtain to reveal a little of what future generations of Prussian militarists had in store for the West. Orders were issued to deal mercilessly with any French communities defending their hearths as guerilla fighters. Truculent civilians were to be shot and offending villages burned. Two were burned within the next forty-eight hours. They were La Chaise and Morvilliers, the first of many. Clausewitz, the Prussian theorist, was fighting in the Allied ranks at that time. He was soon to become the apostle of outrage, promulgating a doctrine of unrelenting and allegedly war-shortening terror that spread like a terrible fungus in the Prussian military mind down through the years. At Sedan, in 1870, patriotic civilians were butchered as *franc-tireurs*. On the road through Belgium, in August 1914, the path of the German Army was milestoned by reeking towns and murdered civilians, and it was given out that the victims of these incidents had fired on German soldiers. In 1940 the teachings of Clausewitz had progressed so far that no special pleading was considered necessary on the part of Nazi executioners. All over Belgium and north-eastern France are rows of headstones with inscriptions reading "*Fusillé par les Allemands, 1914*" and "*Fusillé par les Allemands, 1944*." In the town of Tamines alone there are 384, each bearing the former inscription. There may be older graves bearing the date "1814" in villages between Brienne and La Rothière. Perhaps this is where Clausewitz conceived his theory of pacification. The veterans of the Grand Army had occupied German billets since 1806 and it would be foolish to pretend that there had been no instances of loot and outrage against defenseless civilians. But such instances had been isolated acts, committed by brutalized men far gone in drink, or bloodlust, or both. They had never been part of a deliberate policy, imposed from above. All wars bear heavily upon civilians in occupied territory but the common soldier in the west is not necessarily a murderer, or not until outrage is promulgated as a policy.

Napoleon knew the propaganda value of these acts. Three days after the storming of Brienne he wrote Caulaincourt, still absorbed in the bluff and counter bluff of the Châtillon discussions, "The enemy's troops are behaving abominably. All the inhabitants are taking refuge in the woods . . . the enemy eat up everything, seize all the horses and cattle, and all the clothes they can find, even the poor rags of the peasants; they beat everyone, women as well as men, and commit rapes galore. I have seen this state of things with my own eyes . . . you must draw a vigorous picture of the enemy's excesses. Towns like Brienne, with two thousand inhabitants, haven't a soul left in them!"

II

Brienne was a victory but its effect was even less decisive than Lutzen or Dresden in the Saxon campaigns. Blucher fell back but with his recent reinforcement, and the main Allied army in close touch, he was soon ready to fight again. This he did at La Rothière, a few miles southeast of Brienne.

Napoleon, believing the old Prussian isolated, advanced on him with 40,000 men and at noon, on February 1st, Blucher attacked. The French wings held firm but the center yielded and Marmont, attacked elsewhere by General Wrede, also fell back. A single charge on the part of the Austro-Bavarian cavalry captured seven guns, one of fifty-four pieces lost by the French that day, as well as six thousand men, nearly half of them prisoners. There were familiar flashes of heroism. A battery of the Old Guard, surrounded by the enemy, refused to surrender and cut its way out by forming squadron. The bridge over the Aube at L'Esmont was repaired during the action and the French were able to draw off and make for Troyes, which they reached on February 3rd. It was here that Napoleon encountered General Reynier, one of the senior officers captured during the scramble for the Lindenau bridge, in October. Releasing him on parole the Czar had said, "We shall be in

Paris before you." What then were the plenipotentiaries discussing around the Châtillon conference table?

Snow was falling daily, the first snow, as A. G. MacDonell
remarks, ever to come to the rescue of Napoleon. In the past
it had always helped the enemy. It had checked his descent
from the great St. Bernard in 1800, robbed him of victory at
Eylau in 1807, and made possible the escape of Sir John Moore's
army in Spain almost two years later. It had also destroyed the
Grand Army in 1812 but now it slowed the pace of his pursuers and gave him a few days to regroup. On February 7th
he pulled back to the town of Nogent.

At the Allied Council of War that followed this withdrawal
a new plan was decided upon. Blucher, with 50,000, would take
the shortest route to Paris and Schwartzenberg, with 150,000,
would advance via Sens, thirty-five miles west of Troyes and
twenty miles southwest of Nogent. Again the fatal division, not
only on the field but in council. Terms were still available, even
at this impossibly late hour. France could have her 1791 frontiers
and she owed this miserly offer to the reluctance of Austria to
see a Bourbon back on the throne. The Czar's ambitions fed
upon the leagues over which his army had advanced. He had
now decided to take the whole of Poland and compensate Prussia with Saxony. Even Castlereagh, the British envoy, was
alarmed, seeing no prospect of a permanent peace in the total
reduction of France or the elevation of Bernadotte, still the
Czar's nominee to Napoleon's throne. The arguments of the
British and Austrian delegation were not sufficiently persuasive
to stop the Allied advance on Paris but at least they prevailed
upon Alexander to agree to the French choosing their own
head of state if and when Napoleon was brought to bay.

In the second week of February Napoleon struck again, winning five battles in nine days.

The setting for what was to prove the penultimate display of
the world's most brilliant soldier was a landscape of low, wooded
hills, swampy river bottoms, small towns linked by dirt roads
and isolated, at this season of the year, by flooded ditches and
wide, waterlogged meadows, a landscape intersected by the
Seine, the Aube, the Marne and the Yonne.

It was not, one would have thought, an ideal battleground for a text book campaign against vastly superior numbers. Snow fell intermittently, leaving the hills white below blue-black crowns of leafless trees. River margins froze but rarely hard enough to bear the weight of a man, much less a gun carriage. On the few days when the temperatures rose the thaw flooded highways and tracks that might have been negotiable in frosty weather. Mist hung in the river valleys and the northeast wind, cheerless as the winds of the Russian plain, soughed across the desolate countryside carrying showers of sleet or thin, persistent rain. Overhead the sun shone fitfully between the brief storms but more often the sky was slate grey, with a hint of more snow to come. There was little or nothing to eat and even the Imperial Guard, accustomed to living on the country, was unwilling to pillage French farms and small holdings. At his Headquarters at Nogent Napoleon had dashed off one of his gusty letters, this time to Quartermaster Daure: "The army is dying of hunger! All your reports that it is being properly fed are pure moonshine. . . . Let me have returns of the amount of rice in the different army corps . . . but let it be an accurate report, don't double the figures of the stock in hand!"

And yet, in spite of shortage of men, shortage of rations, foul weather, and mired roads, it was not an entirely hopeless picture. Blucher, chasing the outnumbered Macdonald down the Marne Valley, was committing a series of military blunders, whereas Schwartzenberg, advancing down the Seine, was behaving in a contrary manner, moving so slowly and cautiously that he could not even pin down Oudinot's 25,000 at odds of six to one. In the temperamental differences of these two professional soldiers lay the solution to the puzzle Napoleon had to solve and solve at once if Paris was to be saved. It was necessary to exploit the headstrong qualities of Blucher at the expense of Schwartzenberg's timidity and in achieving this he fought a campaign superior in conception and execution to any he had waged in his youth.

Writing to his brother Joseph from Nogent he outlined his plan to pounce on the dispersed Blucher, annihilate his scattered corps, then turn on Schwartzenberg's more powerful army. He did not have much hope of defeating the larger force in the field but he calculated that he could block its advance and thus save the capital. "After that," he wrote, vaguely, "I shall await new combinations." Only himself and possibly Talleyrand and Metternich knew what lay behind the phrase "new combinations."

As an opening move Marmont, in glum and pessimistic mood, was dispatched north to Sézanne. His command, only a hundred or two in excess of four thousand, was a forlorn hope but close behind him came the Emperor, with 8,000 of the Old Guard, Ney with 6,000 conscripts of the line, and 10,000 cavalry under such experienced leaders as Grouchy, Nansouty and Doumere, perhaps 28,500 all told, counting in the advance guard.

Victor, with another 8,000 was left at Nogent and ordered to hold himself in readiness to march north or south as the occasion required. Oudinot was still retreating down the Seine before Schwartzenberg's Austro-Russian juggernaut. Macdonald, sick and exhausted after his fighting retreat from the Lowlands, had been pushed as far west as the little town of La Ferté-sur-Jouarre, only thirty miles east of Paris.

In the capital there was panic, not allayed by the fumblings of Joseph, the Emperor's official deputy. He was not wholly to blame for his lack of resolution. Letters from Imperial Headquarters urged him to post two hundred and fifty marksmen at each gate, but he had strict instructions not to risk the capture of the Empress and the King of Rome, even if their safety meant the sacrifice of Paris. Remembering the rout at Vitoria the previous summer Joseph might have wondered what two hundred and fifty marksmen, half of them National Guards, could achieve against 150,000 enemies advancing down the Seine, and another 50,000 advancing down the Marne. He wrung his hands, as he had done so often in Madrid. A British detainee, passing the Vendome column, saw a notice posted on its base: "*Passez vite, il va tomber!*" But all was not lost, even if only one man in the Grand Army kept his nerve. Within days a stream of 6,000 prisoners and several captured stands of colors were to appear at those same gates and pass under the astonished gaze of National Guardsmen who had been drapers, coopers and vintners until the latest conscription.

The first triumph was Marmont's. At Champaubert, between

Sézanne and Épernay, he ran into two isolated corps of Russians awaiting reinforcements. They were commanded by General Alsusieff, who had been thrown out of Brienne and numbered about 4,500, a hundred or so more than Marmont had under his hand. Marmont did not wait for support but attacked at once, his boys charging forward with the same élan as their predecessors at Lutzen and Bautzen a year before. Some of them did not know the rudiments of their new trade. Marmont found one standing steadily under a shower of balls and asked why he did not fire back. "I could aim as well as the next man but no one has shown me how to load," was the reply. Nearby was another, more prudent lad, who passed his musket to his lieutenant saying, "You've been at this job a long time, sir. Take the musket and fire and I'll supply the cartridges."[1] The Russians, who could not have realized the weakness of the force opposed to them, were driven from the field. Alsusieff and other officers were taken prisoner, to dine with the Emperor of France in a wayside cottage that same night.

Napoleon exaggerated the small victory into a triumph. Addressing Marmont and others that evening he said, "Another day like this and we'll be back on the Vistula." He must have been joking but the joke fell flat, as he soon realized from the blank expressions of his staff, so that he added, quickly, "And then I'll make peace on the natural frontier of the Rhine."

"As if he would!" comments Marmont bitterly, in memoirs written when his ducal title, Ragusa, had been added to the French language as a word synonymous with bad faith.

Champaubert had been fought on February 10th. The next day there was another larger and equally decisive encounter at Montmirail nearby. Isolated divisions of Prussians, under Generals Yorck and Kleist, supported by some Russians under General Sacken, were attacked with the same dash and a good deal more skill. Mortier pinned down the main body to the front while Napoleon, moving in on the flank, separated the Russians from the allies. By dusk the enemy were streaming back towards Château Thierry, abandoning guns, small arms, and the spoils of a looted countryside. Here was a splendid opportunity for Macdonald, nearer Paris, to convert a defeat into a disaster that could have destroyed Blucher's army as a fighting force.

He missed it but it was not his fault. Once again the result of a campaign depended upon a mined bridge and again a premature detonation exacted the inevitable penalty.

Macdonald's fighting retreat from the Rhine had been conducted with skill and courage. The garrison of Vitry had been rescued and the Scotsman's corps, despite continued harrying, was still in being. Once, on the road from Châlons, the marshal had only escaped capture by minutes but a series of forced marches enabled him to get to La Ferté-sous-Jouarre ahead of his pursuers. His job, at this stage of the campaign, was to cover Meaux, and after Meaux the road to Paris. He knew something of what was going on south of his line of march but not very much, for the situation was confused. Prussian cavalry were roaming the countryside between his force and the Emperor and it was not easy to communicate with Imperial Headquarters. He fought skirmishes every day, recrossed the Marne by the bridge at Trilport and, anxious to preserve this vital link, made his bivouac among a pile of fagots on the bank. Exhausted, and far from well, he went to sleep to be awakened, like Napoleon at Lindenau, by a violent explosion. A match had been applied to the mined bridge and his only access to the far bank was now the bridge at Meaux, some way downstream.

The accident could not have occurred at a more unfortunate moment. Word came almost at once that Napoleon had just beaten the enemy at Champaubert and Montmirail so that Macdonald, no longer pursued but able to turn on his pursuers, could have marched upstream and cut off the enemy's retreat at Château Thierry. He did what he could, sending his cavalry round by the bridge at Meaux, but they arrived too late to box Blucher's men between two fires.

Finding Château Thierry undefended the Prussian fugitives from Montmirail played havoc in the town. Houses were looted, women raped and civilians butchered but the townsmen fought back with any means that came to hand. Prussian stragglers were killed and with the arrival of the French vanguard, under Marmont, the enemy were hunted into the woods. Marmont's men, storming into the town on the 13th, saw hysterical women dragging wounded Prussians through the streets and throwing them into the Marne. If northeastern France as a whole had shown as much spirit as the townspeople of Château Thierry the invaders would have paid an impossibly high price for Paris but it was not to be. Only where the inhabitants suffered gross outrage was there a flare-up of partisan spirit of the kind that had lost the Spanish peninsula to the French. Marmont, still spearheading the flying advance, took the road for Châlons down which the Prussians were now flying, jettisoning equipment as they went.

On the night of the 13th Napoleon had caught up with Marmont at Vauchamps. By then, however, news had reached him that a situation of mounting desperation was building in the Seine valley, where Schwartzenberg's vastly superior army was pushing the combined forces of Victor and Oudinot towards the capital. Victor had had to abandon the bridge at Nogent and the two marshals were badly in need of help. Napoleon's military instinct told him that it was essential to press his own victories home and destroy Blucher before turning on his stronger but less resolute foe. He sent Macdonald and 12,000 men southwest to Montereau, where Victor was still holding on to the Paris approaches. Then, with his own force, he flung himself at Blucher's battered battalions.

The old Prussian warrior was now in serious difficulties. Practically all his cavalry had been destroyed or dispersed at Champaubert, Montmirail and Château Thierry, but he was still aggressive and met his adversary head-on at Vauchamps. It was a courageous gesture but it could not halt the tide of French victory. To reach the battlefield at all Napoleon had to make a flank march beset by appalling difficulties over half-frozen morasses but he got there before Marmont's advance guard had yielded ground and made certain of victory by sending Grouchy and his cavalry round to the Prussian rear to cut the retreat to Châlons.

Never was Blucher in greater danger of extermination and it is to his credit as a general that he met the challenge and survived, despite tremendous losses in men and material. Forming solid squares he faced front with one while those behind cut their way through the encircling cavalry, the squares retiring in rotation until darkness fell, bringing respite to his hard pressed columns. Notwithstanding their obstinate courage the resumption of fighting at dawn would have seen the end of the Prussians but news from the other fighting front made pursuit impossible. Dispatches arrived announcing that Oudinot and Victor were now pushed back as far as Nangis, some thirty miles from the capital, that the roads were cluttered with refugees (how often in the next century-and-a-half would roads east of Paris witness these processions!) and that scouting parties of Baskirs, Tartars and Kalmucks were already foraging in the neighborhood of Fontainebleau. It was time to double back and deal with Schwartzenberg as decisively as he had dealt with Blucher.

In four days, with less than thirty thousand men under his command, Napoleon had smashed an army of fifty thousand and won three battles at odds of two to one and two-and-a-half to one. If it had been done once it could be done again. Then was the time to talk about treaties.

III

The sham conference at Châtillon was still sitting, its proposals and counterproposals regulated by news from the battlefields. The pacific Caulaincourt, representing Napoleon, was weighed down with responsibility. At one stage his master had given him carte blanche to resolve the future of France, but always when prospects looked promising, he had written last minute notes that qualified his acceptance of Allied terms. The Frankfurt Proposals, the "natural" boundaries of France, the "ancient" boundaries of France, the "boundaries of '91," all had figured on the agenda at one time or another, but how much good faith was present at either side of the table? This is impossible to judge because the men who deliberated to the accompaniment of gunfire were themselves irresolute and confused, whereas the minds of skilled negotiators like Metternich and Castlereagh are far too devious to yield up their innermost secrets to later generations. Their memoirs, and their state papers, tell some of the truth but always less than half of it. Sometimes, as in the case of a romantic like Czar Alexander, or a drill-sergeant like Blucher, it is possible to make accurate guesses concerning their real intentions, but in the case of professional diplomats, Talleyrand and the like, an almost inpenetrable web of intrigue, ambition, and self-interest obscures all but the broadest issues.

Certain it was that the Coalition counsels were still divided. Austria seems to have been won round to Britain's preference for a restored Bourbon. Castlereagh still held fast to the basic principle of a free Antwerp and a free Belgium. Russia was still dazzled by the prospect of Father Moscow paying a return call on Mother Paris. The councils of the Prussians were inspired by motives of revenge against the man who had destroyed the military legacy of Frederick the Great in three weeks. Baron Stein continued to dream of a united Germany under a constitutional monarchy on the British pattern. Bernadotte hovered in the wings, hoping against hope to be summoned by the French as his former patron's successor. The witches' brew continued to bubble as one ingredient or another was added. Perhaps the most potent of them were territorial greed and injured pride.

Napoleon, whose spies served him well, was perfectly aware of these dissensions and was determined to exploit them to the full but he could only do this so long as he continued to triumph in the field. He had no illusions as to the overall intentions of the delegates, i.e. to enlarge their own realms, to root out the heresy of equal opportunities for all, and make Europe safe for the dynasties. For more than fifty years after his death the peoples of European nations, struggling to rid themselves of the shackles riveted upon them by hereditary rulers, saw in Napoleon's rejection of what appeared to be generous terms proof of his arrogance but now we know this to be a fallacy. Metternich's memoirs prove that no terms put forward after the summer armistice were honest attempts at a compromise. If they had been accepted after Dresden or after Leipzig they would never have been honored for more than a year or so. By rooting out her aristocracy in the years between the fall of the Bastille and the end of the Terror, France had rejected once and for all the theory of absolution. As long as she remained powerful no hereditary prince could sleep safely in his bed. Behind and beyond all the parleying at Prague, Frankfurt and Châtillon this was the single major issue that kept the documents rustling. Napoleon knew this but he was almost alone in taking it into account.

A few old Republicans like Carnot, up in Antwerp, understood it well enough, but it weighed little in the minds of the men of action whom Napoleon had elevated to positions of wealth, dignity and power. The Macdonalds, the Neys, the Victors and the Oudinots were prepared to do their duty as soldiers but as dukes they longed for peace before the ache of wounds became intolerable. In addition they were themselves converts to the creed of privilege.

IV

He set out for Ferté-sous-Jouarre early on the 15th. Now, with events crowding him hour by hour, he was Longboots once again, the twenty-six-year-old blade of Lodi and Arcola with his way to make in the world. The passage of years, that slow most men down, had no such effect upon him, a man of forty-four, a poor horseman and inclining to corpulence. He covered a journey of fifty miles over winter roads in thirty-six hours and his men kept pace with him, not merely the Guard but also the conscripts for whom his presence guaranteed victory. On the evening of the 16th he was poised to strike south at Guignes. On the 17th he appeared in strength at Nangis and fell like a meteor on Schwartzenberg's vanguard, commanded by the Russian Wittgenstein, the man who, a little over a year ago, had swept down from the north in just such a fashion to deny his passage over the Beresina during the great retreat.

The Russian general could do little to oppose the onrush. Leaving six thousand prisoners behind him he was saved by the speed of his horse. Like Johnny Cope after Prestonpans he was the first to bring news of his own defeat and was engagingly frank about it. "I have been beaten," he told Schwartzenberg, "and have lost two divisions. In two hours you will see the French!" His estimate was accurate. Before the Allies could rally Victor, Oudinot and Gerard were upon them, and the slow tide that had been flowing towards Paris began to ebb, through Villeneuve-le-Comte to Montereau, at the confluence of the Seine and the Yonne.

Here was another moment when disaster for France might have been converted into a triumph capable of achieving splendid and even permanent results. This time the opportunity was lost by Victor, more blameworthy than the bridgeless Macdonald at Trilport a few days before. Orders came to him from Imperial Headquarters at Nangis to storm the Montereau bridge, imperative orders designed to put Schwartzenberg into a position of extreme difficulty, with his vanguard captured or driven in, and his main body falling back in confusion. But the urgency of the situation failed to communicate itself to Victor, a good enough corps commander advancing on limited objectives but one of the worst strategists among the marshals and having a record of consistent failure as an independent commander. Finding fourteen thousand troops from Bavaria and Wurtemberg in the vicinity of the bridge Victor halted his drive and bivouacked for the night, while the main body of the Allies fled across the Seine and headed for Bray and Nogent.

To Headquarters at Nangis came yet another plenipotentiary, this time a herald with a personal message from the Allied sovereigns. They expressed surprise and pious disappointment at the latest attack, declaring that orders had been issued to their representatives at Châtillon to sign the preliminaries of a peace. Napoleon was by no means taken in by this approach but the flag of truce, and the tacit request for an armistice now that the threat to Paris had been turned aside, was useful as propaganda. He wrote to Joseph in Paris, using that bewildered man as an emotional safety valve. "At the first setback these wretches fall on their knees. . . . I shall never grant an armistice until they have cleared out of my territory. . . . I have hopes that I shall soon secure a peace on the lines of the Frankfurt Proposals. Give it out that the enemy is in difficulties and has asked for an armistice or a suspension of arms and that this is absurd because it would deprive me of the advantages my maneuvers have won." And then, a prudent afterthought, "Don't print this but see that everyone talks about it." It is not recorded what Joseph made of this letter, one among so many conflicting dispatches to reach a capital where the civic temperature shot up and down like the blood count of a patient in the grip of a fever.

On the morning of the 18th, to make good Victor's fatal delay, Generals Gerard, Pajol and Chateau fell upon Montereau and hacked their way to the bridge. Chateau, Victor's son-in-law, was killed outright. Pajol, whose horse was struck in the breast by a cannon ball, had a miraculous escape, the general flying high into the air but descending without mortal injury. After six hours' fighting the town and bridge were won and defenders who failed to escape across the Seine were captured or drowned.

Halfway through the action the Emperor arrived in person, galloping into range of the artillery like an impetuous subaltern and dismounting to lay one of the guns. For a few minutes the French artillerymen had a glimpse of the gunner-cadet of more than twenty years before and when someone suggested that he should leave this kind of work to the juniors and not risk the fate of the army by exposing himself, he said, with a touch of bravado, "Don't worry! The bullet is not yet cast that will kill me." He was still convinced he would die the death of "a damned coglione."

His mood of elation did not last for long. No sooner had the enemy retreated than he began dealing out reprimands right and left. Victor was the most heavily censured for failing to storm the bridge the previous night and not merely censured but removed from his command, his corps being given to Gerard, the surviving hero of the assault. Victor admitted his fault but pleaded that he had already been punished enough. His son-in-law, Chateau, had paid with his life for the marshal's slackness. Relenting somewhat, for Victor was numbered among his oldest friends, Napoleon gave him command of two divisions of the Guard but placed him under the orders of Ney.

Victor was not the only high ranking officer to be cuffed. One general was reprimanded for losing guns and another court-martialed for failing to supply his batteries with ammunition. There was praise for lesser men. The National Guardsmen of Brittany were complimented, the Emperor commenting that "the men of the West had always been faithful to the Monarchy." Was irony intended here? The West had kept the Bourbon cause alive throughout the course of the Revolution. In Brittany and La Vendée civil war, stained with atrocities on both sides, had raged from the day the king's head fell into the basket until Napoleon, as First Consul, made peace with the intransigents.

On the night of the 18th he slept at the castle of Surville and remained there the following day. Among the letters he dictated before leaving was a brief one to M. de Champagny, Duke of Cadore, who was concerned with what has since been dignified or debased as "psychological warfare." More than any of the decrees and bulletins he issued at this time this letter reveals the value Napoleon placed upon propaganda. "The Empress has sent me a very interesting portrait of the King of Rome in Polish costume, saying his prayers. . . . I should like to have the picture engraved, under the title, 'I pray to God for my father and for France.' . . . If this little engraving could be produced within forty-eight hours, and put on sale, it would have an excellent effect. . . ."

There were other letters, at least one that would have an important effect on the future. It was a command to Caulaincourt, still negotiating at Châtillon, revoking the carte blanche he had been given and insisting on the terms embraced in the Frankfurt Proposals. That same day he received Allied proposals drafted in advance of his descent upon Montereau. They demanded a retraction of France to the frontiers of '92 and hinted at his abdication. Events were moving too fast for the pens of Châtillon clerks.

The tone of this last offer enraged him more than it should have done, for he had known for a long time what was in their minds and had himself just witnessed what a series of victories could do to mellow Allied councils. Instead of replying directly he addressed a lengthy letter to his father-in-law, Francis of Austria. It was a flat refusal to yield Belgium and Antwerp and was drafted with the object of driving a wedge between the Continental Allies and their paymaster, Britain. Whatever else it did this letter produced a prompt suggestion for another armistice to which Napoleon at once agreed, providing that hostilities should not cease during the preliminaries and that the Châtillon Conference should go to work on a formula resting upon the Frankfurt Proposals. It was now the Allies' turn to bluff and they had ten counters to his one. A commission met to arrange armistice terms. In the meantime it was agreed among them to raise an Army of the South and send word to Blucher that, no matter what he heard to the contrary, "a suspension of arms would not take place."

In the meantime Napoleon had occupied Bray and then Nogent while Schwartzenberg put on a bold front outside Troyes.
He was sixty miles east of the spot where, a few days before,
he had announced that his army was "almost under the walls of
Paris." Only one general of the five nation Coalition kept his
nerve and he, Blucher, had been the hardest hit. With all his allies except Wellington passing over to the defensive, the Prussian septuagenarian was ready to try again and at once. In response to an urgent appeal from his allies to make a diversion,
the indefatigable old man suddenly appeared at Méry, in the elbow of the Seine where it sweeps in a wide southerly bend.
Méry was approximately equidistant from Nogent and Troyes.
His appearance there at that time and in comparative strength
was a military miracle. Napoleon himself could have done no
better.

When he turned west and south to check Schwartzenberg's advance on Paris Napoleon had left Marmont to watch "General
Vorwarts." But troops were scarce, and every musket was
needed to check the Russo-Austrian advance, so that Marmont's
command was unable to do much more than observe the beaten
enemy. Somehow Blucher scraped together a fighting force capable of issuing from Châlons and marching south over the area
of his recent defeats and his sudden appearance on the right
bank of the Seine was an unpleasant surprise to the French. He
was not, however, in sufficient strength to worry them much
and Oudinot was detached to drive him back and regain that part
of Méry that lay on the left bank of the river. The Prussians retired, as usual sacking the town. Napoleon then continued his
advance on Troyes, leaving the Prussian rogue elephant to be
contained by Marmont's 8,000, covering Paris from Sézanne,
and Mortier's 10,000, stationed further north at Soissons.
Schwartzenberg with 70,000 faced front outside Troyes. It
looked, for the moment, as though he was preparing for battle.

If he had contemplated fighting he changed his mind. Mask-
ing the town he suddenly withdrew as far east as Bar-sur-Aube
and the victorious French pushed on to reoccupy the key town
they had evacuated just over a fortnight before.

The situation was utterly transformed. Then, in what had

seemed an irresistable tide, the Allies were advancing on Paris by two routes and the countryside, getting wind of Prussian excesses, was emptying and taking the roads to the capital. A few royalists in Troyes hoisted the white cockade and a deputation of them called upon the Czar representing French willingness to restore the Bourbons to the throne. "Gentlemen," said Alexander, who had been trying conclusions with Napoleon since 1805, "you are a little premature." The small royalist faction fled when the French reconquered the city but they left one of their number behind. He was the Chevalier de Goualt, one of the aristocrats Napoleon had encouraged to return in the heydey of the Empire. Now he paid forfeit for his partisanship. Condemned to be shot he was led out with a placard round his neck, "I am a traitor to my country." He died bravely, protesting his loyalty to the Bourbons to the last.

The Allies were now in such disarray that something on a grand scale might be attempted. The moral worth of the victories at Champaubert, Montmirail, Vauchamps and Montereau were out of all proportion to their military value although this was not inconsiderable. The main body of the Allies was more than a hundred miles from the capital, Blucher was contained, thousands of prisoners entering Paris witnessed the reality of French superiority, and much valuable war material had been captured. The means of turning all this to account, however, rested with a man outside the orbit of battle, fifty-six-year-old Augereau, Marshal of France and Duke of Castiglione, a title derived from his brilliant work in Napoleon's first Italian campaign eighteen years before.

As early as the second week in February Napoleon had recognized the tremendous possibilities inherent in Augereau's army of reserve in Lyons and had ordered him to march his 25,000 men across the Allies' communications. These orders were received by Augereau on the 13th, when Blucher was getting hammered at Vauchamps but he did not respond to them. On the 16th Napoleon wrote again, almost begging him to co-operate, but Augereau made all manner of excuses and remained inactive near Lyons. At Nogent, in hot pursuit of Schwartzenberg, Napoleon wrote a third time and there is something almost piteous in the urgency of his appeal to an old comrade-in-arms with whom he had shared so many triumphs. Brushing aside Augereau's excuses he cried, "I won the fight at Nangis with a brigade of dragoons from Spain which had not unsaddled since it left Bayonne. The six battalions of the Nîmes division, you say, are short of uniforms and equipment and are untrained. That is a poor reason for Augereau to give! I have annihilated 80,000 of the enemy with conscript battalions that had no cartridge pouches and uniforms in rags. . . . You have no money, and where, pray, do you expect to get any? You can't have any until you have recaptured our receipts from the enemy. You are short of transport animals? Commandeer them from any source you like. You have no food depots? That is really too ridiculous. I order you to start within twelve hours of the receipt of this letter, so as to take part in the campaign. If you are still Augereau of Castiglione you may keep your command; if your sixty years lie heavy on you give it up and hand it over to your senior General Officer. The country is threatened and in danger. It can be saved but only by daring and devotion, not by idle temporizing. You must have got a nucleus of over 6,000 picked troops. That is more than I have, yet I have destroyed three armies, taken 40,000 prisoners, captured 200 guns, and thrice saved Paris. . . . It is no question now of the kind of conduct which has served during the last few years; you will want your old boots and the resolution that carried you to victory in '93. When Frenchmen see your plume leading the line, and yourself the first to face musket fire, you will be able to do with them what you will. . . ."

It was a stirring plea but it did not move the duelist-dancing master from Lyons nor induce him to send a deputy to cut Allied communications with their supply and reserve bases east of the Rhine. Augereau had seen enough action to satisfy the most adventurous of men. He was tired and disillusioned, far beyond the lure of fresh honors or a glorious death on the field. He had no desire to share the fate of Lannes, Bessières and Poniatowski. Neither did he love fighting for fighting's sake, as did men like Ney and Oudinot. He was used up, cynical, stiff jointed from many wounds, and satiated with glory. He stayed where he was until February 28th and then it was too late.

At Bar-sur-Aube Schwartzenberg was also dictating and explaining, to his own satisfaction if not to his sovereign's, where his carefully timed plan to capture Paris had gone wrong. "A defeat would have meant retreat not behind the Aube but behind the Rhine," he argued, referring to his swift withdrawal from Troyes, and went on to describe the terrible hazards of fighting a victorious enemy in a country where all the peasants were hostile and supplies and reinforcements were readily available to the enemy. It made some kind of sense to the autocrats and they do not seem to have lost faith in the general. Patiently they kept negotiations boiling while regrouping their forces and making renewed appeals to Blucher to keep up the pressure between the Seine and the Marne.

Realizing that something would have to be done to contain the new Prussian threat Napoleon left the task of pursuing Schwartzenberg to Macdonald and Oudinot, and he turned north once again. The diplomats went on talking, one eye on their maps and the other on the latest bulletins from the battlefield. With the disappearance of Napoleon a measure of confidence returned to them. At Chaumont, in the first days of March, they drew up a new treaty with Britain. In exchange for five million pounds sterling, to be delivered annually and divided equally among them, each sovereign undertook to maintain 150,000 men in the field "for twenty years if necessary," provided Napoleon would not settle for the ancient boundaries of monarchial France. The energy and initiative of Napoleon had proved a catalyst for their fears and jealousies and history has applauded the short term effect of their resolve to make common cause against Napoleon. But one should not overlook the long term effects of the decision taken at Chaumont in March, 1814, for they included the Congress of Vienna that condemned Europeans then unborn to suffer another century of absolution. The conquests of Napoleon had speeded the birth of nationalism but the overthrow of Napoleon by force of arms stunted its growth in the greater part of the territory over which his armies had marched. The ultimate victory of the Czar and his Allies prevented the domination of Europe by a single man of genius but it was followed by piecemeal domination by the dull, the vicious and the incompetent. What followed was peace of a kind but a peace imposed by the gallows and the whipping posts, the end-

less shuffle of political offenders into Siberia, the rape of Poland, the Cossack pograms, the barricades of 1848 and, more catastrophic than any of these, the march of the Prussian jackboot
that led to the holocaust of the Western Front and, ultimately,
to Dachau. For all this the Habsburgs, the Hohenzollerns, the
Bourbons and the Romanoffs must answer and John Bull, their
paymaster, must stand beside them in the dock.

12

EVEN A MILITARY genius has to make contact with the enemy before he can demonstrate his superiority. This, with speed and efficiency, Napoleon had succeeded in doing between February 9th, when he moved north against Blucher, and February 18th, when he stormed across the thirty mile gap between Marne and Seine to smash Schwartzenberg and push him back on Troyes and Bar-sur-Aube. But there were now four widely separated fields of conflict where distances and inadequate communications prevented him from exerting a personal influence upon events, or even assessing a situation by any method other than guesswork.

The most remote and inaccessible of these areas were his fortresses east of the Rhine, some of which had surrendered before he began this whirlwind campaign. Hamburg, the most important of them, was still safe and Davout, the marshal to whom personal loyalty was a religion, would never let it go, despite the grumblings of civilians, shortage of rations and the extreme improbability that he would ever be relieved. Glum, but punctilious, even under the terrible conditions of a sustained siege, Davout held on, knowing that nobody would lift a finger to help him but resolved to do his duty to the last.

Bernadotte, who had not yet abandoned hope of being installed in the Tuileries as Charles, Emperor of France, spent the winter reducing Denmark and keeping an eye on Antwerp, defended by the Republican, Carnot, but the Emperor could do

Dying Gladiator

nothing to help Carnot now. Neither could he influence, except indirectly, the fate of men like Captain Barrès, shut up in the ruined suburbs of Mainz. Along the Rhine generally fighting had ceased, both French and Allies, soldiers and civilians, needing all their hardihood to survive a series of terrible frosts (the Rhine froze that year as did the Thames) and a virulent outbreak of typhus. During the siege of Mainz 30,000 soldiers and civilians died and were buried in trenches filled with quicklime. Food, however, was plentiful and despite the frightful mortality the cafés and theaters remained open and balls and concerts were frequent. "I often went to the theater," Barrès recalls, "in order to forget the preoccupations of the moment." For all the news that reached them of what was occurring elsewhere Frenchmen defending Hamburg, Antwerp and Mainz might have been in Timbuctoo. Rumors abounded, cheering and otherwise, but they received no reinforcements and no fresh orders.

As for Eugène, Viceroy of Italy, still holding the line of the Mincio against a superior Austrian army, his situation was almost as desperate. He was in touch with Imperial Headquarters but he dare not pursue anything but a strictly defensive policy, for King Murat and his Neapolitans were moving north to the River Po and had now almost certainly enlisted with the enemy. Almost certainly; that was the nub of Eugène's problem, for as yet the king of Naples had struck no actual blow against his countrymen and the viceroy's orders were positive. "Defend Italy as long as Murat does not declare openly against you. If and when he does, cross the Alps and bring your Franco-Italian army to my aid."

The situation placed a terrible strain on a conscientious commander such as Eugène Beauharnais. He had under his command 36,000 men, 24,000 of them French (mostly Italian-born) and 12,000 Italians. Ranged against him, on the other side of the Mincio, was the Austrian General Bellegarde, with upwards of 70,000, a small Anglo-Sicilian army of 8,000 and, as Bellegarde was now informed, Murat's 24,000 Neapolitans. Eugène was beset by domestic as well as military problems. His devoted wife, Augusta of Bavaria, was seven months pregnant and isolated with her children in territory occupied by the enemy. Fortunately for her the Austrian commander was a chivalrous soldier. Eugène wrote to him asking for permission to cross into hostile territory and collect firewood for his half-frozen troops. It was granted as was a request that his wife would be left unmolested in Milan.

Despite these polite exchanges events were moving rapidly to a climax in Italy. On January 31st Murat marched into Bologna, not far from Eugène's right-wing anchor at Mantua, and on February 8th Bellegarde attacked Eugène's seventeen mile river line between Mantua and Peschiera on Lake Garda.

The terrain favored the French. The ground on both sides of the river was cut up with vineyards, steep banks and canals but the odds against the French were more than two to one and Bellegarde was relying on the support of Murat, now only thirty miles away. It seems that he did not know the Gascon king as well as he supposed. Murat awaited the outcome of the fight and when, after a day's bloody combat, the Austrian attack failed, he began making tentative overtures to Eugène.

Eugène's position was then strengthened by the arrival of some Italian troops from Spain and as the weather began to improve better news came from the north, a dispatch rider bringing details of Napoleon's victories over the Prussians on the Marne. On the night of the 17th (only four days after the battle of Vauchamps) the Austrians heard a salute of guns from the French lines. They were celebrating the Emperor's successes in France.

Tascher, Eugène's aide-de-camp, had ridden full speed to the Marne with news of the Viceroy's victory on the Mincio. He found the Emperor at Nangis, preparing his descent on Montereau, and was ordered to return at once telling Eugène to hold fast. Tascher reached Mantua again on February 25th. He had made the round trip, in midwinter, in seventeen days, an indication of what was expected of Imperial dispatch riders, but he found the Viceroy in a rage. Letters had just arrived from his mother Josephine and his sister Hortense, begging him to "obey the Emperor's orders, abandon Italy and march to the aid of the mother country." It was clear that both had written at Napoleon's insistence. Josephine added, "France has need of all her children."

Eugène did not take kindly to this sort of prodding. Like Ney he was excessively sensitive concerning his honor and elected to read into this petticoat approach Imperial doubts concerning his loyalty. His suspicions were seemingly confirmed by the arrival of a second letter on the heels of Tascher's dispatches. Napoleon ordered him to send his wife and children to France and the vicereine interpreted this to mean that she was to be regarded as a hostage to her husband's fidelity.

Eugène was not a man to nurse a grievance in silence. He at once put his resentment on paper, pointing out that his original orders had been to hold Italy *unless* Murat attacked and that, far from doing so, Murat was now hinting that, under certain circumstances, he would return to his allegiance! Declaring that his orders had been positive in this respect, and that those conditions had not yet been fulfilled, Eugène went on to describe what would have occurred had he withdrawn. His Italians and Italian-born Frenchmen, he said, would have deserted en masse and the price of the remnant arriving to contribute to the defense of Paris would have been the loss of the whole of Italy! Studying Eugène's situation with the benefit of hindsight one cannot but conclude that Napoleon was wrong and his loyal lieutenant was right.

Augusta, equally offended, defied the Imperial order to qualify as refugee or hostage. Heavy with child she made her way to Mantua in order to stay beside the man she loved to the end. Her child, a daughter, was born in the ducal palace on April 13th. As she lay in childbed she heard salvoes of artillery from the enemy lines. The Austrians were celebrating the entry of the Allies into Paris. Soon an envoy from Francis of Austria arrived at the palace with proposals for a convention. He was a suave, persuasive man whose handsome appearance had been enhanced rather than otherwise by the loss of an eye in action. He wore a black patch over the socket and seemed to get on very well with the ladies. He was Count Neipperg and he has a niche in history. Within months of his appearance at Mantua he was to seduce Napoleon's second wife, the twenty-four-year-old Marie-Louise. As the seducer of a former Empress he had a unique advantage. He approached the young woman's bed with her father's blessing.

The fourth area of conflict over which Napoleon could exercise little, if any, control, was the beleaguered southwest corner of France, where Soult, with his fifty thousand, was at bay.

Since posting down to the Pyrenees in July, Nicholas Soult, the son of a provincial notary who had once hoped to be a village baker, had done as much as could have been expected of a man commanding a dispirited, demoralized army facing a triple alliance commanded by the second best soldier of the age.

Pushed back from the Nivelle and now fighting on the soil of France, Soult had fortified Bayonne and temporarily barred Wellington's progress north. Down here the weather was not as cold as in the river valleys of northeastern France but it was wetter and just as windy. The rivers of the Pyrenees were brimming and the roads were morasses over which it was impossible to move a column of men or a convoy of supplies. For a long time, in early winter, the war bogged down as Soult dug in on the right bank of the Nive, and Wellington's Peninsular veterans camped in what one Allied officer describes as a cul-de-sac, with the swift flowing river on their right, the sea on their left, and the Pyreneean range at their backs. They had one coastal town in their possession, St. Jean de Luz, but before them was the strong fortress of Bayonne, its resilient defenders and a sizeable garrison.

Rifleman Kincaid, as was his nature, made the best of the stalemate, settling himself and his men in the local chateau of the D'Arcangues family and helping his hosts dispose of all the claret in the cellar.

Wellington's problem, now that he had crossed the frontiers of France, was twofold. He had, in some way, to dislodge Soult and open a way into the vast French plain. He had also to win the goodwill of the local inhabitants so that there was no danger of a popular uprising.

His vast experience in Spain had taught him that no invading army, no matter how strong or well equipped, could operate successfully in territory where every woman, child and old man was either a potential assassin, a thief, or an informer. It was this factor more than any other that had defeated the French

west of the Bidassoa and a hostile countryside would mean that
every cart would need a powerful escort. He had numerical superiority. With his Spanish and Portuguese allies he considerably outnumbered the enemy but after mature consideration
(Wellington never, in the whole of his life, acted on impulse)
he decided to send most of the Spaniards home, retaining only
the best disciplined of them.

Explaining his reasons for thus reducing his fighting strength
he said that his Spanish contingents were so ill-found in matters of pay and food that they would be obliged to pillage, and
that nothing was more likely to recruit French partisans. For
himself he was all for conciliation. "I have not lost thousands
of officers and men getting here in order to rob the French,"
he added and proceeded to take the sternest measures to secure
the good behavior of his own men. Squads of military police
ranged the "cul-de-sac" twenty-four hours a day, and any looter
caught in the act was strung up on the spot. Wellington's army
contained a very high proportion of professional picklocks and
smugglers and there were some murmurings among the looters
of Badajaz and San Sebastian at this display of summary justice. One poor devil, about to be hanged, protested that he
could not understand why he was not allowed to plunder now
that he had arrived in the enemy's country.

The policy paid a handsome dividend. The Basques were understandably surprised when they found themselves entertaining
an army of jovial foreigners who not only fed themselves, and
respected private property, but paid black market prices for
goods displayed in a shop window. Like any population invaded
by free spending tourists they made the most of the opportunity but some of them, particularly those who had campaigned
with the Grand Army, were slow to recover from their astonishment. An ex-service innkeeper, having served a British officer with a dinner, was speechless with amazement when his
guest asked for the bill. Others adjusted more quickly. The
price of poultry soared like one of Congreve's rockets and of
the shops in St. Jean de Luz Kincaid says: "They were too
small to hold their consciences and their goods. . . . I have often regretted that the enemy never get an opportunity of having the run of their own shops for a few minutes, that they

might have been, in some measure, punished for their sins, even in this world." As might be expected the civilians soon ceased to regard the British as their enemies. The British soldier has a penchant for making friends in occupied territory. In the century ahead it was to happen again in wars waged as far apart as the Ganges and the Rhine.

But Soult was far from being a spent force. When Wellington, carefully balancing the risks, transferred part of his depleted force to the right bank of the Nive the marshal attacked, launching his whole force first on Hope's 30,000 between the river and the sea, and then, when this failed, against General Hill's 14,000 on the right bank on the heights above St. Pierre d'Irube. Hope had a hard struggle and was himself twice wounded, losing 1,700 men of whom, surprisingly, over 500 were prisoners. It was a rarity for Wellington to have this number of men captured in a single engagement. Fortified in their chateau the Light Brigade troops had no trouble beating off the attack. Kincaid records that one officer and one NCO were shot in the open and that their men sniped at French trying to reach their bodies all day. Finally a French officer appeared waving a white flag and pointing to some men carrying spades. It seems that the enemy were bent not on robbing but on burying. All firing ceased in that quarter. Down there it was still that kind of war.

Red faced "Farmer" Hill came much closer to being overwhelmed by the fury of the French attack. The flooding river made reinforcement hazardous and either mismanagement or cowardice on the part of two colonels added to Hill's difficulties. It is recorded that this was only the second occasion that Hill was heard by his men to swear and that Wellington, informed of this uncommon occurrence, remarked: "If Hill is beginning to swear we had better get out of the way." The "Farmer" held on, however, and when Wellington arrived with reinforcements the French drew off. The two attacks had cost them nearly 5,000 men, apart from the desertion of 1,400 Germans who, like their compatriots at Leipzig, passed over to the enemy while in action.

Vile weather kept both sides inactive throughout the rest of December and January. It was not until February 14th, when

Napoleon, having beaten Blucher, was turning on Schwartzenberg on the Seine, that Wellington moved again, this time
marching east with the object of widely outflanking his watch-
ful antagonist. River line after river line was turned and Hope,
crossing the Adour, invested Bayonne while Soult's field army
maneuvered against Wellington's main force, finally attempting
another stand at Orthez.

Soult was now at a numerical disadvantage again for during
the lull Napoleon had robbed him of three cavalry brigades,
two infantry divisions and five batteries, whereas his Italians
had gone to help the hard-pressed Eugène on the Mincio. Notwithstanding this he fought a hard, skillful fight and exacted a
high price for the ground yielded. Among the British wounded
that day was the almost invulnerable Wellington, struck in the
leg by a spent musket ball. Bayonne held out to the end of the
war but Bordeaux, always a hotbed of Bourbon intrigue, welcomed the invader with enthusiasm. Doggedly, and with a certain fatalism, Soult headed for Toulouse and there, with his
usual caution, Wellington followed him. The back door of
France was now wide open.

II

His lunge at Blucher, the third in a little over a month, and
the last of this storming campaign, conformed to the pattern of
much earlier strategic designs in the days when he had led
his ragged army against the Sardinians and detached them from
their Austrian alliance in a running fight that lasted sixteen
days. This had always been his favorite way of waging war, a
pounce on the weakest of his adversaries, swift exploitation of a
victory and a renewed attack upon those left in the field. His
watchwords on these occasions were speed, surprise and concentration at one narrow sector of the line. The method had been
applied with spectacular success not only in Italy but at Ulm,
Austerlitz, Jena and Friedland, and later in the Danube campaign of 1809, when he turned his back on Spain and rushed
across Europe to crush the Austrian revolt. To a degree he
had used the same design (if on a far grander scale) in 1812,
striking what he hoped would prove a knockout blow at Rus-

sia, the most formidable of his enemies, in order to discourage others. The theme had persisted in Saxony up to the time of his reluctant concentration on Leipzig. Now, fighting against impossible odds in defense of his capital, he saw no reason to adopt more cautious methods. The same principles held good, to concentrate, to divide and defeat in detail.

The surprising thing is not that Napoleon was predictable but that the Allies, so much more powerful in men, money and guns, continued to allow him to practice on them, and made no attempt to unite and cut their way through to Paris. Wellington, far removed from the main theater, was contemptuous of their dispositions. "I would not," he said, "march a corporal's guard in such a manner!" But the autocrats, their vision blurred by conflicting interests and by a sense of personal inferiority, did not see it that way. Alone among them gallant old Blucher continued to make his clumsy, costly attempts to catch the crocodile by the tail, while his allies danced a gavotte around the periphery of the battle area, leaving him to take most of the hard knocks. Bernadotte, looking with growing suspicion on the favor the Allies were showing the Bourbon princes, continued to skulk in Brussels with his 23,000 Swedes and even began inconclusive negotiations with his brother-in-law, Joseph Bonaparte. Britain, apart from acting as paymaster, had all she could do to contain the elusive Soult, now concentrating on Toulouse. It was a sorry picture of divided councils, indecision and sometimes what looked like cowardice on the part of men like Schwartzenberg and his staff.

Blucher's renewed drive on Paris via Meaux was an act of desperate courage on his part. Crossing the Ourcq he tried to move on Meaux from the north but Marmont and Mortier parried the blow and he retreated up the valley of the Ourcq, moving in the direction of Soissons. Napoleon, maneuvering northeastwards, then crossed the Marne in expectation of making a devastating flank attack upon the Prussian columns. With Soissons securely garrisoned by the French it was a logical move, for Blucher could only retreat eastward so long as Soissons blocked his progress north. Mortier and Marmont followed him, reinforced by 6,000 recruits sent out from Paris.

Then occurred one of those chances in war that make non-sense of plans hatched over charts and parade states. Soissons was *not* closed against Blucher, and instead of being a stumbling block it proved a sanctuary and a source of much needed recruitment. Defended by an inexperienced commander and 1,400 Poles it had surrendered in the interval at the summons of two enemy corps under Bulow and Witzingerode. Here, after his profitless wanderings in snow and slush, Blucher found unlooked for rest and refreshment.

If Napoleon despaired when he was told of the changed situation he did not show it. On March 5th he led his scarecrow army over the Aisne and occupied Rheims. His modified plan now was to widen the wedge between the Prussian and his allies further south and perhaps, even at this stage, there was forming in his mind the outline of a plan he had conceived before Leipzig, of turning his back on the long columns of invaders and marching directly east to the Rhine hoping to draw the Coalition out of France in a long straggling pursuit.

If such a project suggested itself he did not act upon it, or not at this stage, but continued to regard Blucher as his principal antagonist. Once more he acted like a swordsman who, finding himself assailed by a pack of brigands, seeks out the most aggressive of them with the intention of killing him and, by so doing, putting the remainder to flight. When Blucher moved north from Soissons, heading for Craonne and Laon, he advanced against him, making contact with part of Blucher's force, mainly Russians, at the former town, where he found it posted in a strong position on a plateau and in no mood to retreat.

Ney and Victor went in to attack at eleven A.M. and the engagement, a murderous one, lasted until four P.M. when the enemy drew off, having inflicted as much damage as they had received. The cavalry of Grouchy and Nansouty and the artillery of Drouot did their best to consolidate the victory but their efforts availed little, except to leave the battered French infantry masters of the ground. Both Victor and Grouchy were wounded at Craonne, the former seriously.

That night the Emperor slept at an inn called *The Guardian Angel* and it was here that Caulaincourt's last Châtillon messenger found him with a stale proposal—peace, at the price of a retreat to France's "ancient" boundaries. He hardly bothered to read it. "If I am to be flagelated let it at least be compulsorily inflicted," was his comment.

As always, as soon as word reached them that Napoleon was not personally opposed to them, the sovereigns plucked up heart. Leaving Bar-sur-Aube, the limit of their retreat after the pounding they had received at Montereau, they advanced cautiously against Macdonald and Oudinot on the Seine.

The two marshals gave ground, first to Troyes and ultimately to Provins, Macdonald doing everything in his power to prevent the capture of the river crossings and block a renewed advance on Paris. He was still too ill and exhausted to be fighting a winter campaign and on arrival at Troyes was obliged to go to bed. But there was no rest for the clansman. Oudinot marched off with his men, grumbling that the Young Guard were not designated to be used as a rearguard, and a growing exasperation with the trend of events can be seen in this attitude, for Oudinot's loyalty had never been in question. Now even he and Ney were becoming frustrated to the point of mutiny, seeing nothing to be gained from this endless series of empty victories and all the marching and countermarching that accompanied them. If Napoleon forfeited their support the game was indeed lost. One by one the band of brothers who had conquered Europe had fallen away. Lannes, Bessières, Poniatowski and Duroc were dead; Victor, badly wounded, was out of the fight; Bernadotte and Murat were in arms against their old comrades; Soult and Eugène were cornered; Augereau in Lyons was contemplating treachery; St. Cyr and many others were prisoners of war; Ney, Oudinot, Mortier and Macdonald were sick, disillusioned and dispirited. Now it was the turn of Marmont, Napoleon's oldest friend, the gunner-cadet of his early youth.

The quarrel that led to a rupture between the two men occurred under the walls of Laon. Napoleon survived the incident by seven years, and Marmont by half a lifetime but henceforth, whenever they thought of one another, it was with acrimony. History has judged Marmont a scoundrel and Napoleon a megalomaniac. To some extent both these judgments were influenced by what each said of the other in retrospect.

Pushing forward from Craonne the Grand Army, or what remained of it, made its dispositions to storm the town. Laon stands on a terraced hill and Blucher had established himself both in and on each side of the town. With the two corps he had picked up at Soissons he now had a strong numerical advantage, was well posted and protected by fortified outlying villages, notably the village of Athies, opposite Marmont. General Gourgaud drove in the enemy pickets on the night of March 9th and on the following day the French mounted their general assault. It made good progress, particularly on the enemy's right but Marmont experienced great difficulty in clearing more than half of the village of Athies. During the battle a considerable force of Cossacks interposed between his corps and the French center and when night fell Marmont was cut off from his comrades.

This, in itself, was by no means disastrous. The attack would be renewed in the morning and there were excellent prospects of the Allied right being driven back, when pressure on Marmont would be relaxed. Then the whole army could move forward, drive Blucher from Laon and perhaps inflict upon him irreparable loss. Some such moral success was vital before Napoleon could turn once more on the timid Schwartzenberg and who could say what might result from the destruction of one Allied army and the repulse of another? One thing was certain. Bickering on an increased scale would break out between the partners of the alliance and from bickering, cleverly exploited, better terms than France's ancient frontiers could be secured. It was a chance that would never come again and it was Marmont's carelessness or psychological weakness that lost it.

After attaining only half of his objectives the marshal retired to rest in a chateau three miles behind the front line. In the middle of the night of March 10th–11th the Prussians mounted a surprise night attack that caught him completely off balance. He was not only routed but bundled out of his position and compelled to abandon all his guns.

Two fugitive dragoons brought the news to Napoleon as he was drawing on his boots, preparatory to renewing the combat. This time he did not react calmly, as he had done when they told him Soissons had surrendered. He stormed and raved against his old friend, and some of the men around him, Berthier among them, seem to have thought his anger justified for later, when the two men met, the chief-of-staff said, "The Emperor would have been justified in cutting him down where he stood!" But curses and reproaches did nothing to repair the situation. With his right flank in the air there could be no prospect of advancing on Laon and Napoleon took the only course open to him. He remained where he was, thus preventing the enemy from pressing the pursuit of the routed corps. Marmont fell back in disorder as far as Fismes and here, with more luck than he deserved, he managed to rally about 8,000 men.

In his memoirs Marmont gives a graphic picture of the state of the army at this juncture. It is one of utter confusion and demoralization, of men lacking not only the rudiments of training but clothes, shoes and hats. He speaks of artillery served by sailors who did not know how to load and aim a field-piece and of the discovery of a supply of captured uniforms so infested with vermin that his conscripts preferred to retain their own rags rather than wear them.

Early on the 13th the French main body fell back on Soissons, cheated once more of a victory that would restore civilian morale in the distracted capital. Blucher, although battered, was still intact and still capable of taking the road to the capital. Macdonald and Oudinot were being edged north by Schwartzenberg and their commands were scattered about the area north of the Seine between Provins and Arcis-sur-Aube. Nothing was to be expected from Augereau or Eugène in the south, or the hard-pressed Soult in the southwest. And in the meantime came another, more immediate piece of bad news. Rheims, not much more than thirty miles east of Soissons, had fallen to the French emigré, St. Priest, offering a means of direct communication between the two main armies of the Allies.

If the union of Blucher and Schwartzenberg was to be prevented something had to be done at once. Orders went out from Soissons to concentrate for the recapture of the town and Marmont, as the nearest, moved on it at once, hoping perhaps to atone for his dismal failure outside Laon. The main body followed by forced marches but the artillery lagged behind and Napoleon arrived with the vanguard to find a desperate struggle for the city already in progress. The French, gallantly led by Marmont, stormed in from the west. St. Priest was killed—it is said by the same gunner who shot and killed Moreau at Dresden—and the population greeted the Emperor with a storm of cheers. They were the last civilian cheers he was to hear until his return from Elba a year later and Rheims was the last town he was to take, the end of a string of victories that began at Toulon, in 1793, and included, through the years, the capture of Milan, Vienna, Berlin, Warsaw, Madrid and Moscow. Says W. M. Sloane, in his impressive survey of Napoleon's life, "The movement on Rheims was the dying stroke of an exhausted gladiator."

The two friends met the following morning. Marmont was the hero of the fight but his recapture of Rheims did not earn him Napoleon's forgiveness. Instead the Emperor called him sharply to account for letting himself be surprised and driven back at Laon and Marmont, whose exertions in this campaign and the last had been tremendous, may well have considered himself harshly treated and left in a temper. Like all the soldiers of fortune who had won fame and riches by their own efforts, and with little to help them make their way in life but courage, Marmont found it almost impossible to overlook criticism that involved his honor and professional skill. In the old days, when one success had followed another, and personal failures were soon forgotten and forgiven in the excitement of a triumph, a rift between men who had fought side by side for so long might have healed in a few days. Now, seeing treachery and incompetence on all sides (often where it did not exist) Napoleon was as sensitive to failure as the most inexperienced officer in his ranks. What he said to Marmont at Rheims was to have consequences out of all proportion to the loss of a position and a few guns. In seventeen days his rebuke was to cost him dearly.

13

THE CAMPAIGN HAD opened with Blucher's crossing of the Rhine on New Year's day. It was now March 14th and no decision had been reached. For seventy-three days, over a tract of country from Holland to the Seine, armies had marched and fought and died. The bleak countryside was strewn with the bodies of Frenchmen, Germans, Russians and Austrians, and by no means all the French dead were soldiers. According to Allied propaganda the war was being fought to deliver France from the grasp of a tyrant but currently Uhlans and Cossacks of the sovereigns were committing deliberate outrages against the civil population that had been comparatively rare during the period France had dominated Europe.

Response to the Emperor's December call-to-arms to the French nation had been disappointing. In the center and south of the country it had made no impact at all and few civilians, if not manifestly pro-Bourbon, were disposed to shed blood on behalf of the tottering Imperial dynasty. But here in the northeast, where the realities of occupation by the Prussian and the half-savage Asiatics of the Czar were apparent in every hamlet, the French were resisting with the fanaticism of the Spanish peasant. Allied stragglers were slaughtered, small convoys attacked, and prisoners brought in in droves. Outrages such as those committed by Blucher's Prussians at Château Thierry were answered with others so that the wheel of horror spun faster and faster as the snow melted and the east wind dried the marshy fields beside the Aisne, the Marne and the Aube.

"Embrace My Boy . . . !"

The problem of how to exploit this popular fury had occupied
Napoleon for some time and during his three-day stay in
Rheims, where his civic reception had been tumultuous, a plan
began to mature. He could beat the enemy, notwithstanding the
odds, whenever he met them in person. That built-in inferiority
on the part of Schwartzenberg, Blucher, Bulow and Witzingerode was demonstrated by their collective and individual blunders, and in the fatal indecision they showed in handling their
vastly superior forces. But it was not enough to waste his
strength, and the valor and hardihood of his boys, marching
and countermarching between the Marne and the Seine, par-
rying clumsy thrusts at his capital. Some more ambitious plan
would have to be put into practice that would have the effect
of removing or neutralizing the recurring threats to Paris. He
pondered the possibilities, trying to base his decisions upon
known facts concerning the present position of his enemies and
the morale of their rank and file and this was by no means easy.
Reports were conflicting and the sum total of reconnaissance in
an area swarming with enemy columns, provided little on which
to form a clearcut resolve. Would Blucher try for Paris again?
Was he in a condition to mount a third advance down the valley of the Marne? Could Schwartzenberg's timidity be due to
the restraining hand of Austrian diplomacy or was it proof of
the General's incompetence and cowardice? Could Talleyrand
and others in Paris be trusted, even temporarily? Was Augereau,
in Lyons, beset by actual difficulties, or was he a traitor like Murat? How long could Soult hold on in the southwest? What were
the prospects of the powers quarreling over war aims and part-
ing company? What was in the mind of the inactive Bernadotte
in Liége? The questions were numerous and complex. He had
to guess always and one wrong guess would cost him the future.

To a degree, at Rheims, the situation clarified itself. Assuming that the recapture of the town, following hard upon Blucher's latest failure, would induce Schwartzenberg's main force to
retreat, three courses suggested themselves. One, the most obvious as well as the most prudent, was to fall back on Meaux
and cover the eastern approaches to Paris. The second was to
take a more southerly route and march by way of Sézanne to
Provins, where he could block a renewed advance by the Allied

main army along the Seine. The third, offensive where the other courses were defensive, was to march due south on Arcis-sur-Aube and cut into Schwartzenberg's flank as he marched towards Vitry and St. Dizier and surely, being Schwartzenberg, and being eager to effect a junction with his Prussian ally, he would do this.

The guess, as we can see today, was a shrewd one. The failure of Blucher's diversion, and the easy recapture of Rheims by the French, had dismayed the Allies out of all proportion to the importance of the events. The Czar, notwithstanding the grandiose plans he had been making for a triumphal entry into Paris with himself cast in the leading role, was now counseling a halt, whereas Schwartzenberg would have liked to have retreated as far as the Rhine. All the Allied captains feared a general uprising of the civilian population, particularly in Alsace and Lorraine, where their communications would be cut and they themselves isolated in a hostile country with a man-eating tiger outside their lines. Nothing immediate could be expected from Blucher and even less from Bernadotte's Swedes. Encouraging messages came from the south but up here, in the main battle area, very few Frenchmen had mounted the white cockade of the Bourbons. Instead came stories of murdered sentries and dispatch riders, of bands of partisans at large in the woods and of plundered convoys at country crossroads. The autocrats had had one experience of a resurgent France and it had led to twenty years of humiliation and defeat. The more judicious among them were prepared to go to almost any lengths to avoid a repetition of '93 and '94, when the professional armies of the Habsburgs and the Hohenzollerns had been flung back across the frontier by columns of artisans and peasants. An orderly withdrawal, and a long pause to await more propitious times, seemed infinitely preferable to another Valmy, another Jemappes, and perhaps another Austerlitz. In the meantime the Czar and Schwartzenberg dithered, their columns strung out along the southwestern approaches to Paris, their options more or less open but dependent upon a variety of factors, chiefly information concerning Napoleon's next move.

He did not leave them in doubt for long. Ordering Marmont and Mortier to counter any move Blucher might make he chose the third and most perilous alternative, marching due south towards Arcis-sur-Aube. He had made up his mind that the main Allied force was retreating and was going to try his luck in a flank attack.

The guess was half-correct. The Allies were contemplating retreat, had even begun withdrawing in dribs and drabs, but no general movement northeastward had begun and when news arrived that the French were assembling at Arcis a decision was forced upon the Allied command. It must give battle and hope that its overwhelming numerical superiority would decide the issue while Blucher kept Marmont and Mortier occupied further north. These were the movements that gave rise to the muddled but curiously decisive battle of Arcis-sur-Aube, on March 20th–21st.

On the first day there was no major engagement. The French numbered only 16,000 and the Allies in the field no more than 24,000, mostly cavalry. During the night, however, both armies were strongly reinforced, Napoleon by 11,500 men. On the 21st, still convinced that he was engaging no more than the rearguard of Schwartzenberg's host, Napoleon sent Ney and the cavalryman Sébastiani to occupy the plateau behind the town. What they saw, looking east, amazed and appalled them. Drawn up as on parade, with both wings covered by large forces of horsemen and a frontage of 370 guns, was the Austro-Russian army, totaling 100,000 men. Odds of four to one were too great, even for the victors of Montereau. Grimly Napoleon ordered a withdrawal over the Aube towards Vitry and such was the paralysis of will produced in the enemy's mind by his presence that two-thirds of the French force crossed before an attack was launched.

Sébastiani's cavalry came into action as a screen and Ney and Oudinot covered the rear. That night the French set out for Vitry, expecting the Allies to follow, for Vitry was already in Allied hands.

What now? The plan that had suggested itself at Rheims began to take shape until it became so clear in outline that he was more than half-resolved to act upon it. Eastward lay the country of the Meuse, the Moselle, and the Ardennes, and beyond were French-held fortresses where munitions and men could be obtained and plans developed to raise the countryside and strike hard and repeatedly at Allied communications. For the time being Paris would have to look to itself.

II

Word had gone to Marmont to march on Châlons and from Rheims a letter had been dispatched to Joseph in Paris to evacuate with the Empress and the King of Rome should the enemy enter the capital. Napoleon's instructions regarding the precautions to be taken to avoid the capture of his son were adamant. "I would sooner see him in the Seine than an Austrian prisoner," he wrote, adding, "The fate of Astyanax has always seemed to me the unhappiest in history."[1]

But Marmont did not march on Châlons. Nor did he obey the Imperial command to keep the road to Châlons open. Marmont, and Mortier too, had other more urgent matters on hand for on the 18th, the day after Napoleon's main force had marched on Arcis, Blucher, the indefatigable, had rallied yet again and begun groping south from Laon for his allies. For the time being he had had more than enough of solo attempts to storm the capital. What he sought now was a junction and a sharing of hard knocks and responsibility. There were limits to the amount of punishment that even he could take and his losses, in the battles beginning with Champaubert and ending outside Laon, had been terrible, notwithstanding a constant flowing of reinforcement.

Between them Marmont and Mortier had only 17,000 men to oppose Blucher and defend the capital. They joined forces at Fismes, less than twenty miles west of Rheims, between the Aisne and the Marne. They were to fight one more field, and then, for both of them, their lives of active service were over. Behind them Rheims and Épernay fell, and soon afterwards Soissons was invested, to be defended with the greatest gallantry until the end.

Things were no better in the south, where Augereau seemed to be playing a game of double-bluff with both sides. On

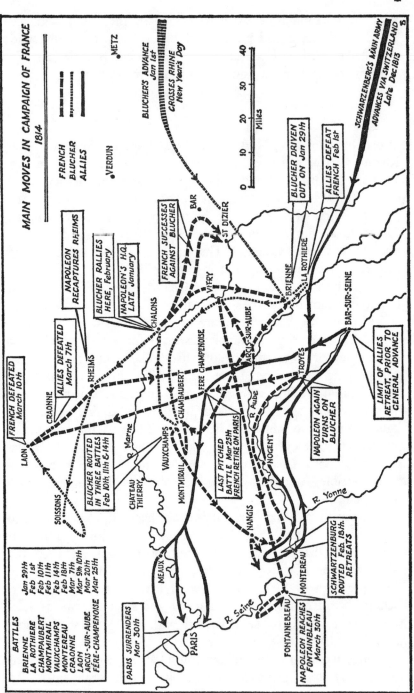

MAIN MOVES IN CAMPAIGN OF FRANCE
1814

FRENCH
BLUCHER
ALLIES

• VERDUN

• METZ

BLUCHER'S ADVANCE
Jan 1st

CROSSES RHINE
New Year's Day

BLUCHER DRIVEN
OUT ON Jan 29th

ALLIES DEFEAT
FRENCH Feb 1st

SCHWARTZENBERG'S MAIN ARMY
ADVANCES VIA SWITZERLAND
Late Dec 1813

Miles
0   10   20   30   40

NAPOLEON
RECAPTURES RHEIMS

FRENCH SUCCESSES
AGAINST BLUCHER

BLUCHER RALLIES
HERE, February

NAPOLEON'S H.Q.
LATE January

ALLIES DEFEATED
March 7th

FRENCH DEFEATED
March 10th

BLUCHER ROUTED
IN THREE BATTLES
Feb 10th,11th & 14th

BAR

ST DIZIER

LA ROTHIERE

BRIENNE

VITRY

CHALONS

RHEIMS

CRAONNE

LAON

SOISSONS

CHATEAU
THIERRY

MONTMIRAIL

VAUXCHAMPS

FERE CHAMPENOISE

CHAMBAUBERT

ARCIS-SUR-AUBE

TROYES

NOGENT

R Aube

R Marne

NAPOLEON AGAIN
TURNS ON
BLUCHER

LIMIT OF ALLIES
RETREAT, PRIOR TO
GENERAL ADVANCE

BAR-SUR-SEINE

R. Yonne

NANGIS

LAST PITCHED
BATTLE Mar 25th
FRENCH RETIRE ON PARIS

MEAUX

PARIS

R. Seine

PARIS SURRENDERS
Mar 30th

FONTAINEBLEAU

MONTEREAU

NAPOLEON REACHES
FONTAINBLEAU
March 30th

SCHWARTZENBURG
ROUTED Feb 18th
RETREATS

BATTLES

BRIENNE	Jan 29th
LA ROTHIERE	Feb 1st
CHAMPAUBERT	Feb 10th
MONTMIRAIL	Feb 11th
VAUXCHAMPS	Feb 14th
MONTEREAU	Mar 7th
CRAONNE	Mar 9th,10th
LAON	Mar 20th
ARCIS-SUR-AUBE	Mar 25th
FERE-CHAMPENOISE	

March 20th his bluff was called. At Lyons he had 21,500 men opposing a scratch Allied force of 32,000 but substantial French reinforcements were on their way. Augereau did not wait for them. He dug no fortifications and abandoned his heavy artillery at Valence. While the assault of Lyons was in progress he called a conference of civic dignitaries and asked their advice as to what course he should take. Should he hold on, or should he evacuate? What answer did he expect from propertied civilians under fire? It was an odd question for a man who had been numbered among the most audacious of Napoleon's marshals. The civic authorities gave their answer and the second city of France opened its gates to the enemy.

There were still men around Napoleon, however, who not only possessed the courage to fight but the honesty to speak their minds. One such man was Macdonald, now covering the rear of the Grand Army. Ordered to assault Vitry he politely refused, pointing out that his men were exhausted, that the town was strongly garrisoned, garnished with pointed stakes, and surrounded by a moat. "Fill the moat with bales of straw," Napoleon suggested but the Scotsman replied, "Ask tired men to attack across a straw bridge? Try it first with your Guard, Sire!"

The incident would seem to suggest that, at this stage of the campaign, Napoleon's mind was so clouded that it was unable to assess the hopelessness of his situation but this is not really so. No man who was not in full possession of his faculties could have achieved what he had accomplished since January 25th, when he rejoined the army at Châlons and now, with his customary grasp of the overall possibilities, he perceived that his chances had narrowed to one—to link up with isolated pockets of veterans on the Rhine, weld them into a single striking force, rouse Alsace-Lorraine, and wreak such havoc in the enemy's rear that the capture of Paris would prove an empty gesture. He knew by now that Italy was a spent force, that Augereau was a deserter, that Soult could not hold Wellington in check indefinitely, and that the Allies might bicker and fall out over details but would never disperse to the extent that he could defeat their main army in the field. If their own territory was menaced, however, that would bring them tumbling after him in sufficient numbers and he had little doubt but that he could smash them in detail once their invasion of France had been exposed as a failure.

The situation was desperate but no more so than on the road back from Moscow, or Leipzig, or, indeed, a few weeks before he had shown what could be achieved with a small, devoted band led by men with tactical skill. Davout was still maintaining himself in Hamburg and even making regular night sorties in the enemy's lines. Eugène was still unbeaten on the Mincio, and Soult continued to engage the attention of Wellington's forces. Bernadotte, inactive throughout this campaign, might be persuaded by an impressive Imperial foray to change sides, whereas Murat's allegiance could be purchased by anyone who could guarantee him retention of the crown of Naples. There were, in addition, potential allies in Saxony, in Berg, in Poland, in Denmark, in a hundred and one places where men feared the despotism of Prussia and looked upon the savage horsemen of the Czar as brigands. There were also, in France itself, many who stood to lose everything they possessed if the Bourbons returned and put the clock back to July 13th, 1789.

Weighing all these factors he cautiously sounded the opinion of the men still around him. They were unresponsive. Only Macdonald urged him to carry his plan into effect. The others, men whom he had raised to high positions, who owned large estates in the departments and were proud, as upstarts usually are, of high-sounding titles, were noncommital. He marched on into St. Dizier, brushing aside the resistance he met there and then turned north in the direction of Bar-le-Duc.

The country was strangely deserted. Cavalry patrols found no sign of the enemy but they captured some of the marathon debaters from the recently dispersed conference at Châtillon. At Bar-le-Duc French patrols came close to catching the Emperor's father-in-law, Francis. Napoleon was puzzled and concluded that the main Allied army, which he was certain had been in hot pursuit of him since Arcis, had now abandoned Troyes and Brienne and were concentrating on the strongly-held Vitry. All the way to St. Dizier a mob of Russian horsemen had been following him at a safe distance and this, he concluded, must be Schwartzenberg's vanguard. Irritated by their presence, and hoping to bring on a general action, Napoleon suddenly turned and struck at his pursuers, overturning them with ease and killing or capturing 2,500. Only then did he learn the truth. His pursuers were not a vanguard at all but a decoy force of 8,000 detached by the Russian Witzingerode. Schwartzenberg was not pursuing him at all. At last, after weeks of futile maneuvering that had enabled Napoleon to defeat the Allies in detail, the Austrian general had united with Blucher and both made a momentous decision. They would march directly on Paris, treating the main body of the Grand Army as if it did not exist. After so many setbacks and humiliations each had made an accurate assessment of the value of the ragged band manipulated by a genius. It was a thing of straw that did not constitute a real danger to united adversaries. Danger lay not in going forward but in going back, in allowing themselves to be hoaxed into believing that the grey devil on horseback was a serious challenge. Paris, the seat of his central government, was the goal. Without its prestige the Emperor Napoleon would cease to exist.

They had not arrived at this obvious decision without a little prompting by Fate. On March 23rd, when they were still undecided what to do, a Cossack patrol brought in two Imperial dispatches. One was a message from Berthier to Macdonald and seems to have contained little that its interceptors did not know, i.e., the whereabouts of Napoleon. The shorter of the two messages was of prodigious importance to men awaiting a sign. It was a letter dictated by Napoleon to the Empress and in a few sentences it laid bare his plans.[2] It ran, "My friend—I have been all day in the saddle. On the 20th I took Arcis on the Aube. The enemy attacked at eight in the evening. I beat him, killed four thousand men and captured four cannon. On the 21st the enemy engaged in order to protect the march of his columns toward Brienne and Bar on the Aube. *I have resolved to betake myself to the Marne in order to draw off the enemy from Paris and to approach my fortifications. I shall be this evening in St. Dizier. Adieu my friend; embrace my boy."*
Now they not only knew where Napoleon was but what he

intended to do next. The note resolved the last of their doubts. Orders were given for the entire Allied army to advance directly upon Paris.

It seems odd that an experienced general like Napoleon should have committed such vital information to paper and then attempted to send it through the enemy lines, so odd, indeed, that one cannot help wondering if the story of the note is false, or at any rate apocryphal. The actual piece of paper has not survived and one can only judge its authenticity from the terms in which it is couched. These have a ring of truth for they say precisely what was in Napoleon's mind at that time, whereas the postscript, "Embrace my boy," is thoroughly characteristic. Possibly it was in cypher that was broken down but there seems no doubt but that its capture played a vital part in determining the course of the invasion. From this point on the Allies paid no attention whatever to Napoleon's main force, out on the eastern periphery of the battle area. Horse, foot and guns they smashed through the thin screen of French troops between themselves and Paris and within six days of the capture of this dispatch they were within cannon range of the city's outer suburbs.

They did not get there without a fight and of all the clashes in the campaign of France the battle of Fère-Champenoise about ten miles east of Sézanne and fifteen north of the Aube, was the most ill-matched and the hardest fought. It provided an example of heroism rarely equaled and never surpassed in the annals of the Grand Army.

Marmont and Mortier, with considerably less than 20,000 men at their disposal were now facing odds of something approaching seven to one, and by far the greater proportion of their troops were half-grown youths with almost no experience of war. Fère-Champenoise was no set piece of a battle but a disorderly, straggling affair, fought between dispersed bodies of troops, the attackers part of a vast, disciplined force marching on the capital, the defenders a loose formation of Frenchmen struggling to halt the tide. Step by step, suffering severe losses in men, guns and materials, the two marshals were forced back first on Sézanne, then on the Marne, and finally to the gates of Paris but never, during this final onrush, did the Allies lose contact with the defenders. There were clashes every day until all that remained of the marshals' forces had reached the approaches of the city.

The story of one such isolated combat, fought on the day Marmont and Mortier stood at Fère-Champenoise, has come down to us. It is a miniature epic. More than any other eyewitness' account it demonstrates the desperate courage of boys whose fathers had thrown back foreign invasion on these same fields and whose elder brothers had shared in the glory of Austerlitz, Jena, Friedland and Wagram.

It concerns two divisions of Macdonald's corps, some 4,300 men in all, charged with escorting a convoy of munitions and food from Châlons to Fère-Champenoise under the command of General Pacthod. They had sixteen guns and almost every man in the ranks was a teenage National Guard. On the morning of March 25th the convoy was resting at the crossroads of Villeseneux when it was attacked by masses of Russian cavalry. Pacthod formed his men into six squares, with wagons in the center and batteries of four guns between the squares. Then, moving very slowly in this unavoidably clumsy formation, the little army moved across country to Fère-Champenoise expecting to join up with Marmont and Mortier.

Scenting plunder the Russian cavalry moved in, blasting the squares with horse artillery at close range, but although they inflicted many casualties they could not break the formations and every attempt to do so cost them casualties. Realizing that none would survive if they were hampered by the wagons Pacthod gave the order to cut the traces and harness the draft animals to the guns. Approaching a village, and still fighting off four times their number, the French found the road blocked by artillery and two regiments of dragoons. They cut their way through and the retreat continued. They had now been engaged in close combat for five hours, without a moment's respite. Renewed cavalry attacks were pressed on both flanks but the squares closed up and moved on, and as the afternoon waned they came within sight of the hills above Fère-Champenoise. Here were troops in formation and a glimpse of gilded staff officers, standing together on high ground. Pacthod's conscripts supposed them to be French and gave a rousing cheer.

They were not French but the staff of the Czar and the king of Prussia, who had just driven Mortier and Marmont from the field.

Pacthod's six squares, shrunken but still intact, were now engulfed by the Allied Army. Artillery fire belched down on them and fresh masses of cavalry charged out of the setting sun. Pacthod gave the order to change direction and make for some adjacent marshes where the cavalry could not follow them. A summons to surrender was rejected.

The boys had now been under attack for ten hours and almost every man in the division was wounded. An infantry battalion was ordered up and 20,000 cavalry joined the assault but still the squares did not dissolve. Only after another five miles did one crumble away and then an additional forty-eight guns and fresh regiments of enemy cavalry appeared from the direction in which Pacthod was marching.

There was now no hope of reaching the comparative safety of the marshes. The French commander, feeling that he had no right to condemn the survivors to death, stepped out of the ranks to answer another demand for surrender. "I don't discuss terms under fire," he said. "Give the order to stop firing and I will do the same." The firing died down and Pacthod yielded up his sword. In an adjoining square surrender followed expenditure of the last cartridge. A third refused to yield and the survivors reached the sanctuary of the marshes as night fell on the scene of the heroic combat. Of the original 4,300 more than 2,000 lay along the road to Villeseneux. Of the 1,500 who surrendered almost all were wounded, including the gallant Pacthod.

Two days later Napoleon, studying accounts Russian prisoners gave him of the combined march on Paris, was shown an Allied bulletin captured by one of Macdonald's patrols. It was the first indication Macdonald had received that two of his divisions had been cut to pieces and all the artillery and stores at Sézanne (in addition to Pacthod's convoy) had been captured. The fatal bulletin was handed in by the marshal himself who silently awaited the Imperial comment. To the Scotsman's amazement Napoleon smiled. "What day of the month is it?" he asked. Macdonald said it was the 27th. "This bulletin is dated the day after tomorrow, the 29th" Napoleon said. "It is not true, the enemy is always doing this kind of thing."

Nonplussed, for he had been convinced by the rank and names of prisoners that the bulletin was genuine, the marshal returned to Drouot of the Artillery.

"What did the Emperor say?" asked the veteran.

"That it wasn't authentic," replied Macdonald.

"It's authentic all right," said Drouot, "the numeral 'six' has been printed upside down as a 'nine'."

Macdonald returned with the information but Napoleon, while accepting it at its face value, did not seem overwhelmed. He said quietly, "So you don't think we can carry Vitry?"

"I thought you were convinced of it," grumbled Macdonald, to which Napoleon replied, "Quite true, let us go away."

It was then that the Scotsman, unlike the silent Berthier, the exasperated Oudinot, and others who were telling their Chief only what he wished to hear, spoke out boldly. "If I were you I would go into Lorraine and Alsace, collect the garrisons from there and wage war to the knife upon the enemy's rear, cutting off their communications, intercepting their convoys and reinforcements. They would be compelled to retreat and you would be supported by our strongholds."

Unknowingly he had spoken the Emperor's thoughts, putting into simple words the plan that had been recommending itself to Napoleon ever since he had driven the enemy from the field of Dresden as long ago as September the previous year. March east. Forget the enemy's field force as he has forgotten yours. Carry the fight back to the Rhine, to Saxony, to the Oder if necessary. It was a good plan, indeed, it was the only plan left and by not putting it into execution he lost the war.

III

On a grey January day more than twenty-one years before a somber procession had passed down the Rue Royale between thousands of silent spectators. It centered upon King Louis, now styled Louis Capet, who was going to his death at the hands of the public executioner. To some extent it was this needless act of

cruelty that had begun this fearful hullabaloo and now the same
thoroughfare was to provide the stage for another theatrical
display. On March 31st, about midday, a cavalcade of forty
banner waving horsemen rode down the Boulevard de la
Madeleine shouting "Vive le Roi! Vivent les Bourbons!" To
those who looked on, saying nothing, the significance of the
demonstration was not lost. They saw it as not merely the end
of the Empire but the end of an epoch. For here were Frenchmen, some of them in uniform, shouting for the gouty brother
of the blameless man whose head had been shorn away a stone's
throw from this same spot, and they were doing it under the
windows of two foreign autocrats who had just entered the
capital at the point of the bayonet.

"Paris," said General Clarke, Minister of War, "is indefensible,"
and enough people believed him to make it so. In 1870 and 1914
history was to prove the opposite but again, in 1940, the inertia
of Parisiens was to bring about an almost exact repetition of the
muddle, halfheartedness and treachery that characterized the
1814 debacle. Neither in 1814 nor in 1940 did Paris fall by force
of arms. On both occasions it was sacrificed to bad faith, incompetence, and nervous exhaustion on the part of those responsible for its defense.

Reading eyewitness accounts of those last catastrophic days
one is struck by the strange and shaming contrast between the
conduct of Pacthod's conscripts and the selfish scuttle of the
men and women for whom they had died.

With the wreck of his battalions Marmont, smarting under
the Imperial rebuke at Rheims but still a long way from contemplating betrayal, fell back on the heights of Romainville
and Belleville outside the capital. With Mortier's survivors he
had, perhaps, about 8,000 men to add to what could have been a
powerful and well organized garrison of National Guardsmen
and other volunteers under old Marshal Moncey, long since retired and remarkable for his honesty rather than his military
talent. There were arsenals stocked with guns, small arms and
powder and there was no immediate difficulty in feeding the
population. A spirited resistance, along the lines of what actually occurred a generation and a half later, would have placed
the victorious Allies in an untenable position. Behind them—

with Napoleon in command no one could ever really be sure where—was the main field army of France, and behind that were the frontier fortresses from Antwerp to Verdun, all well garrisoned and all commanded by experienced officers. And even this was not the limit of France's potentialities. Davout still clung to Hamburg, Soult was still in the field against Wellington, the brilliant Suchet was undefeated and Eugène was still under arms at Mantua. All hopes, if hope did exist, rested on Paris and on the stiffening Marmont's battlehardened men could bring to a hundred thousand amateurs in the capital. The only ingredient lacking to provide an epic defense was resolution and of that there was none, neither among the soldiers, the citizen army, the legislators, or the professional schemers for whom Talleyrand was both rallying point and policy maker.

Historians have argued for a century and a half concerning Talleyrand's motives in the spring of 1814. Was he bent on insuring his own amnesty or was he, deep down, acting in what he sincerely believed to be the best interests of France? It is not possible to buttress either theory with convincing evidence. Talleyrand was Talleyrand, just as Metternich was Metternich. Both men possessed minds of infinite subtlety and neither was hampered by unselfish idealism that exists, somewhere, in almost every human being. They had their own codes and made their own rules, mostly as they went along, picking their way like a pair of fastidious cats among the broken bottles and the slime of power. They loved intrigue for its own sake but this does not necessarily mean that their intentions were wholly base. They juggled with combinations of circumstance as dedicated scientists juggle with formulae, mathematicians with figures, poets with words. Problems of the kind that faced them at this moment of time so absorbed them that they were able to think of men and nations as chessmen and it did not detract from the lure of the game that many lesser minds were at work upon the same problems in the same conference rooms.

Waiting in Paris, as conflicting reports poured in from the battle areas between Marne and Seine, Talleyrand sifted and examined every eventuality and now, as March drew to a close, he thought he had the right answer. The Allies, two hundred thousand strong, were at the barriers. Napoleon and his remnant were far away to the east, trudging down some miry river valley. The bovine Marie-Louise and the former King Joseph presented no problems. One came close to being a halfwit and the other was a man whose turgid brain had never once enabled him to make use of his splendid opportunities. Of Marmont, Mortier, Moncey, and the other soldiers, Talleyrand took little account. He had always regarded soldiers as grownup little boys who needed shining weapon-toys to exercise authority. Of the autocrats themselves, the handsome, shallow, half-mystic Czar, and his slow-thinking junior partner, Frederick William of Prussia, he had nothing but contempt of the kind he had always had for His Imperial Majesty, Napoleon the First, and this contempt extended to Royalists, Jacobins, Constitutionists and Legitimatists. In all that concourse of braggarts, buffoons and honest men there were only two men who commanded his respect—Metternich, the Austrian Chancellor, and Castlereagh the hard-bargaining Englishman. For they alone were cast in his mold.

There was a battle of sorts. On the 29th and 30th the suburbs echoed with the roar of cannon and the sputter of small arms but every man who fell on either side sold his life worthlessly. The real decisions had been made, not on the field but in the Council Chamber.

On the evening of the 28th Marie-Louise and Joseph had conferred with the civic authorities and a majority had voted in favor of her leaving the capital at once and heading west for Rambouillet, taking her son with her.

To understand the mood of fashionable Paris in the last days of March, 1814, it is helpful to read eyewitness accounts of three women, each of them more perceptive and more responsive to atmosphere than the inbred Habsburg girl Napoleon had accepted as the price of peace with Austria four years before. Lodged in the capital at that time were Hortense, daughter of the discarded Josephine and estranged wife of his brother Louis; the recently widowed Madame Junot, wife of his old companion-in-arms; and La Maréchale Oudinot, wife of the Corps Commander still fighting for the Empire.

The sudden advance of the Allies, together with the prolonged absence of Napoleon in the field, temporarily deprived all three of their nimble wits for each was a sophisticated, intelligent woman. At the height of the Empire they had been leaders of fashion, courted and fawned upon by place seekers, the possessors of immense wardrobes, innumerable jewels, and considerable wealth. Now, almost overnight, they were turned into refugees, sewing jewels into their corsets, secreting their valuables against Cossack pillage, and generally submerged in the ground swell of a distracted capital. Each owed everything she possessed to the man shadow-maneuvering at St. Dizier, many leagues to the east, and each had less inclination to desert him now than had his family or the soldiers and politicians he had raised to eminence.

Hortense wondered how the fall of the Empire would affect her mother, who was in receipt of a substantial pension from her former husband. She also wondered about the fate of her beloved brother Eugène, isolated in Italy and surrounded by enemies. As to herself and her children, where could she go and what could she do? Unhappily she sought advice from the Empress as Marie-Louise was coming away from a discussion on her future movements. "I am leaving," said Marie-Louise, with a smiling expression that suggested the decision brought her relief, "and I advise you to do the same." "I am glad to see Your Majesty loses the crown with a smile," replied Hortense, who had a sharp tongue and a spiteful disposition. But Hortense realized what a panic evacuation of the Empress and the heir to the throne would do to morale in the city. The garrison and the allies would see it as an admission of defeat and Hortense tried, without success, to get the Duchess of Montebello (chaperon to the Empress and widow of Marshal Lannes) to persuade her to change her mind. Failing in this she sought advice from Joseph, who was even less helpful. Gruffly he told her to shift for herself. There had never been love lost between the Bonapartes and the Beauharnais.

One can see here the fatal flaw in Napoleon's government, a weakness that afflicts all personal dictatorships. Ever since the Coup d'État, in 1799, the Emperor had exercised personal control over the hands, hearts and minds of all his subjects, high, low and bourgeois. Now, at a crisis in his fortunes, the selfish deserted and the potentially loyal were robbed of initiative. Men and women whose influence would have been decisive scuttled about asking one another rhetorical questions and even trained soldiers were unable to see their duty clearly through a fog of propaganda, counterpropaganda and rumor. Only the cool and detached like Talleyrand and his fellow-plotters could find a path and pursue it step by step, unhampered by conscience and guided by self-interest. In the end, informed by her sour husband Louis that their children would be regarded as hostages, Hortense followed the example of Marie-Louise and fled to the west, wondering how soon it would be before this last avenue of escape would be closed by British advancing northeast from Toulouse.

In the last mad moments before her departure she heard the muted clamor of the Royalists emerging from hiding or obscurity after a quarter of a century. She heard also the pitiful story of the little King of Rome, his mind bewildered by all this confusion, clinging desperately to the draperies and door knobs of the Tuileries in an effort to delay the flight of his mother and her suite. Hortense's principal weakness, an inclination to indulge in maudlin self pity is exposed by her own pen. Awakened twice on her final night in Paris she complains: "Such a restless night in addition to my delicate health, was not calculated to prepare me for the difficulties and dangers that lay ahead." Later, at Glatigny, she heard the roar of cannon and reflected that hitherto this familiar sound had been associated in her mind with the celebration of Imperial victories.

Madame Oudinot passed through a similar agony of indecision. She left Paris at four P.M. on the same day as the Empress, taking the crowded road to Versailles and Rambouillet, to which all the exalted were flying without the least notion of what they would do or where they would go when they arrived. That first night, halting at Versailles, the Marshal's wife obtained a lodging in the Rue de l'Orangerie. All night long a procession of refugees flowed past under her windows. "What we saw passing, my children," she records in a memoir written for her family, "was the Empire, with all its pomp and splendor . . . the ministers in their coaches and six, taking with them portfolio, children, wife, jewels, livery; the entire Council of State, the archives, the Crown diamonds, the administration. And instalments of power and magnificence were mingled on the road with humble households who had heaped up on a barrow all they had been able to carry away from the houses which they were abandoning, as they thought, to the pillage that was about to burst forth over the country." Possibly it occurred to her that here was an exact repetition of scenes that had occurred along roads leading to almost every European capital since the Paris mob had gathered in this same street to clamor for bread at the locked grilles of the great chateau. Before she left the window that overlooked this chaotic scene someone gave her a copy of Joseph's proclamation urging Parisiens to stay and fight. It ended with the words, "Parisiens, I remain in your midst!" In the act of reading it she looked up and saw the author in the midst of his staff. He too was heading for Rambouillet.

Madame Junot, whose husband had recently gone mad and committed suicide, did not fly. The reason that prevented her was not loyalty to the man who had elevated her husband from sergeant to duke, but a letter of advice from another old friend, Marmont, then the senior military officer in Paris. Left alone with her staff and her four young children she also sewed diamonds into a girdle that fitted over her corsets, and being undecided what to do next wrote to Marmont who was then negotiating terms with the Allies. Notwithstanding his manifold responsibilities he somehow found time to reply and his letter helps to explain what afterwards came to be regarded as his betrayal of Napoleon. He wrote, ". . . I would recommend you not to quit Paris, which tomorrow will certainly be more tranquil than any place within twenty leagues around. After having done all in my power for the honor of France and French arms, I am forced to sign a capitulation, which will permit foreign troops to enter our capital tomorrow! All my efforts have been unavailing. I have been compelled to yield to numbers, whatever regret I may have felt in doing so. But it was my duty to spare the blood of soldiers confided to my charge. I could not do otherwise than I have done and I hope that my country will judge me as I deserve. My conscience expects this justice."

IV

That was how Marmont saw his duty and perhaps history has judged him too harshly. After all, the Imperial cause was seen to be lost. With the Empress and Joseph gone, most of the notables fleeing down the road to Versailles, and shopkeepers digging holes in their gardens to bury valuables, the morale of the National Guard had slumped to zero. There was no one with sufficient military prestige to rally Parisiens to the defense of the capital. Fear of Cossack pillage hung over the homes of the bourgeois and fear of Bourbon reprisals dwelt in the slums. In the fourth year of the Revolution, when the kings of Europe were advancing on Paris, a royalist proclamation had promised every regicide a noose. Now the armies of the autocrats were here, and who could say that the threats of twenty years ago would not be carried into effect? And yet, without a Danton or a Napoleon to rally them, few of those who feared pillage or the hangman would risk their lives at the barricades. Neither Marmont, nor Mortier, nor old Moncey possessed sufficient personal magnetism to inject Paris with the will to resist and in his heart Marmont, shouldering most of the responsibility, realized as much. The Bonapartes were gone. Joseph reappeared briefly but then disappeared again in the train of the Empress and his brothers, former King Louis and ex-King Jerome. All their adult lives the Imperial family had made a poor showing but never so poor as in the last week of March, 1814. Even Josephine, once hailed as Our Lady of Victories, had fled from Malmaison to her chateau in Navarre, seeing imaginary Cossacks behind every tree.

On March 30th there was fierce fighting in the suburbs. The Prussians advanced on Montmartre, the Wurtemberg troops and the Russians on Romainville, the Austrians on Vincennes and Charenton. At four in the afternoon the Prussians took Montmartre and began to fire heavy guns down on the city. Further resistance seemed useless and Marmont had been given power to negotiate by Joseph before his final departure.

Negotiations were opened that evening and Marmont, sick at heart and physically exhausted, found Orloff, the sovereign's emissary, surprisingly generous. If the regular troops withdrew from the city they could march away with their arms and equipment. The National Guard were to be disarmed, all arsenals and military establishments were to be left as they were, and all wounded and stragglers left behind were deemed to be prisoners-of-war. The terms were accepted. The battle of Paris, culmination of bloody campaigns lasting a little short of a year, was over in a few hours but, short as it was, it had not been bloodless. The brief engagement in the suburbs had cost the Allies over 9,000 men.

All that night there were diplomatic comings and goings at Marmont's house in the Rue de Paradis. Talleyrand was among the visitors. Meeting Count Orloff there he did not neglect to send "his profound respects to the Czar." Marmont felt he had done all that a man could do. Bourrienne, one of Talleyrand's plotters, saw him come in from the street fighting. His tunic skirts were riddled with shot holes, his face black with powder, and he had eight days' growth of beard on his chin. One eyewitness of the fighting at Montmartre says that he saw six men bayoneted beside the Marshal. Another claims Marmont lost five horses that day and was wounded in hand and arm. From this point on the soldiers withdrew from the scene and the politicians moved in. By the morning of March 31st, Talleyrand was already at work drafting a constitution. On one point the Allies' representatives were adamant; they would not treat with any member of the Bonaparte family.

It was at this stage, noon of the 31st, that the mounted demonstration was made on the Boulevard de Madeleine. The royalist fervor of the group was contagious. White scarves fluttered down from windows. A few National Guardsmen tore off their tricolor cockades and replaced them with white ones. To the scattered shouts of "Vive le roi!" and "Vivent les Bourbons," were added three new battlecries, "Vive l'Empereur Alexandre!" "Vive le roi de Prusse" and, more surprisingly, "Vive notre Liberateurs!" Inside his hotel Talleyrand must have smiled, reading the public pulse as a surgeon checks the progress of a fever. Round him dedicated conspirators were joined by the waverers, men who had remained hesitant and uncommitted until now, most of them Napoleon's lackeys until a week ago. Confidence warmed the group like the spring sunshine. From the suburbs, first as a trickle, then as a flood, the liberators moved into the heart of the city, perhaps the most cosmopolitan army that had come this way since the Roman legionaries had named the collection of huts on this stretch of the Seine "Lutetia"—The Muddy. Curiosity brought the Parisiens flocking into the streets and the procession they witnessed had a sobering effect upon men and women who had grown to maturity in the years of Napoleonic triumphs. For here, in the flesh, were a hundred and eighty thousand armed representatives of the countries where those victories had been won, sons of towns and villages made familiar by the long roll of French battle honors and Imperial titles. From the heights of Montmartre came Blucher's veterans, pigtailed hussars, grenadiers and infantry in their low crowned shakoes who had fought their way step by step from Silesia. From Vincennes and Charenton came the Austrians, compatriots of the absent Empress, rank after rank of Croatian infantry and Hungarian horsemen, enjoying their first real victory after more than fifty defeats at the hands of Republican, Consular and Imperial armies of France. But it was the Russians who excited the most astonishment, for here was an army that looked as if it had spilled from the pages of medieval history, bearded Cossacks on their shaggy, piebald ponies, Circassians in chain mail, Bashkirs with their short bows slung behind their backs, Tartars and Siberians in their native furs, and mingling with them, cohorts of Swedes, Bohemians, Bavarians, Saxons, and men of Wurtemberg, many of whom, until a few months before, had marched beside the veterans of the Grand Army to the last of their victories.

At the head of this host rode the two original partners, Czar Alexander and Frederick William of Prussia, and with them the comparative latecomer, Schwartzenberg, representing the Emperor Francis of Austria then at Dijon. All three were respectfully greeted by the municipality and respect became servility when it became known that the greatest of the conquerors had issued an edict; Paris would be occupied pending a general peace but Paris, unlike Moscow, would not be burned. It was not even to be pillaged. For this the city fathers had the word of a Czar.

Paris was conquered but the future of France was far from being settled. Even at this stage the powers had yet to agree upon
a common policy. Austria (though secretly) still hoped for a
solution that left Marie-Louise regent. Prussia, and especially
Blucher, was determined to make an end to Napoleon and there
were several half-baked schemes for encompassing his assassination. Czar Alexander, upon whom every major decision
now centered, remained unconvinced by Britain's sponsorship
of a Bourbon restoration, now urged by Talleyrand and his
conspirators. Chateaubriand, one of the most celebrated writers of his time and, under the Empire, the high priest of French
literature, added his considerable prestige to this view. He had
withdrawn from Napoleon after the judicial murder of the Duc
d'Enghien in 1804 and had spent the last winter of Imperialism
writing a pamphlet essay, subtitled *Of the necessity of attach-
ing ourselves to our legitimate princes for the salvation of France
and of Europe*. Events had overtaken him. It was still at the
printers when the Allies entered Paris.[3] The general feeling in
Paris would seem to be royalist but the Czar, although a romantic, was not a fool. He could sense rather than see something contrived in the sporadic demonstrations of Bourbon
cliques appearing at street corners. There was no malice in the
man. He did not hate Napoleon and certainly did not wish his
death. Rather he was conscious of the tremendous importance
at this moment of doing the right thing for France, for Europe,
for history and his reputation. There had been more than enough
bloodshed and he had no desire to shed more on behalf of a
family who had been pensioners-in-exile for a quarter of a
century. If France sincerely wanted a Bourbon they could
have one. If not then some compromise must be found, a prolonged regency, even a Bernadotte. Talleyrand balked at this
last proposal. "If we need a soldier we already have the finest
in the world," he said, adding that no other military figure in
France could rally more than a hundred men to his side.

Caulaincourt, the sincere friend of Napoleon, now reappeared
urging a regency but the provisional government was packed
with Talleyrand's creatures and dedicated royalists and neither
faction would accept the continuation of the dynasty. A decree

was issued by this rump government releasing soldiers from their allegiance to Napoleon and softly but insistently Talleyrand continued to advance the claims of the Bourbons as the only possible solution.

It could have been put into effect then and there had the close of the campaign been tidier, and had Napoleon been brought to bay inside his capital but this was not the case. He was still at large at the head of an army, some sort of army, and just across the Seine, at Essonnes, was Marmont with fourteen thousand disciplined men capable of giving battle. Nor was this all. The garrisons of some of the frontier fortresses were said to be marching west to join their isolated leader. Soult was still in the field against Wellington. Augereau had not yet declared himself. Suchet's Catalonian army was intact. And Eugène in Italy had refused to emulate Murat. Napoleon had achieved many miracles in the past and might achieve more if he could assemble these widely scattered forces and fight on west of Paris or south of the Loire. He was not alone with his rank and file. Berthier, Oudinot, Ney, Lefèbvre and others were still loyal, as was Mortier, the other defender of Paris. All these factors had to be taken into consideration for the Czar did not want to prolong the war, particularly a people's war. In this consideration vanity played a part. He now saw himself not as a victorious general who had entered and subdued his enemy's capital but as a European father figure, omniscient but just, moderate and merciful.

And so, in Talleyrand's house, the talking and bargaining went on and the Czar presided, mostly silent, the guest of a relapsed priest with a crippled foot and a mind with more fissures than a splintered plate of glass.

14

A HUNDRED MILES to the east, at the town of St. Dizier, whence he had marched after Macdonald had insisted that it was impossible to storm Vitry, Napoleon knew nothing of these great events.

On March 25th, having at last discovered that the 8,000 Russian cavalrymen shadowing him from Arcis-sur-Aube were only decoys, he had reverted to his plan of harrying the rearguard of the enemy and would have put it into operation by now had he not realized that all save Macdonald were opposed to such a desperate course. To some degree it was already operating, for the countryside, in this area, was thoroughly roused and armed peasants brought in prisoners and materiel every day, some of their engagements with the enemy assuming the proportions of miniature battles. Such was the case at Bazoches, near St. Mihiel, where that unlucky man Colonel Viriot (he who had been so victimized by Fouché's secret police) put his frustrated military ardor to work on the invaders.

Colonel Viriot's little action is typical of what was happening all over that part of France and demonstrates the practicality of the Imperial plan. Borrowing six guns from Verdun and harnessing them to plow horses, the colonel attacked a Russian army corps and cut it to pieces, taking 1,800 prisoners, eighty wagons, five hundred horses and eight guns. Fate, however, continued to dog him. The corps he defeated was commanded by Prince Biren of Courland, a close friend of Louis XVIII, and

A New Word Is Coined

the luckless Viriot was to be called to sharp account for this victory when all was over.

By now Napoleon had learned details of the Marmont-Mortier defeat at Fère-Champenoise and clearly understood that Paris was about to be invested but this had been foreseen. He must have known that the marshals, with a few thousand exhausted conscripts, could not hold back the united armies of the Coalition and could never have regarded their force as more than a screen. Without the enthusiastic backing of his senior officers, however, he was unable to mount a counterattack and the mood at Headquarters was clearly for peace and peace at any price. Large scale guerilla tactics behind the enemy's lines would prolong the war indefinitely and at St. Dizier, between the 25th and 28th, it became obvious that his dream of setting the heath on fire across the Allies' lines of communication would never be translated into reality. Making the best of what could not be altered he marched west, aiming roughly at Fontainebleau to the south of the capital, a line of march that would keep the Seine between his right wing and the left wing of the Allies in and about Meaux. The route also had the advantage of traversing a region where food and fodder could still be found for his men and horses.

Some have interpreted this march and abrupt change of plan as a panic measure. Emil Ludwig claims "he set out for Paris like one who hears his house was on fire" but this is not certain. The march was certainly forced, and was accomplished at phenomenal speed, but it was in his nature to move quickly, to decide upon a maneuver then carry it out without a moment's delay. Paris would resist no doubt but its defenders would need help. No one knew better than Napoleon that their stocks of arms were mostly antiquated, that the city's fortifications were weak and decayed, and that it sheltered any number of traitors. Fixing Talleyrand with his keen gaze before leaving Paris in January, he had said, "I am aware I have enemies here as well as those I go to meet." He could not have hoped for much in the way of a prolonged defense in his absence.

He set out from St. Dizier early on the morning of the 28th and his progress down the valley of the Seine was meteoric. Every step of the way the specter of impending calamity ac-

companied the doomed army. Among the prisoners taken en
route was an Austrian diplomat on his way to London. He
was promptly paroled, turned round, and sent back to his Imperial master with letters and appeals. At Doulevant Napoleon
was handed an urgently worded dispatch from Postmaster Lava-
lette, a man to be trusted. It was an unequivocal demand for
more haste if catastrophe was to be averted. The pace of the
march was stepped up and at nightfall on the 29th the exhausted
columns staggered into Troyes.

A few men could travel faster than an army, even when that
army was Bonaparte's. With a small escort he pressed on to
Villeneuve and then, almost alone, by post chaise towards Paris.
Beside him sat Caulaincourt, his sole companion throughout the
sleigh and coach ride from Smorgoni to Paris. Behind them
trundled a tiny staff, including General Gourgaud and Marshal
Lefèbvre.

There was a special reason for Lefèbvre's presence. His name
had been included in the list of marshals ten years before in
order to placate the diehard Republicans after Napoleon had
assumed the Imperial title. Now, with so many royalists coming
out of hiding and making their mocking bon mots, a man of
Lefèbvre's stubborn disposition would prove invaluable in raising the faubourgs on behalf of the tricolor. To this extremity
then had he been driven, a man who, all his life, had hated and
feared the mob but now looked to it for rescue.

Lefèbvre's slumbering republicanism was never put to the test.
At Essonnes they learned that a battle was raging and the Empress had fled across the Loire. At the next stage, a dismal posting house ten miles from Paris, the little procession of chaises
encountered a dismounted chasseur who said he was attached
to Mortier's staff and had been sent ahead to secure billets. For
a moment the man's mission puzzled the Emperor. He could
not comprehend why Marmont and Mortier's troops should
need billets here. The officer told him the marshal's corps were
being withdrawn, that his brother Joseph had followed the
Empress and that Paris, the capital of the world as some had
thought of it until a week ago, was already billeting Bashkirs,
Croats and Prussian hussars. In short that the war was over.

For a few moments he was stupefied. Then he began to rave.

Tomorrow the Guard would arrive! The National Guard of Paris would welcome him with cheers! Once inside the city he would only leave it as a conqueror or a dead man . . . !

Caulaincourt was familiar with the mood. He had sat beside this man as they were whirled a thousand leagues across a wilderness of snow and ice and had learned the trick of sorting the grain of genius from the chaff of hysteria. He waited for the storm to blow itself out and then counseled a swift return to Fontainebleau and a pause during which the new situation could be studied.

Even Caulaincourt, however, was shaken by the Emperor's vehemence on this occasion. He cursed Joseph for a coward, Marmont for a bungling fool, and the deputies for their incipient treachery. Embarrassed officers and men, standing in the windy darkness about the tumbledown buildings, saw this man for a few moments not as a general and administrator of genius, or even as a comrade who had shared their hardships and triumphs over the years, but as an adolescent with a foul mouth and an ungovernable temper. He refused to accept the evidence of his eyes and actually set out on foot, followed by the protesting Caulaincourt, down the road towards Paris. Luckily for him he ran into Mortier's vanguard who confirmed the billeting officer's statement. Regular troops had withdrawn from the capital under an agreement signed that evening and were now falling back to find new positions.

At once he regained control of himself and, as always, his genius for improvisation reasserted itself. He gave orders for the troops of Marmont and Mortier to take up a strong position between the Essonne and the Seine, with the river Yonne protecting their rear. He dispatched Caulaincourt to seek an interview with the Czar and make a final plea for the dynasty. He himself turned about and made his way back to Fontainebleau, arriving there at six A.M. on the morning of March 31st.

II

Two men emerge with credit from the maelstrom of intrigue and bad faith surrounding the crash of the Napoleonic Empire in the first days of April, 1814. They are Caulaincourt, friend and envoy-extraordinary of the stricken Emperor, and Czar Alexander, his most powerful enemy. Now, to the chagrin of those Frenchmen who sought to profit from the collapse, they were to meet and confer.

In what passed between them lay the final hope of the dynasty. If the thread snapped—as Talleyrand and so many others were resolved that it should—all hopes of the house of Bonaparte would crumble. In the charm and persuasiveness of Caulaincourt there reposed no prospect of Napoleon continuing as head of state—that was already a dead letter—but he was considering the possibility of his son mounting the Imperial throne of France fourteen years in the future. Caulaincourt was an honest, dedicated man. As he rode towards the twinkling watch fires of Cossacks and Uhlans, bivouacked on the far side of the Seine, he was resolved to do his utmost on behalf of the man he loved.

His entry to the capital was fraught with difficulty. Pickets had strict orders to turn away any messenger from Napoleon and the presence of Caulaincourt in Paris was feared above that of any envoy, for he had once been Ambassador in Moscow and was known to stand well with the Czar. Had it not been for a chance encounter with the Grand Duke Constantine, the autocrat's brother, he would have returned to Fontainebleau without an interview. Constantine recognized him and conducted him to the Czar's presence at the Elysée Palace, where the Allies were in congress. There, physically exhausted, he was shown into a small room that Napoleon had used as a study when he was in residence. The desk was still littered with maps of Russia. Tactfully Caulaincourt burned them and then went to sleep on a sofa. He was confident now that the Czar would receive him and he was right; Alexander not only accepted the validity of his embassy but also agreed to see him in private.

At first there seemed little hope. "You are too late," the Czar told him, kindly. "It is all over. I can say nothing to you at present." Caulaincourt persisted and there was a second, more promising interview. What passed between these two men is not known with any accuracy for both, in later years, were reticent on the subject. What is known, however, is that Caulaincourt made progress, accepting the fact that Napoleon must go but continuing to plead the cause of his son and a regency. He had two strong cards to play. One was the doubt in the Czar's mind (in less than a year this doubt was to be resolved into certainty) that France did not really want a Bourbon restoration and that Talleyrand and his jackals were either lying or exaggerating. The other was Napoleon's ability to carry on the struggle either from Lorraine, as he had planned, or south of the Loire. Caulaincourt played his hand very skillfully and when he left the Czar's mind was still unresolved. Talleyrand, Prussia and Britain would have to work that much harder to bring him round to accepting their counsels unreservedly. With this crumb of comfort Caulaincourt left for Fontainebleau.

In the meantime events were gathering momentum. On April 1st, under Talleyrand's tutelage, a Provisional Government had been appointed and its membership left a sour taste in the mouths of French patriots. Bourrienne, who hated Napoleon, was the new Postmaster. The Abbé de Pradt, a Talleyrand nominee who had been the first to greet Napoleon at Warsaw at the end of the first stage of his flight from Russia was Chancellor of the Legion of Honor. General Dupont, whose shameful surrender at Baylen in Spain had sent 8,000 Frenchmen to die of starvation in a desert island prison camp, was Minister of War. The rest, with few exceptions, were nonentities, possessing either genuine or self-seeking royalist sympathies.

On the next day, April 2nd, the Senate published a decree in which Napoleon was accused of almost every misdemeanor a head of state could commit and backed it with accusations that might have been leveled against a barbaric Roman emperor, indicted by the Praetorian Guard as a prelude to assassination. Among other things he was charged with abandoning wounded without dressings and deliberately causing famine and pestilence in the country. That same day the Municipal Council openly declared for the Bourbons and sanctioned overtures to the remaining marshals and generals to desert the tricolor. As an inducement they were all offered continued enjoyment of their pensions, positions and honors. No one seems to have commented on the absurdity of reaffirming titles like "Prince of the Moscowa" or "Duke of Danzig," upon men who had earned them defeating the armies of the sovereigns who were now backing the appeals.

The Paris political scene changed hour by hour. When Caulaincourt returned to Fontainebleau on April 2nd his assessment of the situation was already out of date but he had no hesitation in declaring to Napoleon that, in his view, the very best he could hope for now was a regency. He was by no means alone in this judgment. Ney had already been heard to mutter in Napoleon's presence that only an abdication could save them, and others, including Lefèbvre, Oudinot and Macdonald to name only three, were sounding one another on the prospect of a deputation demanding this solution.

Yet even now, with a half-million invaders in France, the military situation was not hopeless. After marching fifty leagues in three days the relics of the Grand Army were approaching from Troyes and within call were something like fifty thousand men. How many times had Napoleon worked wonders with fewer? There was anxiety but no despondency among the rank and file. From colonel downwards the majority continued to trust him and look to him for another masterstroke, this time under the walls of Paris. But heart and hope had ebbed from their chieftains. General Gérard, in conversation with Macdonald, told him the men of property among them feared that further resistance might mean Paris would suffer the fate of Moscow. Macdonald promised to pass on these fears to the Emperor as soon as he reached the chateau.

In the meantime the decree of the Provisional Government, releasing the army from its Imperial allegiance, was doing its deadly work, particularly upon one man who held a key position. Talleyrand rarely made mistakes in picking accomplices and he made none now. His man, as he saw it, was Marmont, Duke of Ragusa, the Emperor's oldest friend and among his most trusted.

Marmont's reputation just then was riding high. After a lifetime of honorable service, and a personal association with Napoleon that went back to the days when they were cadets, he had displayed great gallantry in the battle for Paris and had, moreover, wrung unexpectedly favorable terms out of

the victorious Allies. What was passing through Marmont's mind
just then can be pieced together from the memoirs of men engaged in detaching him from his allegiance and also in the recol-
lections of his friend Macdonald, who was the most dispassionate
eyewitness of what followed. Marmont was beginning to see
himself as a General Monck, who, in reconciling civil and
military interests in war weary France, would earn the plaudits
of his countrymen and the accolade of history. Like Ney, Macdonald and other leaders, he was mentally and physically exhausted. His body was seamed with scars received in the service
of his country and his soul was sick of war. He could see no
prospect of a Napoleonic recovery. The bravery of his men
at Fère-Champenoise and at the barriers of the capital had
achieved nothing. By now it was manifestly clear that the Czar
had no intention of sacking Paris and, what was equally clear,
was that many eminent Frenchmen, not all of them venial,
were prepared to accept a Bourbon restoration as the price of
peace. On meeting Napoleon after the Emperor's glum return
to Fontainebleau following the encounter with Mortier's billeting officer, Marmont had received Imperial congratulations
on his spirited fight against great odds at Montmartre and elsewhere in the suburbs but what availed praise from a man who
was now isolated on a tiny island of vainglory among so many
enemies? Waiting at Essonnes, with his gallant fourteen thousand, Marmont could see no sense in continuing the struggle
and when an envoy of the Provisional Government arrived, with
letters of appeal from his friend Bourrienne, his faith in Napoleon's prospects foundered.

Talleyrand had made a characteristically devious approach.
The authors of two letters addressed to Marmont were old
friends, Bourrienne and General Desolles, but there was also a
third and more important letter from General Schwartzenberg.
All three pointed the path of patriotism and honor. Marmont,
they suggested, should now demonstrate the army's loss of faith
in Napoleon by marching back into the enemy camp. By so
doing he would show the whole of France that the Bourbons
were desired not only by civilians but by the men who had
contributed to the glory of France's victories abroad. Such a
course would preclude the possibility of civil war and bring

instant peace to a nation bled white by Napoleonic ambition.

Marmont's duty as a soldier was clear. He should have burned the letters as Eugène had burned his and sent the emissary, Montessuis, about his business. Instead, however, he asked himself if he did not have another and overriding duty as a Frenchman? Was anything to be gained by shedding more blood in a lost cause? He hesitated and finally returned answers that he was willing to treat. Montessuis returned jubilantly to his masters and the doom of the dynasty was sealed.

Bourrienne's letter has come down to us. It is a moving appeal to Marmont to speak the single word that could secure the happiness of France. It concluded "Your friends expect you, long for you, and I trust will soon embrace you." General Desolles wrote in almost identical terms while Schwartzenberg offered an unimpeded retirement, with the honors of war, to Normandy. He also guaranteed to the man he was urging Marmont to betray "life and liberty in a space of territory and a circumscribed country, to be chosen by the Allied powers and the French Government."

On April 2nd, two days after the incident at the posthouse where Napoleon learned of the surrender of Paris, the Emperor rose in excellent spirits and set about the task of reassessing the situation. The state apartments of the great chateau had not been opened and the Emperor was occupying a private suite. He called for his maps and parade states and began to juggle with figures and distances with the air of a man still in a position of tremendous strength. Possibly he succeeded in bluffing himself, a common practice with dictators on the verge of ruin, but he impressed nobody else, not even the silent Berthier, who handed over muster rolls like a physician humoring a wealthy but deranged patient. There were, Napoleon said, three courses open to them. To march east and throw themselves across the Allied communications as envisaged a week ago; to retreat over the Loire and wage war from central France; or to gather up all their forces and assault Paris. For himself he was disposed to adopt the latter course as the boldest and the only one promising a quick solution. Outside, warming themselves in the early spring sunshine, were veterans who would march into the mouth

of hell if he gave the word and he pointed out that these were
not his sole tools for a reconquest of the capital. Within reasonable marching distance were the garrisons of Sens, Blois, Tours
and Orleans, eight thousand in all, and further off (he apparently
discounted Wellington's army) were Soult's 40,000, Suchet's
15,000 that had now returned to France, Augereau's 16,000 (his
treachery was still unconfirmed at Headquarters) and General
Maison's 20,000 in the north. There were other garrisons at
Antwerp and along the Rhine but he gave no indication as to
how these were to rally at Fontainebleau. Nobody gave him any
tactical advice for there was none to give. Ney did show him a
Paris newspaper, full of descriptions of demonstrations in favor
of the Bourbons, but he dismissed its content as irrelevant non-
sense. That was the afternoon of Caulaincourt's return but the
faithful emissary received no thanks for his heroic endeavors.
Instead he was scolded so severely that later, relenting, Napoleon apologized. So resolved was he on a march on Paris, however, that the little group of marshals about him must have
begun to wonder if the great brain had lost its reason.

On April 3rd Napoleon held a review in the great courtyard
and was received with cheers by battalions of the Old and Young
Guard. In full uniform and decorations he walked among their
ranks with the gloomy Ney and old Marshal Moncey who
had slipped out of Paris during the brief armistice. But all this
was shadow play and among those who saw it as such was
Macdonald. It was the Scotsman, fresh from the duty of commanding the rearguard at Montereau, who was best qualified to
take a detached view of the pantomime at Fontainebleau. An
addendum to the script was in his pocket and now, stepping out
of the muttering group, he produced it.

Napoleon greeted him jovially. "Good day, Duke of Tarrentum. How are you?"

The Duke of Tarrentum said he was very sad. It not only
looked like a pantomime, it was beginning to sound like one.
Macdonald admitted that he felt overwhelmed and humiliated
by the surrender of Paris but before Napoleon could mistake this
as an endorsement of his plans to attack the city, the marshal
said bluntly that his troops were unwilling to expose Paris to the
fate of Moscow. He then went on to give a detailed picture of

the sorry state of his men and suggested what would certainly happen to them if they met vastly superior forces on an open plain. "For my own part," he ended, "I declare that my sword shall never be drawn against Frenchmen. Whatever may be decided upon we have had enough of this unlucky war, without kindling civil war!"

To everyone's surprise there was no irrational outburst, no deluge of facts, figures and gaudy prophecies. This was mutiny but it was not received as such. Napoleon remained calm and reasonable. Macdonald took advantage of the mood and whipped out a letter he had received, passed on to him with broken seals by Marmont. It was signed by Beurnonville, a member of the Provisional Government, and was a kind of circular produced for the benefit of the high ranking officers. Briefly it announced that the Allies, magnanimous in their intentions to all other Frenchmen, would not treat with Napoleon. France, it said, was to have a constitution on the English pattern and the Senate was already drafting one. The Emperor passed the letter to Maret, who read it aloud. When he had finished Napoleon returned it to Macdonald and thanked him for the mark of confidence. "You should never have had any doubt of it," answered the clansman.

It is not often that men of war, assembled to discuss a military predicament, are conscious that they are making history but the men at Fontainebleau on that spring afternoon were exceptions. They knew that what happened here within the next few minutes, would decide the future of France and perhaps the future course of the nineteenth century in Europe and they were not misled. Each reacted to the responsibility according to his temperament. The meeting, begun so casually, had suddenly assumed an importance that none of them could have anticipated. Macdonald was obstinately and icily polite. Ney was red in the face and beginning to fume. Lefèbvre, also excited, was determined on a course that would prevent a repetition of the Terror. Moncey, perhaps remembering that he was the son of an attorney, had himself under control but Oudinot, a front line fighter, was out of his element in this war of wills and could offer little to the discussion. The two civil representatives, Caulaincourt and Maret, were embarrassed, partly because they felt superfluous but also because each was deeply attached to the pale, plump man now confronted with the ultimate realities of failure. Berthier, the man who had leaned on Napoleon ever since he accepted the post of Chief of Staff in the spring of '96, said nothing at all. Everyone was to remember this. He did not so much as follow the progress of the discussion with his eyes. For nearly twenty years Alexandre Berthier had not made a policy decision. Everything he did, and he did most things faultlessly, was done as a co-ordinator, not as an innovator. Technically senior to every man in the deputation he stood aside, letting events take their course. He might have been one of the sentries at the door.

Napoleon's reaction to Beurnonville's letter was to dismiss it as he had rejected the scribblings of Paris journalists and to return once again to the subject of a rally of all available arms. There was one concession. Recognizing the hopelessness of carrying these men with him he threatened to appeal directly to the army. At this Ney's uncertain temper boiled over. "The army," he shouted, "will not march! The army will obey its chiefs!"

In other days this would have produced an explosion that would have emptied the room but today it produced no more than a thoughtful pause. Then Napoleon said, quietly, "What is it you want me to do?"

It was a general question, addressed to them all. They told him, without preamble; "Abdicate, in favor of your son." This, as they saw it, was the only way to save the Empire and every man present in that room recognized this as being of paramount importance, both to them and to France. They did not want a return of the Bourbons. To the younger among them the Bourbons were nothing but a superannuated family of exiles, living on foreign charity. To the elder men, like Lefèbvre and Moncey, a Bourbon dynasty promised a return to aristocratic privilege and retribution. Under a long regency they could look to a comfortable and honored old age in a country at peace.

"Very good, gentlemen, since it must be so I will abdicate," Napoleon said. "I have tried to bring happiness to France and have not succeeded. I do not wish to increase our sufferings.

But when I abdicate what will you do? Will you accept the King of Rome as my successor and the Empress as regent?"

Eagerly the group declared as one man that they would and Napoleon said he would at once dispatch a deputation to Paris. He nominated Marmont, Ney and Caulaincourt and asked if the selection satisfied them. They said that it did and accepted this as a dismissal. The confrontation was over. Of the men assembled there only Napoleon was completely self-possessed. In ones and twos they drifted away leaving him to draft a renunciation of his life's work.

It was a short, dignified document: "The Allied Powers having proclaimed that the Emperor Napoleon is the sole obstacle to the re-establishment of peace in Europe, the Emperor Napoleon, faithful to his oath, declares that he is ready to descend from the throne, to relinquish France, and even life, for the good of his country, which is inseparable from the rights of his son, those of the regency of the Empress, and the maintenance of the laws of the Empire." The deed was dated April 4th.

There was one slight change of plan. Macdonald was named to replace Marmont in the embassy, partly because Marmont was at his headquarters at Essonnes, partly because Napoleon wished to spare his oldest friend, "who had grown up in his tent," the humiliation of carrying such a document into the camp of the enemy, a quaint reservation in the light of what was happening in Marmont's headquarters at that moment. The trio were empowered, however, to call at Essonnes on the way to Paris and include Marmont in their number if he wished to accompany them.

III

In the period between the fall of Paris and the final, unconditional abdication of Napoleon, conspiracies proliferated in the capital like flies on a refuse heap. None was so clumsy and ill-conceived as Marmont's attempt to assume the role of General Monck. Nor did any single intrigue of that period generate more acrimony and discord in the years ahead.

Ney, Macdonald and Caulaincourt, bearing their hard won terms, arrived at Marmont's headquarters at four P.M. on the

4th. The announcement of their presence and purpose caused such dismay that it did not take the Imperial messengers more than a moment to realize that something was amiss. It was indeed. Their mission placed Marmont, and the five generals he had just won over to his point of view, in an impossible position. For by now negotiations with Schwartzenberg were all but complete, and the conspirators were faced with the choice of pushing ahead with their plans to surrender, or risking court martial as deserters. Marmont's only course was to confess and pray that his fellow officers would believe he had acted in good faith, knowing nothing of what was happening at Fontainebleau and this he did but with an important reservation. He lied concerning the extent to which negotiations had already gone, and when Ney asked him bluntly if he had signed anything he replied, with almost pathetic earnestness, that he had not. Ney, a simple man, was relieved to hear this but Caulaincourt, an experienced diplomat, recognized the fearful harm that Marmont's "understanding" with the Allies would cause for surely it knocked the main prop from the structure of Napoleon's proposal. If Marmont, the Emperor's oldest friend, was ready to desert what was to be feared from the Grand Army?

Desperately he and Macdonald, with some help from Ney, set to work to repair the damage as best they could. Marmont refused to write an unequivocal letter to Schwartzenberg, saying that he had changed his mind, and he did not think much of their suggestion to detain the Austrian's messenger—then present in the camp—on the pretext that Marmont had been summoned to Fontainebleau. Caulaincourt's third proposal, that Marmont should accompany them and tell Schwartzenberg to his face that it was now impossible to carry out his original intentions, was more favorably received, if only because it would remove Marmont out of range of Napoleon's wrath. Unhappily he climbed into a carriage with Macdonald and they set out behind the vehicle conveying Ney and Caulaincourt. Behind him Marmont left five unhappy generals—Souham, his second in command; Megnadier, his chief-of-staff; Merlin; Digeon and Landru des Essarts. Souham was instructed to inform the troops of Napoleon's act of abdication but make no other move, no matter who ordered it.

For Macdonald, who had always been a close friend of Marmont, it must have been an embarrassing drive. The Duke of Ragusa was obviously horrified at his situation—on his way to plead the cause of a dynasty he had betrayed in all but fact. Ahead of them Ney and Caulaincourt had plenty to discuss and in the course of that discussion Marmont must have been the subject of some grossly unflattering terms but in Macdonald's carriage there was a prolonged and uncomfortable silence. When the party arrived at the castle of Petit-Bourg, Schwartzenberg's headquarters, Marmont, on Macdonald's advice, remained seated. The Scotsman got out and joined his comrades. Then all three were personally received by the Austrian General to whom they conveyed their desire for an immediate audience with the Czar.

From this point Marmont dropped out of the mission, at all events as a bona fide Imperial ambassador, for while the others were explaining their presence to Schwartzenberg, the Austrian general was called away. He returned after an interval of only fifteen minutes and with him was Marmont. The three Frenchmen noticed at once that it was a very different Marmont from the abject man they had left in the carriage outside the castle for now he was relaxed and smiling. He had, it seemed, made his confession and received absolution from his half-promise to surrender. Under precisely what circumstances, however, they never discovered and neither did future generations for from here on everyone tells a different story. Some stories (his own included) absolve Marmont from the charge of double dealing. Others, a majority, brand him as a scoundrel who, for complex reasons of his own, deliberately snapped the last frail thread between France and the Napoleonic dynasty.

It is unrewarding to guess at the part Marmont played in events after Macdonald had left him, tormented and alone, in the carriage that had taken them from Essonnes to Petit-Bourg. He may well have been released from his obligations by Schwartzenberg. He may also have sent a secret message to Talleyrand, who knew the situation in detail by nine o'clock that night. Or he may have done something much worse—sent orders to his deputy, General Souham, to march the corps into the enemy's lines as arranged. All that we know for certain is that his manner had vastly changed in a brief interval and that he informed his fellow marshals and Caulaincourt (who somehow could not bring themselves to believe him) that Schwartzenberg understood and accepted his inability to finalize the terms of the original convention.

The Czar was in no particular hurry to receive the deputation. He knew how far negotiations had proceeded between Marmont and Schwartzenberg and he needed time to think. Late that evening Talleyrand, his iron nerve shaken by the possibility that Alexander would now decide in favor of a regency, had used every argument at his disposal to persuade him France was predominantly royalist but the Czar remained unconvinced and at midnight, in Talleyrand's house, the deputation was granted an official interview. Significantly Marmont was not among their number. He had slipped away again, this time to Ney's house in the Rue de Lille.

The meeting began with an exchange of flatteries. Alexander complimented the marshals on their gallant defense of France, specifically mentioning the heroic behavior of Pacthod's conscripts at Fère-Champenoise. The marshals returned the compliment by acknowledging the Czar's magnanimity and the moderation of the occupying troops. Then they all got down to business, Macdonald proving the most eloquent and persuasive of the trio. They stressed the fact that the army was not only loyal to Napoleon but ready to mount a formidable counterattack on Paris and there is no doubt that the Czar was impressed. After a long discussion, in which they seemed to make headway, the Czar said he must consult his allies and would give them their answer the following morning.

As they left his presence they met, in an outer salon, various members of the Provisional Government, including Buernonville, author of the letter Macdonald had passed to Napoleon, and also Dupont, the new Minister of War, who had been court martialed for his part in the disgraceful Baylen surrender in 1808. It was an opportunity not to be missed and Macdonald, accosting both, expressed his disgust at their behavior. Voices rose and a violent quarrel seemed imminent but Caulaincourt, reminding them all they were in the lodging of the Czar, suggested they repair to another place to continue the argument. "What use would that be?" demanded the indignant Scotsman. "Ney and I don't even acknowledge the Provisional Government!" All three left for Ney's house where Marmont was awaiting them.

Early next morning the three marshals and Caulaincourt sat down to breakfast together but the meal was soon interrupted. Fabvrier, Marmont's aide-de-camp, arrived in a state of great excitement and the marshal left the table to hear his news. When he returned he looked as pale and distraught as when they had descended upon him at Essonnes the previous afternoon. "My whole corps went over to the enemy last night!" he told them. "I would have given an arm to prevent this happening."

"Say rather a head!" shouted Ney, "it wouldn't be too much!"

Taking his sword, Marmont left without another word. His comrades stared at one another in dismay. Their one remaining card had been trumped.

The defection of the 6th Corps in Marmont's absence is another imponderable in the history of that crowded week. Even if it is admitted that Marmont was blameless, the man responsible for the movement that disposed of any chance that remained of the Czar accepting a regency was General Souham, temporarily commanding Marmont's troops at Essonnes. It is just possible that he acted on his own initiative and contrary to his chief's orders. Possible, but very unlikely in view of Marmont's furtive behavior during the preceding hours.

Faced with the certainty of summary court martial and even a firing squad should Napoleon's embassy succeed, Souham and his four brother officers had awaited the outcome with understandable impatience. When a string of couriers arrived from Fontainebleau, demanding Marmont or his deputy's immediate presence at Headquarters, anxiety became panic. Calling together his divisional commanders Souham advised them that they must all act in concert and without a moment's delay. They must march to Versailles, thus carrying out the first stage of Marmont's agreement with the enemy. They seemed to have concurred with his view and set off in the early hours of the morning before it was light. At first the rank and file thought

they were marching to attack the enemy but this was soon seen
to be a ridiculous supposition for as they advanced they passed
between two bodies of Russian and Bavarian cavalry who
watched them closely but did not attack. As the sun rose word
that the 6th Corps was surrendering passed quickly from
mouth to mouth and the columns were thrown into confusion.
The troops and junior officers were outraged. Squads of men
kept falling out and a body of Polish lancers detached themselves altogether and rode off towards Fontainebleau. By the
time the corps reached Versailles it was in open mutiny and
threatening to hang its generals.

The ugly situation was saved by the arrival of Marmont, who
had driven from Paris at breakneck speed. The marshal was re-
vered by the men of the 6th Corps and his frantic harangue
checked the revolt. The inevitable, he argued, must be accepted.
Napoleon was finished, his dynasty was finished, and their loyalty was now to France. Sullenly, and only half convinced, they
bivouacked where they were inside the invaders' lines, 14,000
men surrounded by three great armies.

Back at Ney's house in the Rue de Lille the deputation could
see a single gleam of hope. If they could win the Czar's as-
sent to a regency *before* word reached him of the 6th Corps'
desertion the situation might still resolve itself in favor of the
dynasty. Hurriedly they set out for Talleyrand's house where
Alexander saw them at once and listened politely to a summary
of the arguments they had used at the first interview. With the
Czar on this occasion was Frederick William, king of Prussia,
and close at hand were the disconcerted members of the Provisional Government. Every man among them was ruined if the
Czar decided in favor of a regency.

They need not have worried. The discussion was still continuing when an aide-de-camp came in and said something in Russian to his master. Caulaincourt caught the single phrase:
"Duke of Ragusa. . . ." and he knew the long game was over
at last. There was a brief delay while the Czar left the room for
consultation. When he returned they saw from his expression that their mission had failed. Like three men on their
way to the gallows they left the Imperial presence and summoned their carriages to take them back to Fontainebleau. To

facilitate their journey the Czar had granted them an armistice of forty-eight hours.

Marmont remained within the enemy lines. "The courage of Marmont saved everything!" exulted Bourrienne, commenting on the events of the day years later. And so it did from the standpoint of Bourrienne, Talleyrand, and all the other Frenchmen who had accepted high office under Napoleon only to betray his interests at the first opportunity. But a majority of Frenchmen of that generation did not share this opinion. Soon after these events a new verb entered the language—"raguser," synonymous with the act of betrayal.

Notwithstanding the patient research and intelligent guesses of historians most public figures are judged on the verdict of their contemporaries. In 1940 the people of Norway invented a word with a similar connotation. By 1945 that word had the same meaning all over the Western World. It was "Quisling."

15

THE DISSOLUTION OF the Empire can be compared to
the tide's obliteration of a child's sandcastle, paper battlements
and matchstick banners being caught up and swept clear of
the ruined keep. Or to the flight of a cluster of needles from
a parent magnet towards other, more imposing, magnets exerting a stronger pull. But a more embracing simile would be
that of a foundering ship of state, shedding its super cargo of
rentiers, position seekers, office holders, concessionaires and
poltroons, so that at last only a few resolute officers remained,
commanding a lower deck of bewildered men.

The ship was settling now, lower hour by hour, and as the
scramble to abandon her increased the heart-searching among
the few survivors was painful and pitiful. Less than a year before the treachery of Bernadotte and Murat had disgusted former
comrades but then, as the plains of Saxony receded, desertion
became commonplace, both individually and en masse. Sometimes, as in the case of the kings of Saxony and Wurtemberg, it was accomplished with dignity and sometimes, as in
the case of the Saxons at Leipzig, under sly and infamous circumstances. By the new year the men around Napoleon had
come to terms with their isolation. One by one the allies and
courtesy kings had stolen away to make their peace with the
autocrats but the virus of betrayal had bypassed the French up
to this moment.

It was otherwise after the Allies had stormed into the Paris

The Guest of Europe

suburbs. The terrible finality of recent events was brought home to all by Marmont's night march from Essonnes to Versailles. Word of his surrender rippled down the lines like a warning flash of lightning, exposing the worthlessness of the cause, and when the present whereabouts of the Sixth Corps became known, deep inside enemy lines (where it had marched with arms in its hands) the most dedicated imperialists began to think in personal rather than patriotic terms. Incredibly the man before whom everyone had flinched was finished, unable to fire one more shot and, what was more to the point, unable to bestow one more meaningful reward. What did one do in this situation? Surely the one thing that remained to be done, to study one's personal future in the light of vastly altered circumstances. After Bernadotte Talleyrand, and after that prince-and-priest Murat, the finest cavalry leader in the world. And after Murat one other prince, the Prince of the Moscowa, bravest of the brave. Within an hour of condemning Marmont's treason Ney was reshuffling his own hand and wondering if it was strong enough to follow suit.

News of Marmont's desertion was brought to Napoleon at Fontainebleau by one of Mortier's adjutants. The news saddened him beyond belief but it did not have the power to stun him, as had his chance encounter with the retreating Paris garrison a few days earlier. By now he had learned where to look for treachery, equating it with high rank and in direct proportion to the honors, wealth and privileges he had distributed. The men who owed him nothing could be depended upon, even to the extent of waging civil war but the others, or all but a very few of them, used a golden slide rule to assess their obligations to him. The more they possessed the less dependable they were likely to prove and this axiom had been demonstrated over and over again in the last few months. Murat had married his sister and mounted a throne. Bernadotte had been chosen king of Sweden on the strength of his reputation as a leader of French troops in battle. Marmont had been his closest friend for more than twenty years. The politicians, now engaged in the task of composing an address of welcome to Louis XVIII, were regicides almost to a man and some of them owed their lives to the rule of law that he had imposed on his return from

Egypt in the final year of the old century. Now the water round the half-submerged ship was black with bobbing heads and he was able to contemplate them all with a certain amount of objectivity. There were no frenzied outbursts, no broadsides of rhetorical questions concerning gratitude, honor and fidelity. Instead there was a kind of repose reflecting the enormous experience he had had of assessing the fallibility of human nature and the amount of strain that can be imposed upon the loyalty of individuals. In a curious way the process seemed to interest him and the answers he gave himself were not measured in terms of baseness, ingratitude or vanity, but in those of a mathematical sum. Sometimes an answer surprised him but more often it did not. Of the men at his elbow only a handful could be trusted absolutely. Of the others some would hesitate a little longer, awaiting a legal release from their allegiance, but a majority, like Marmont, would find the solution in a compromise of their own design. "Only the soldiers and officers who have not been made dukes can be counted upon," he said, when Marmont's gap in the line was being repaired. "I should have sent them all to bed and begun the war with men of youthful, unsullied courage."

There were still thousands of such men available but they did not wear the epaulettes of generals. Twenty-five thousand of them were bivouacked in the forest glades about the chateau but their leaders were no longer with them, preferring to stay within close range of the facts and rumors that bombarded Headquarters as couriers, deputations and commissioners came and went at all hours of the day and night. Their names were known and feared in every corner of Europe and time had been, not so long ago, when any one of them at the head of a column of grenadiers or a few squadrons of cavalry could have captured a city by appearing at its gates. Now they were either deserters or potential deserters, either planning mutiny or preferring to slip away unobserved and see what could be rescued of their fortunes before it was too late.

Jourdan, Kellerman and Lefèbvre were among the former group, too proud to scuttle but determined nonetheless to end the war on this spot. Neither one of them had much to hope for from a Bourbon for all three had led Republican armies to victory before the name Bonaparte conjured up anything more frightening than a shabby young officer with a strong Corsican accent. Augereau, who also belonged to this Republican group, had already made his decision, and Oudinot, the brewer's son, was in the process of making his, talking to Ney and others of forcing an immediate decision in front of the Emperor's desk. The divisional generals were in like mind, proposing to follow the lead of their comrade Souham of the Sixth Corps. Among them were three brilliant cavalrymen, Milhaud, Nansouty and Latour-Mabourg and others in this group were men whose record deserved something better than the choice of the present alternatives—Maison, who had walked beside Ney in the Moscow rearguard; Ségur, whose pen was to make public the horrors of the retreat; Belliard, the man who had informed Napoleon of the fall of Paris; Lagrange, Hulin and many others, whose battle honors would fill a page. This left but three, all famous and all in a class of their own—Macdonald, Ney and Berthier, the Chief of Staff. Nothing in their splendid past reveals the true characters of these men as their behavior did during the next forty-eight hours.

The choice was not a simple one between loyalty to Napoleon and their own interests. It was complicated by so many other factors and dependent upon the answer to so many relevant questions. Was desertion more honorable than conniving at civil war? Could France jettison the glory of the recent past and accept a family whose name was synonymous with the straitjacket of aristocratic privilege? Had the Revolution been no more than an incident, now to be swept under the carpet of history? Had any one of the leaders of the Grand Army the right to ask one more eighteen-year-old boy to die for a ruined adventurer? These were only some of the questions that tormented the minds of men like Ney and Oudinot and Caulaincourt as they walked among the camp fires surrounding the chateau of Francis I. And in the end the choices were reduced to three; to turn their backs on the man who had led them to victory on fifty fields, to hold fast to their oaths of allegiance and pursue their duty as officers to the letter, or to efface themselves, say nothing, and await the moment when their actions would be screened by the dust of a falling empire.

Macdonald had never been an Imperial favorite. He was too outspoken to qualify as a courtier. His baton had been earned by hard work in the field and it had taken him years to build a reputation for dogged, painstaking service, performed without dash. Now, at a time of crisis, his real qualities emerged. He gave honest advice whenever it was demanded and when it was not he went silently about his duties without a thought of what might happen to him in the years ahead. He was not and never had been dazzled by Napoleon. He thought of him as the head of state and his commander-in-chief, much as his father, the clansman, had regarded the Young Pretender before and after Culloden. He was brusque, unsmiling and utterly dependable but his instincts bound him to his allegiance until the last moment. Abdication must come but it must derive from Fontainebleau, not Paris, where the national interests were in the hands of men like Talleyrand.

Berthier, Chief-of-Staff, was cast in a very different mold. He had been Napoleon's man body and soul for twenty years and their reputations as soldiers were inseparably linked. For two decades he had looked to his chief for direction and inspiration. Now for the first time in all those years, he was having to make his own decision. He discovered that he could not do it. Mumbling an excuse he slipped away, promising to return, and Napoleon, who knew him better than he knew himself, was not deceived. "He won't be back," he said and he wasn't. Torn from his anchorage Berthier drifted helplessly in a whirlpool of conflicting loyalties. The effort of adjusting was to cost him his life.

Ney's temperament was different again. He was a man of action with no flair for politics. His courage was a byword, not only in the Grand Army but among its enemies although his temper was uncertain and all his judgments were emotional. If he had realized this and come to terms with it his record would have remained unsullied but he was not sufficiently introspective to evaluate his motives. As always, on the battlefield or away from it, he relied on impulse, and this time his impulse led him to pursue a course that seems to us, at this distance, unworthy and uncharacteristic.

Accepting the impossibility of persuading the Czar to support a conditional abdication, the Imperial deputation—consisting of Ney, Macdonald and Caulaincourt—made preparations to return to Fontainebleau and wrest from Napoleon a surrender of sovereignty that ignored the claims of his infant son. They did not return in a body. Ney set off first, riding at full gallop and arriving well ahead of the others at some time on the night of the 5th. He at once sat down to write a letter that placed him in the same category as Marmont. In it he pledged himself to give unreserved support to the Bourbons on the grounds that this was the only course likely to avert civil war and if this, in fact, was his true motive his private capitulation was his own concern. But he did something else that is inexcusable, implying that he was the man who had persuaded Napoleon to consent to an unconditional abdication and adding that he "hoped to receive the vital document within a matter of hours." This was a lie for it is certain that he did not see Napoleon that night, or indeed at any time until his letter was well on its way to the Provisional Government. One cannot escape a conviction that, in saying this without consulting his two colleagues, he was hoping to claim the credit for ending the war and sharing the honors with Marmont, the hero of the hour. Neither did he inform Macdonald and Caulaincourt of his action when they arrived back at Fontainebleau at one A.M. that same night. They were to find out later, in embarrassing circumstances for all three of them.

In the early hours of the 6th Napoleon was awakened and informed of the failure of the mission. News of Marmont's desertion had prepared him and he understood now that nothing short of unconditional abdication would satisfy his enemies. For all that he made a final appeal, suggesting a retreat behind the Loire or, alternatively, a second march over the Alps to establish an independent kingdom in Italy. The same tired old arguments were employed—Soult's army in the southwest, Suchet's army of fifteen thousand now north of the Gironde, Davout's resolute defense of Hamburg, the inviolability of the Rhine fortresses, and Eugène's presence in Northern Italy. When they told him that a courier riding to any one of these centers would be captured he said, "Fifty thousand men can march on roads that are not open to couriers."

It was a dream and he knew it, even though he did not know that the remaining marshals, including Macdonald, had agreed not to obey any order for general troop movements that he might issue. He realized from their expressions, however, that he could not carry one of them with him, that this indeed was the very end of a journey that had begun eighteen years ago when, in a carriage crammed with maps, he had traversed this forest en route to Nice to take command of the Army of Italy. He said, briefly, "Very well. You deserve repose—take it!" and dismissed them to draw up the document for which everyone in Europe was waiting. It read: "The Allied Powers having declared the Emperor Napoleon to be the sole obstacle to the re-establishment of peace in Europe, the Emperor Napoleon, faithful to his oath, declares that for himself and his heirs, he renounces the thrones of France and Italy, because there is no personal sacrifice which he is not ready to make for the welfare of the nation." The last six words were erased and "in the interests of France" substituted. With this document, at midnight on April 6th, the weary trio again took the road to the capital.

II

Imperceptibly the center of gravity was shifting from Fontainebleau to Paris. For many years now all the major policy decisions of Europe had been Napoleon's and wherever he happened to be—Paris, the Low Countries, along the upper Rhine, or the lower Danube, in Spain, or beyond the Niemen, the pivotal point was his tent or lodging, from which the threads of government ran out along routes of a thousand miles or more. Now, in the first mild days of spring that followed the dismal winter, he operated on the periphery of affairs, feeding on rumor and out-of-date newspapers. By the time official bulletins reached him they had been overtaken by events. Men like Maret, Caulaincourt's predecessor, and a few of the faithful like the big, jolly Mortier, continued to present themselves for orders, and outside in the glades the old moustaches brushed their bearskins and cleaned their weapons, awaiting the order to march, but it was all like a play presented by a forlorn company of players in the presence of a thin, scattered audience, and even the players themselves were half convinced that they should be giving their attention to the more ambitious drama in the Tuileries and Place de la Concorde.

He had been told of arrangements for his future. He was to become Emperor of Elba in the Mediterranean, ninety square miles of territory for a man who had held a continent in thrall. Henceforward he was to be the guest of Europe. Learning this his curiosity concerning Elba had been aroused and he sent for an officer who had served there. He was told the inhabitants were mostly fishermen and possibly his face was lit for a moment by one of his pale smiles. He had been fishing in and about Mediterranean waters since he was a boy but in those days his dreams had centered on an island a few days' sail east of Elba. Provision had been made for his financial needs, a revenue of six million francs chargeable to the great book of France. The Empress Josephine was to share another two and a half millions with dethroned Bonapartes living within prescribed areas. He was to keep his Imperial title. His wife and son were to have the duchies of Parma, Placentia and Guastalla. All things considered the terms were generous, generous that is for anyone who had not acquired and administered the largest and most populous empire since the days of the Caesars.

In Paris itself diplomatic activity was mounting to the point of frenzy. The work of the soldiers was done. Cossacks, Uhlans, hussars and grenadiers stabled their horses and piled their arms, strolling along the boulevards to take a look at the monuments of the capital of the world but for the clerks and couriers there was no respite. Pens scratched industriously in government departments and cobbles rang with the hooves of dispatch riders carrying the great news to the furthest corners of Europe. So much to be done and all in a hurry lest the man at Fontainebleau should change his mind.

The new king was proclaimed, Louis XVIII, a gouty, amiable successor to the boy—the lost Dauphin—who had never been crowned and had died in circumstances that have remained mysterious down to this day. He was brother to the man in the puce coat who had struggled with his executioners within sight of the same palace where now Talleyrand's agents, armed with the necessary documents, were pilfering Napoleon's personal savings, together with his snuffboxes and handkerchiefs.

In twos and threes, in family units crammed into berlines and cabriolets hired with borrowed money, the emigrés and the irreconcilables began to converge on Paris, appearing like reassured citizens after a typhoon that had kept them in cellars for a generation. Men who fled from burning chateaux when they were young bucks returned with double chins and paunches. With them were wives and children acquired in exile, all curious to discover what this cartoon character had made of Paris in their absence. Not all of them were bitter and revengeful. The more patriotic had watched with secret pride the high tide of French imperialism, sniggering when one coalition after another had been overturned by Murat's cavalry and the bayonets of Ney's grenadiers. Louis himself, asked to celebrate the Allied triumph at Leipzig, had replied, with dignity, "Neither I nor any of the princes of my family can rejoice at events which are so great a sorrow to our country." Auguste de la Ferronays, another exile, could not be dragged from the maps during the Allied progress across eastern France. When they told him of the fall of Paris he said, bitterly, "They have conquered without us!" The Prince Regent, suddenly aware that he had a royal family instead of a packet of royal beggars on his hands, invited Louis to Queen Charlotte's birthday ball in Carlton House, where the Bourbon found the walls decorated with tapestries embroidered with the fleur-de-lys. With him went many other exiles but more than twenty years had passed since French aristocrats had attended functions of this kind and the ladies had to borrow dresses from their English friends. Fashion was kind to those who had no friends. Highwaisted gowns were in vogue and old ball dresses could be pinned up to the requisite length.

The first to take advantage of the Allied occupation of Paris was Charles-Phillipe, Comte d'Artois, the king's youngest brother. As a rake in the last days of the monarchy, and a reactionary during the very earliest days of the Revolution, he was the most unpopular of the Bourbons. Tall, distinguished looking and passing as handsome, he had behind him the longest period of exile. Hated by the Paris mob he had left France within four days of the fall of the Bastille, in July, 1789, but now, shielded from any possible brickbats by an escort of Cossacks, he rode back into the capital on April 12th. "The jubilation at his appearance," commented an observant witness, "was confined to those in his presence." Parisiens watched his entourage pass but few of them cheered. Why should they? He and all his kind were strangers and standing in the crowd were middle-aged men who remembered the man who had advocated bloody measures to contain the Revolution in its first tumultuous days so long ago.

The comte had left Yarmouth in January, 1814, and landed in Holland where he at once immersed himself in an occupation dear to all royal exiles. He issued a manifesto urging "all true Frenchmen" to recognize the benefits of legitimacy. For the time being it fell upon deaf ears. He was not even welcomed by the Allied leaders to whom his presence was an embarrassment. When Paris fell, however, and a restoration was decided upon, they mounted him on a white horse and dressed him in the uniform of the National Guard. It was odd that he should have chosen this regalia. The National Guard was a product of the revolution and in the last days of the monarchy the Bourbons had preferred to rely upon Swiss mercenaries. On April 12th, in brilliant sunshine, he trotted into Paris surrounded by numerous followers. He had been absent a few months short of a quarter-century.

He was officially received in the Place de la Concorde, a forum that had seen a very great deal since July, 1789. Many others had died there besides Louis and even now it is difficult to pass this spot without acknowledging the plaintive ghosts who haunt the site of the guillotine. Marie Antoinette, Artois' sister-in-law had been among them, grey haired and half-blind at thirty-seven. Charlotte Corday and all the Girondins who had tried to steer a revolution with pious platitudes had perished here, and after them the authors of the Terror, Danton, conscious of failure, and Robespierre, glaring and wordless under a dirty bandage hiding his shot away jaw. Now the tricoteuses who had watched the fall of heads were replaced by kings and princes and their bawdy revolutionary chants by the intoning of priests.

The same day the treaty formally disposing of the Emperor Napoleon was signed and the Imperial representatives, Caulaincourt, Macdonald and Ney were asked by Talleyrand to pledge their own allegiance to the new government. Caulaincourt and Macdonald refused, claiming that they were still emissaries of the Emperor with duties as yet undischarged. Ney was obliged to admit that he had already given his assurances, a blushing reminder of his letter of submission written on the night of April 5th. The difference of opinion among the three men touched off a lively exchange of views. Already the stubborn, honest pair had been humiliated by seeing Ney treated as the leader of the deputation and being warmly congratulated by the Czar. Now, in the face of Ney's explosive self-justification, they demanded their passports. Ney burst out, "I'm not going back there looking for a reward!" but Macdonald was equal to the occasion. "*I* am going back," he said, "to keep the promise I made to the Emperor." Together with Caulaincourt he left.

III

The period of waiting between the 6th and the 12th of April was probably the most wretched week in Napoleon's life. No answer came to his letters to Blois, where chaos reigned over the raggle taggle mob of fugitives who had fled there on the fall of Paris. He had just signed away his own rights and the rights of his son, an heir procured by putting aside a graceful and affectionate wife. None of the great called to comfort him and only one old friend, his former mistress, the blonde Countess Walewska, who had also borne him a son. He did not receive her. Even a hint of a renewal of their old association would place a deadly weapon in the hand of Metternich and others who sought to alienate him from his second wife. Walewska wrote a letter and left. She was to see him again at Elba and thus qualify as "the only woman who loved and was loved by Napoleon." It is a romantic title but it has too many pretenders to have much significance. It was not of romance that he thought during these interminable days but of his dynasty and of all the plans he had had of modernizing France and federalizing Europe that had somehow gone awry. He thought of assassination too, for the word was in the air he breathed. The old ruffian Blucher had not abandoned the project and a rascal in Talleyrand's pay was already plotting an attempt during the Emperor's impending journey to the Riviera. He thought of many other things, of lost opportunities, military midjudgments, broken friendships, and anemic loyalties, and the sum total of these thoughts spelled out a word that was alien to everything in his nature.

For years now, since 1808 according to some authorities and since that retreat from Moscow according to others, he had worn a little leather sachet round his neck. It contained a deadly poison, prepared for him by a well-known French physician named Pierre Cabanis, brother-in-law of the Marquis Condorcet, a mathematician who had committed suicide in prison with poison supplied by Cabanis.[1] The actual prescription has never been established. It was probably a compound including strychnine. Napoleon always declared that he kept it as a last resort should he fall alive into his enemies' hands. Now then was the time to take it and on the night of the 12th–13th, after he had signed papers brought to him by Caulaincourt and Macdonald, an official at the palace tells how he caught a glimpse of the Emperor sitting alone in his study, staring into space with vacant eyes.

The next few hours were to witness one of those sudden deviations that occasionally occur at a crisis point in history and are never wholly explained or even verified. Although the circumstances are well vouched for no one can ever be certain that the sudden and violent illness of the stricken man was the result of an attempted suicide or an accidental overdose of opium, taken to induce sleep that had evaded him during his long vigil.

Constant, his valet, is the most reliable reporter of the story that came to be accepted by all but the most obdurate partisans of Napoleon and after Constant, Baron Fain, his secretary and author of *The Manuscript of 1814*. From the accounts of these two men, both devoted to their master, it is clear that Napoleon was very ill after retiring to bed at 10:30 P.M. when he had said of Ney's defection, "I know him. He was against me yesterday and he'd give his life for me tomorrow." This would seem to preclude an assumption that the desertion of yet another old friend had pushed the Emperor over the abyss of despair.

Pelard, another valet de chambre who had gone into the bedroom to feed the fire, says that when he came out leaving the door ajar he saw Napoleon open a chest of drawers and pour something in a glass and drink it, whereupon the servant hurried up to Constant's room immediately above. Together they ran to the Emperor, finding him in bed but clearly in great distress, twitching, groaning and vomiting. At this point, however, comes the passage in the narrative that encourages doubt, for Constant goes on to say that Napoleon made a dramatic, declamatory speech.

A man who has just swallowed strychnine does not talk of his eagles being dragged in the mire, or croak "My good Constant, they will be sorry when I'm gone. . . ." like the misunderstood hero in a mid-Victorian novel. Doctor Yvan, the Imperial physician who had accompanied Napoleon to Moscow (according to Fain it was Yvan who had procured the poison during this campaign) was summoned and an antidote was administered. After a time the vomiting ceased, the Emperor was able to drink tea and presently he slept, not awakening for several hours when he appeared to be recovered although, according to Macdonald (who saw him at nine A.M.) "his complexion was yellow and greenish." He told Macdonald that he had been taken ill during the night.

Taking note of all subsequent accounts, most of them written years later, an aura of doubt surrounds the suicide attempt. On balance, and in spite of Constant's declaration that he saw the remains of the sachet in the fireplace, one is inclined towards the theory of a carelessly-mixed sleeping potion, taken at a time of extreme nervous tension and physical exhaustion. It should not be forgotten that the man's mind was in a turmoil and that he had ridden or driven hundreds of miles in severe weather during the previous ten weeks.

Sick or not Napoleon seemed composed on the morning of

the 13th, when Caulaincourt told him Macdonald was ready to leave for Paris with the signed acceptance of the Allied terms. He took this opportunity to thank the Scotsman for his services and bestow upon him a gift of a kind that touched the marshal deeply. Expressing his sincere gratitude for Macdonald's devotion he said, "I have done so much for so many others who have abandoned and neglected me and you, who owed me nothing, have remained faithful. I appreciate your loyalty all too late and I sincerely regret that I am no longer in a position to express my gratitude to you except by words." But there was, after all, to be a more material reward although not of the kind Ney had envisaged the day before. On impulse Napoleon presented the Scotsman with the sword of Murad-Bey that he had worn at the battle of Mount Tabor in the Holy Land, in 1799.[2] "Keep it in remembrance of me and of my friendship for you," he said. No gift could have pleased Macdonald more. After a warm embrace the two men parted. They never met again. Macdonald rode to Paris to make his peace with the new regime, Napoleon turned his attention to packing for the journey into exile.

I V

Couriers who had left Paris with the momentous news made good progress along fast drying roads. Far and wide they fanned out, the early arrivals taking ship at Calais. A few hours later their dispatches set beacons blazing along the English coast and attracted queues of excited Cockneys to the newspaper offices. The Lord Mayor of London ordered fireworks. Easter congregations, emerging from church after morning service, embraced one another. The war that, with a single short break, had lasted from January, 1793, to April, 1814, was over and *The Times* headline of the previous year, "He's falling! He's falling!" had been translated from wishful thinking into fact. Other couriers made their way across devastated country towards Brussels and the Netherlands and to the garrison towns along the Rhine where Imperialist troops were still holding out. Reception of the news in these strongholds was mixed. Some of the veteran officers, Captain Barrès among them, wept with rage but there were others, like Barrès' battalion commander, who were prepared to pledge their allegiance to the Bourbons without hesitation. "Don't worry about the future of France," this officer told Barrès, "it will be happier under the paternal scepter than under the rod of iron of this adventurer." "You thought differently three months ago!" replied the Captain, who admits that he was "choking with grief and shame" for his country.

Barrès' loyalty came near to getting him into serious trouble a week later. Seeing a colonel displaying the emblem of the Bourbons he exclaimed to a group of officers, "See, there's a white cockade!" whereupon the colonel marched up to him and demanded, "Well, Sir, what have you to say about this cockade?" Barrès could have said a great deal but the habit of discipline, plus a ready wit, saved him from court martial. "It's the first I have ever seen in my life, sir!" he replied, innocently. He was less discreet when leaving civilian friends at Mainz. "You are glad to see us go," he said, "but before a month is out you will regret our power and our institutions."

Down in Hauterive, near Castres, in an area where Soult was still fighting it out with Wellington, the Marquis de Villeneuve lived quietly with his family. On Easter Tuesday, sitting reading near a window, his eleven year old daughter Léotine remembered a horseman clattering into the courtyard shouting, "We've got peace! We've got peace!" and in a few moments everyone was clustering round him. He had just ridden in from Toulouse with the news that the Bourbons had come home and that henceforth the new master of France would be Louis XVIII. The immediate response was a chorus of *vivats* on behalf of the king.

At Limoges there was a different reaction. A boy serving at one of the many quasi-military lycées established by Napoleon had recently written to his father that Spanish prisoners detained in the town had started a riot that resulted in all of them being locked up in a church. When news of the abdication arrived at the college the pupils refused to acknowledge it and marched through the town shouting "Down with Louis XVIII," a protest procession that ended in their fencing master slapping the face of a royalist and challenging him to a duel.

In Italy there was family strife, Murat's Neapolitans chasing Napoleon's eldest sister Elisa from her Tuscan domains, in spite of the fact that she was far advanced in pregnancy. At a mountain tavern during her flight Elisa gave birth. Soon afterwards she was taken prisoner at Bologna.

Maximilian Joseph of Bavaria, Eugène's father-in-law, had passed the Viceroy news of Marmont's surrender and of the attempt of the Imperial emissaries to secure the succession for Napoleon's son, adding, as a postscript, "The Allies wish you well, my dear Eugène; profit by their good intentions and remember your family. A further holding-out would be unpardonable." Josephine had also written, telling her son that further resistance was useless. ". . . there is nothing more to hope for. All is finished; he is abdicating." Eugène accepted the inevitable, signing a convention under which French troops were to return home at once. He had some hopes that he would be chosen to rule an independent Italy but the forces of reaction were too strong for a solution as wise as this. Italians were to wait another generation for unification as a nation. Sadly but proudly Eugène de Beauharnais, one of the few incorruptible men who served Napoleon in high places, withdrew to Bavaria. The Vicereine, nine days out of childbed, accompanied him but the devoted couple were parted again the night they arrived in Munich. A letter from Eugène's mother was awaiting him and it said she was ill and begged him to come to her. He did not suspect, and neither did anyone else, that she was dying.

V

Colonel Ponsonby, of the Light Dragoons, the man who brought the news of the abdication from Bordeaux to Toulouse rode as hard as the other couriers but he was too late to save the sacrifice of nine thousand lives—English, French, Spanish and Portuguese. On Easter Sunday, the day that witnessed the official Allied thanksgiving in the Place de la Bastille and only two days before the Comte de Artois rode his white charger into Paris, Soult and Wellington met in the final battle of the campaign.

Stripped of some of his best units by the demands of Napoleon during the battle for France Soult continued to fight stubbornly and brilliantly. His retirement to Toulouse in late March presented his cautious opponent with one of the most formidable military problems of the Peninsula War.

Standing on the east bank of the Garonne, Toulouse was also protected on the north and west by stretches of a canal. The only side open to attack was the south and with the intention of assaulting from this quarter Wellington ordered a bridge to be built across the Garonne out of range of the enemy. Hurriedly the pontoons were launched and strung together. The bridge was too short by eighty feet.

Wellington could have had few doubts concerning what this error (his own, since he had been warned in advance) could cost in terms of casualties. By now he had a wary respect for his adversary and it was a compliment Soult had earned. Ever since the summer truce in Saxony the marshal had contested every defensible position, fighting with dwindling forces against one of the keenest military brains of all time, and although Wellington can be said to have won the game on points there was no repetition of the French rout at Vitoria. Everything that could be done to hold the backdoor of France was done, so that the man who had once aspired to be the village baker of St. Amans-la-Bastide emerges from this onesided contest with a military reputation that most of his fellow marshals lost between the summer of 1813 and spring the following year.

In some ways the two men were alike. Both were defense minded, cautious in all their judgments and unfashionably sparing with the lives of their troops. Each regarded war as a science and practiced it as such but Wellington's supreme advantage lay in his unbroken record of success. For six years he had emerged victor of every encounter, even though, on many occasions, he had had to withdraw from a contested field, and his men, as well as his Portuguese and Spanish allies, had learned to equate his presence with the certainty of victory.

It was otherwise with Soult. He had taken command of a demoralized army forever on the defensive and now fighting on its native soil, with a disloyal civil population in the offing. There was never a hope of mounting a full scale counter offensive. All the French could do to delay the march of Wellington's men was to find a good position, dig in, give as good as they got, and then retire to fight again.

Toulouse was a classic battle of this kind and to win it Wellington was obliged to take risks that were alien to his nature. Unable to cross the broad Garonne below the town he began to cross it above but when 18,000 of his men were on the right bank the bridge collapsed and for three days his vanguard was exposed to attack by the entire French army of 35,000 infantry and 7,000 cavalry. No attack came. Soult, with a lively awareness of the fighting qualities of the British, preferred to sit tight behind his water defenses and the long, fortified ridge of Mont Rave, that rose to a height of three hundred feet between Toulouse and the river Ers between ridge and city.

It was Mont Rave that dominated this final trial of strength. Wellington made provision for two separate assaults on it, north and south, while feint attacks were launched on the canal bridge from the north and on the fortified suburb of St. Cyprien, on the west bank of the Garonne.

It was a sharp, bloody contest. Wellington's 10,000 Spaniards (he had 50,000 men in the field) claimed the honor of launching the first assault up the slopes of Mont Rave, while Beresford's men worked their way over a slough to attack the southern end of the eminence. The Spanish attack, launched too precipitously, was a fiasco. The attackers gained the road that crosses the ridge but despite the heroic example of their leaders could not be induced to go further. Soult's counterattack by voltigeurs drove them back down the hill at such a pace that Wellington remarked, "Well, damn me if I ever saw 10,000 men run a race before!"

In the meantime Picton had converted his feint attack into a real one but he too was repulsed, with a loss of 400 men. The situation was saved by Beresford's stubborn, superbly disciplined advance from the swamplands up the southern end of the long ridge. By darkness the British had worked their way along the summit and outflanked all Soult's strongpoints and the French withdrew into the town. The battle had cost the victors 4,568 men and the defenders 3,236. Two Highland regiments lost approximately half their strength.

Soult withdrew the following day, groping south for Suchet's

15,000, and on the 12th Wellington entered the city to learn, from Colonel Ponsonby, that all was over and there had been no need of a battle. Even Wellington was moved to shout "Hurrah" but that night, at dinner, when he proposed the health of Louis XVIII, he sparked off a demonstration that resulted in what must have been one of the most embarrassing moments of his life. A Spanish general proposed "The Liberator of Spain" and then someone else hailed him as "The Liberator of Portugal." Presently every foreigner was on his feet calling him "Le Libérateur de la France" and "Le Libérateur de l'Europe!" There is no record that the Duke blushed but he brought an end to the demonstration by bowing swiftly and calling for coffee.

Even now, however, the strife had not ended. On the night of the 13th the French governor of Bayonne, still under siege, made a successful sortie and several hundred men who had survived so many battles lost their lives in this idiotic fray. Soult had more sense. Convinced at last that his chief had indeed abdicated he followed Marshal Suchet in laying down his arms, the last but one among the paladins to surrender. The last of all, Davout, Duke of Auerstadt, would not believe Russians who told him what had occurred at Fontainebleau. At last a curt note arrived signed by Dupont, the new king's Minister of War, informing him that an amistice had been declared and that General Gérard was to supersede him. With arms in their hands the unconquerable garrison of Hamburg marched out, their leader in deep disgrace and warned to await trial on charges of seizing the bank of Hamburg, destroying a suburb to make a glacis, and rendering the word "French" odious by his severity. Davout was not impressed by these threats. As he saw it he had done his duty. Like his comrade Macdonald it was all he ever sought to do.

In the pleasant country around the little town of Castel-Sarazin in Languedoc, Johnny Kincaid and his riflemen, who had fought their way from Lisbon, were enjoying the hospitality of a predominantly royalist civil population. One and all, Kincaid included, fell in love with the pretty brunettes who fêted them as liberators and when the time came to say good-by "buckets full of salt tears were shed by men who had almost forgotten the way to weep." The sight of his lady love riding his horse astride showing a fine pair of legs cooled the young Scotsman's ardor. Notwithstanding the fact that he had literally laughed his way from Portugal to France, Kincaid was too conventional a Scotsman to overlook such immodesty. Castel-Sarazin, however, never forgot its British riflemen. When, a year later, a rumor reached the town that every officer in the battalion had been killed at Waterloo, and that the regiment had been brought out of action by a volunteer, a communal letter signed by every citizen of the community was sent to the commanding officer, "lamenting our fate and expressing a hope that it had been exaggerated." It never took the British Tommy long to win the affection of civilians in occupied territory; if Blucher's Prussians had borrowed his tactics, and applied them to the people of northeastern France, the campaign of 1814 would have been shorter and far less costly.

16

THE MAN'S NERVES were taut as fiddlestrings. The least incident, the most trivial remark that touched his pride, set them twanging so that he seemed to those who shared his vigil as temperamental as a prima donna.

He had always been prone to irrational outbursts. When something displeased him he would sometimes revert to the gestures and vocabulary of a street urchin but in the past these lapses had been prompted by an act of incompetence on the part of an underling. However much they belittled him, they could, to some extent, be excused for few men carried a greater weight of responsibility. It was different now. Until he got his second wind, and adjusted to obscurity, he behaved like an irritable oaf.

From April 13th, when Macdonald saw him after his alleged suicide attempt, until April 28th, when he stepped on board the British frigate *Undaunted* at Frejus, his vitality ebbed and flowed along with his courage and authority, so that if these sixteen days are isolated from his life he cuts a pitiable figure, a man without dignity, drained of physical and moral courage. It is his misfortune that the bulk of this interval was spent under the scrutiny of four commissioners appointed by each of the warring powers, all of whom committed their impressions to paper, or passed them on in great detail by the spoken word. Having said this one must add, in justice, that when the most shaming of these accounts reached him during his St. Helena exile he was man enough to vouch for it as truth.

Spring Journey

The four men who were to be his escorting jailers south were
Sir Neil Campbell for Britain, General Schuvalov for Russia,
General Köhler for Austria, and Count Waldburg-Truchess for
Prussia.

The quartet arrived at Fontainebleau on the 16th with instructions "to treat him with the respect befitting a deposed sovereign." His reception of them was pettish. To Campbell he was
affable, even to the extent of discussing Wellington's strategy,
to the Austrian and Russian representatives he was coldly polite,
but to the Prussian he was very rude, demanding to know why
his presence was necessary, since no Prussian troops were to accompany them south. The wretched commissioner mumbled
that he regarded attendance upon the former Emperor as an
honor but this did not mellow Napoleon's approach. As their
enforced companionship continued his liking for Campbell
increased and he learned to trust the Austrian, but he remained
unbending towards Waldburg-Truchess and distant in his approach to the Russian. It was the behavior of a sulky child
rather than that of a mature man of affairs, for he must have
known all four men had been detailed for what was clearly going to prove an embarrassing and dangerous assignment.

The four men arrived at Fontainebleau under the impression
they were to leave for St. Tropez almost at once. They were
soon enlightened. Napoleon, without realizing it at this stage,
was already flexing his muscles for martyrdom. Far from being
ready to leave he declared that the Allies had broken the terms
of the agreement by preventing the Empress from joining him
and accompanying him as far as the coast. He would not stir,
he said, until she appeared and he might not go at all!

The commissioners' position was delicate. Around them the
Imperial Guard was still under arms and their handling of the
situation was inhibited by their instructions to treat the prisoner with respect. They applied for fresh instructions and received them but their hand was not strengthened by the sovereigns' command that Napoleon might choose his route but was
to start for St. Tropez with or without Marie-Louise. Napoleon was a past master at this game of protocol poker. He quarreled with their proposed route and made a number of altera-
tions in it. He took his time packing up, filling no less than a

hundred wagons with furniture, books and objets d'art to solace his exile; he bullied, rumbled, strutted and argued. Campbell tells us that his personal appearance during this interval left a good deal to be desired. On one occasion he presented himself with traces of snuff adorning his waistcoat, his chin and his upper lip. His favorite trick was a game of Imperial jack-in-the-box. He would emerge from his study causing servants to throw wide the doors and announce him, whereupon, when everyone had risen, he would turn on his heel and return to his study again. Under different circumstances, and with a different leading actor, it would have been an amusing farce and perhaps, in his heart, he was play acting in order to revenge himself upon the powers for the humiliations they had heaped upon him. Even so it was a degrading business for everyone concerned, not least the patient Caulaincourt who loved him.

He made the most of his farewells, giving Caulaincourt, his valet Constant, and his Mameluke Roustan large sums of money. Generals Bertrand and Drouot of the Guard were to accompany him to Elba, together with a hand picked four hundred of his old moustaches, among whom there was fierce competition for the honor or act of penance, according to how one views the gilded martyrdom that was being prepared for him.

The ranks of the Imperialists thinned a little every day. Maret was still there, with Generals Belliard, Gourgaud (who was to share his second exile), Flahault, lover of his stepdaughter Hortense, Baron Fain, his secretary, and a handful of others, but all the legendary figures had gone and most of them had made their peace with the Bourbons. The fugitive court at Blois was breaking up, scattered far and wide by the avalanche of events. Marie-Louise and her son had drifted back to Orleans and then Rambouillet, where she met her father, Francis of Austria. It did not take a great deal of persuading for her to go on to Vienna under a guard of honor. Dr. Corvisart, the distinguished surgeon who had delivered her child under the greatest difficulties in 1811, was retained in her service. This served as an alibi to support a claim that her health was unequal to the strain of opposing her father's determination to disassociate the Habsburgs from the fallen adventurer.

His mother, Madame Mére, seeing her prophecies of a general collapse more than justified, departed for Italy with the worldly Cardinal Fesch, her half brother. Lucien, his second brother, who had been a paroled prisoner in Worcestershire for years, was soon to join them. Elisa, his eldest sister, driven from her Tuscan domains, also made for Rome, and the three ex-kings, Joseph, Louis and Jerome, made their way to Switzerland. So much for the Bonaparte clan. One and all they had a wonderful capacity to adjust to circumstances and do so in comfort. They were not cast in a heroic mold and saw no reason why they should not make the best of the years ahead, just as they had exploited the splendid period that was past.

General Köhler, the Austrian commissioner, at length succeeded in convincing Napoleon that he could not count upon Marie-Louise as a traveling companion and on the morning of the 20th they told him that the Grand Marshal of the Palace wished to inform him that all was ready for departure. At once he erupted. "Am I," he roared, "to regulate my actions by the Grand Marshal's watch? I will go when I please! Perhaps I may not go at all! Leave me."

At twelve o'clock, however, he reappeared, crossed the gallery and descended the staircase. It was the moment for launching the legend and his intuitive knowledge of stage management had chosen it with exactness. In the courtyard outside the Guard was drawn up as for review, men who had followed him down into Italy, across the Sinai Desert, over the Alps, down the Danube, to Warsaw, to Spain, to Dresden, to Moscow and back again. There was not a man among them who was unmoved by the occasion and some of them, tall, sunburned, professional killers, were in tears. He rode out to meet them on horseback, dismounted and passed along their ranks. The commissioners and the survivors looked on, knowing they would never see a pageant like this again. Phrases of the final address reached them.

". . . for twenty years I have constantly accompanied you on the road to honor and glory . . . with men like you our cause could not be lost but the war would have been interminable . . . continue to serve France . . . I intend to write the history of the great achievements we have performed together. . . ," stock-in-trade jargon for soldier-politicians down the ages but, coming from him, and in that setting, invested with what the poet Yeats might have called "a terrible beauty." He embraced the commanding officer, General Petit, and kissed the eagles. Then, knowing the precise moment to bring down a curtain, he announced his readiness to go.

II

The long cavalcade set out for Briarre, the first stopping place, Napoleon sharing a carriage with Bertrand. On this first stage he was escorted by the Guard. The terrible journey had begun. It was to last eight days that left upon his memory, and the memories of those who shared it with him, a bitterness and moral squalor that had not attached itself to the 550 mile withdrawal from Moscow to the Niemen, or the long retreat from Leipzig to the Rhine.

They traveled via Nevers and Rouanne to Lyons. It was bright spring weather and over the first stages progress was swift and uneventful. At all towns and villages he passed through he was greeted respectfully and sometimes enthusiastically. At Nevers he heard the familiar "Vive l'Empereur!" and at Lyons an old lady clung to his carriage window frame and blessed him. But as the cavalcade began to descend the Rhone the atmosphere changed from cordiality to surliness and then to a hostility so spiteful that he was bewildered and bruised.

Near Valence those riding ahead had an unexpected encounter. They met Marshal Augereau, the traitor of Lyons, riding in the opposite direction and warned him that the Emperor was within hail. Augereau took no steps to avoid an encounter and when the carriage stopped and Napoleon descended he met Imperial affability with churlishness. The two men walked apart and Napoleon, perhaps mischievously, asked, "Where are you going? To Court?" Augereau replied gruffly that he was on his way to Lyons and then the exchanges became acrimonious, Napoleon saying that the marshal had behaved badly during the final campaign, Augereau retorting that Napoleon owed his present plight to his own insatiable ambition. When Napoleon returned to his carriage the marshal did not uncover but remained glowering, his hands clasped behind his back. To the

Emperor it was a foretaste of the kind of reception he was to receive on the road ahead. Augereau expressed himself forcibly to Colonel Campbell. "He should have marched up to a battery and died in action!" he said. Curious advice from a man who had said to Macdonald on the banks of the Elster, "Do you think I am such a fool as to die for a German suburb?"

So far Napoleon had been composed, even jocular. He said to one of his traveling companions, as they traversed areas where he had served as a young lieutenant, "I began the game with a six franc piece and I have come out of it very rich." But early morning sunshine on the orchards and vineyards must have evoked more sentimental memories. It was here that he had fallen in love with sixteen-year-old Caroline Colombier, a shy, pretty brunette whose mother had shown him kindness when he was a penniless boy far from home and without friends or resources. "No one could have been more innocent than we were," he was to write on St. Helena, describing his early morning trysts with Caroline more than thirty years before. "It may not be credited but our sole delight consisted of eating cherries together."[1]

The first open demonstration of Provençal hostility occurred at Orange where a mob surrounded the carriages shouting, "Vive le Roi!" and general abuse. There was no actual violence but the mood of the mob was sufficiently ugly to prompt the commissioners to pass through Avignon without changing horses at five o'clock in the morning. An hour later, at St. Andiol, a stop was made for this purpose, and Napoleon, now showing signs of depression and physical exhaustion, walked up the hill with Campbell and Bertrand, a valet-de-chambre walking a short distance ahead. It was the valet who met a post office courier, who asked if the carriages lower down the hill were Napoleon's entourage. In an attempt to prevent another demonstration the valet denied that they were but the courier would not accept the statement as truth. Declaring that he was an old soldier who had served Napoleon in Egypt, he warned the valet of the reception that was being prepared for the Emperor at Orgon, the next village on the route. "The wretches there have erected a scaffold and hanged an effigy dressed in a French uniform smeared with blood," he said. "I daresay I shall get into a scrape by warning you but profit by it." He then rode off at full gallop and the valet retraced his steps to confide in General Drouot.

A discussion was held on the roadside and a strategem agreed upon. Napoleon, dressed in a blue cloak and a round hat (he refused to wear a white cockade) was mounted as an outrider and sent on ahead with one courier, a man called Amandru. The two horsemen arrived in Orgon to find that the veteran's fears were justified. There was the gallows and the blood smeared effigy, and round it seethed the villagers, howling for the blood of the tyrant "Nicholas," a derisory nickname for Napoleon. The pair cantered quickly through the village and nobody seems to have suspected that the outrider in the round hat was the man who had dominated Western Europe for close on a generation.

It was otherwise with the following entourage. Led by the mayor, the same man who had fallen on his knees before General Bonaparte when the latter passed through the village going north after his return from Egypt, the crowd surged round the commissioners shouting, "Down with the Corsican!" The mayor, freely admitting his mistake in 1799, declared that he would like to hang the villain with his own hands. Then someone drew a saber and ordered the Emperor's coachman to shout "Vive le Roi!" Courageously the man refused and was saved by the order of the commissioners to start. The carriages moved on, their occupants badly shaken by the incident. At this rate, they felt, they would be fortunate to bring their prisoner alive to the coast.

Cantering some distance ahead Napoleon and Amandru alighted at the inn of "La Calade," a miserable highroad hostelry. As he entered the kitchen the landlady asked Napoleon "if the tyrant was soon to pass this way?" In view of next year's events she must have been something of a prophetess for she went on, "It is all nonsense to say we have got rid of him. The Directory sent him to Egypt but he came back. I always have said and I always will say that we shall never be done with him until he is at the bottom of our well in the yard, covered over with stones!" It has been alleged by some that Napoleon Bonaparte had no sense of humor but this is proof that he had. He agreed with her heartily and derived a certain satisfaction from her embarrassment (and bustling attentions) when the commissioners arrived and she discovered his real identity.

The carriages were driven into the inn yard and the gate locked, the entire party sitting down to a meal. One report says that Napoleon, fearing poison, would not touch the food. It is more likely that he lacked appetite.

Word came that a hostile crowd was assembling at Aix, the next town on the route. The commissioners, taking no chances, sent a strongly worded letter to the mayor, warning him that the town gates must be closed and that any demonstration would be met by force. The warning had its effect, the mayor replying that he would obey instructions and hold himself responsible for the behavior of the townspeople.

In the meantime, however, a crowd was assembling outside "La Calade," where the curious were clutching five franc pieces in order to compare the minted likeness to the stocky figure in the blue cloak and round hat. The same comparison had led to the identification of Louis XVI and arrested his flight to Varennes in 1791, an irony that may not have escaped the fugitive, toying with his food at the table. At all events he was learning the true value of popular acclaim. Dozing on the shoulder of his valet-de-chambre he was awakened by the clamor outside the locked yard. He said, quietly, "If the crown of Europe was offered to me now I would decline it. . . . I was right never to esteem mankind." Then, worn out with the tedium and excitements of the journey, he slept.

The commissioners did not sleep. They were too busy making plans to deliver their prisoner alive. It was now proposed that Napoleon should be disguised as an Austrian officer and to this subterfuge the Emperor agreed, borrowing a spare uniform of General Köhler. It served to get him clear of "La Calade" but the entourage was recognized as it passed under the walls of Aix and there were more shouts of "Down with Nicholas! Down with the tyrant." Napoleon, hearing them, made a scathing comment on the instability of the Provençals. "They committed frightful massacres down here during the Revolution," he recalled. "Eighteen years ago I came to this part of the country with a thousand men to rescue two royalists they were going to hang. Their 'crime' was that they had been seen wearing the white cockade and I saved them, not without difficulty. Now you see they are ready to resume the same excesses against people who don't wear it!" Beyond Aix the group met an escort of gendarmes who conducted them safely to the castle of Luc.

It was near here, in the home of a prefect, that Napoleon had the one pleasing encounter of the journey. His sister Pauline was there, prettiest and most amiable of the Bonaparte girls. She was distressed to find him wearing an Austrian uniform and he changed it to please her. She told him that she would share his life in Elba, a promise she later kept. It was April 26th, the seventh day of his journey into exile.

III

Bernadotte, crown prince of Sweden who had dreamed of occupying the vacant throne, did not prolong his stay in Paris. He soon decided that it would be inadvisable to test Parisien reaction to his act of leading Swedes into battle against the men who had elevated him. He thought of himself as a much misunderstood man. Demonstrations against his person during his brief stay puzzled him, for he could see nothing wrong in helping to butcher old comrades all the way from Saxony to the lower Rhine. Bourrienne, himself a traitor, was mildly astonished at his attitude, particularly when Bernadotte admitted that he was confused by the apparent readiness of the French to accept a Bourbon prince. "I was surprised," Bourrienne says, in a rare moment of candor, "that Bernadotte, with the intelligence I knew him to possess, should imagine that the will of subjects has any influence in changes of government. Not very well satisfied with his residence in Paris," Bourrienne continues, "after a few days he set out for Sweden."

Paris, at this time, was entertaining an assortment of crowned and uncrowned heads that is surely unique in the history of any city. The Emperor Napoleon was leaving Fontainebleau, the Empress Marie-Louise with the King of Rome was on the point of leaving for Vienna. The divorced Empress Josephine was entertaining the ruling Czar of Russia, the emperor of Austria and the reigning king of Prussia, assisted by Hortense, her daughter, who was now the former queen of Holland. The Comte d'Artois was in the capital as the accredited representative of the restored king of France awaiting the official summons at Stanmore, in Middlesex. The average Frenchman can be forgiven a certain amount of confusion as he picked his way among the claims of old and new loyalties.

The call for Louis came on April 20th, the very day that his rival quitted Fontainebleau. Watched by an approving crowd of Cockneys the tightly corseted Prince Regent set out with a glittering military escort to conduct his brother sovereign to the metropolis. White Bourbon favors were everywhere, the walls of Devonshire House were hung with the colors and arms of France and England, and Londoners whistled the popular hit of the season, *The White Cockade.* The two fat sovereigns met and embraced outside the "Abercorn Arms" in Stanmore, the exile having been drawn there by cheering Englishmen, harnessed between the shafts of his carriage. It is a pity that the caustic Duke of Wellington was not present to witness this act of reconciliation between the two countries. Had he been history might have been enriched by another of his sardonic witticisms. The grinning Francophiles having been replaced by bay horses, the procession set out for Grillon's Hotel in Albemarle Street, Piccadilly, where the Duke of Kent's band played *God Save the King* in honor of host and guest. The Lord Mayor and Aldermen crowded into the reception and behind them came a swarm of emigrés (including Fanny Burney) anxious to ensure that the fatigued Louis would remember them as having been among those who had not been tempted home by Napoleonic amnesties. A few days later, as the fallen Emperor was speeded on his way out of the realm by the execrations of southerners, Louis stepped ashore to acknowledge the cheers of equally vociferous northerners. The emigrés accompanying him were in a state of emotion. After twenty years' absence they were at last retreading the soil of France and the minds of most of them were assuredly fixed on the future. There was one, however, who did not forget to acknowledge the past. Leaving his British sanctuary at Somers Town the Abbé Carron addressed a farewell letter to "noble and sensitive souls who had . . . treated as a brother and cherished as a son, this poor stranger, obscure citizen in his own country who was, and ought to have remained unknown in yours." His letter ended, "Providence condemns me to this great sacrifice which to me is like a new emigration. . . ." In 1814 political refugees could be absolutely certain of safety and hospitality in Britain. There was no likelihood of them being arrested on the strength of a pigeonholed treaty, tossed into a waiting aircraft and delivered up to their executioners. In that direction we in Britain seem, as a nation, to have retrogressed. Perhaps a copy of the Abbé Carron's letter should be framed and hung in the study of successive Home Secretaries.

The long journey to the Mediterranean was all but over. On the 27th the travel weary entourage reached Fréjus, the little port where, less than fifteen years before, General Bonaparte and the more fortunate among his personal following stepped ashore at the end of their Egyptian adventure and rode north to make an end of the revolution. No enthusiastic Frenchmen, begging to be delivered from a corrupt and incompetent government, pressed round him now but Captain Usher, commanding the British frigate *Undaunted*, fired a twenty-one gun salute, perhaps in acknowledgement of him, perhaps as a compliment to the commissioners. Whichever it was he was rapped over the knuckles by his superiors.

Riding at anchor close by was a French brig, aptly named *Inconstant*, but she flew Bourbon colors and Napoleon preferred British hospitality. Thankfully the Russian and Prussian commissioners took their leave. Colonel Campbell and General Köhler, a pair of gentlemanly watchdogs, representing Britain and Austria, were to accompany him to Elba.

At eleven P.M. on the night of the 28th he embarked and at once began to display the cordiality and affability that he had used so often to convert enemies into allies. His first conquests were the tars of the lower deck, who were soon calling him "a capital fellow," all but Boatswain Joe Hinton, who was proof

against his charm and growled "Humbug!" whenever he over-
heard his messmates praising their distinguished passenger. Hinton's crustiness endured until, on leaving the vessel, he received
his share of the gold napoleons the Emperor distributed among
the crew.

By then he had recovered his second wind. Composed,
reasonable, mentally alert and politely conversational, he was
the Jekyll of Tilsit, with the Hyde of the last four weeks subdued. He was also very tactful. On board, by a curious coincidence, was a nephew of Sir Sydney Smith, the English adventurer of whom Napoleon had once said, referring to Smith's
stubborn defense of Acre, "That man made me miss my destiny."
Now all he said was, "Ah, that's the man I encountered in Egypt."

For everyone the voyage was a pleasant, relaxing experience
and for a privileged few, dining and conversing with the State
prisoner, it was a revelation, not only of his astonishing powers
of resilience but of his secret thoughts.

To the Austrian Köhler he warned of the dangers of a tri-
umphant Russia and what her enlargement would mean to the
Habsburg Empire. To Captain Usher he spoke of his dream to
build a navy of three hundred sail of the line and when the
skeptical sailor asked how they were to be manned he said he
had intended to conscript crews from all the seacoast towns of
France and train them in the Zuyder Zee. Smiling indulgently
the British captain replied that a naval conscript would cut a
sorry figure in a gale. Possibly he had forgotten that half his
own crew had been recruited by the Press Gang. Without rancor Napoleon prophesied a stormy future for the Bourbons and
made some disparaging remarks about the fighting quality of
the Austrians, Russians and Prussians who had just toppled him
from his throne but he had, it seemed, great respect for Blucher.
"That old devil," he acknowledged, "gave me the most trouble.
If I beat him in the evening he was there next morning. If I
routed him in the morning he rallied and fought again before
night." It was almost as though he could project his vision a
year ahead, calculating Blucher's contribution to the ultimate rally of June 18, 1815.

By May 4th, when the *Undaunted* dropped anchor off Port

Ferrajo, Boatswain Hinton had succumbed to the Imperial charm and joined in the British tars' valediction of "Good health, Your Honor, and better luck next time."

From all parts of Europe, as summer succeeded spring, long files of footsore men in patched, threadbare uniforms, trudged towards the frontiers of France. They were prisoners of war, released under the terms of the peace, begging their way home to the land they had left as seasoned fighters or conscripts in the string of campaigns that had convulsed the Continent in an almost unbroken succession of wars. They moved south from the Channel ports, set ashore from British ships after their release from the hulks in English estuaries, from the new prison shrouded in Dartmoor mists that still does duty as a Golgotha, and from parole towns as far apart as Edinburgh and Ashburton, a generous exchange for a lesser number of Englishmen detained since 1803 in the fortress towns of Bitche and Verdun.

They came over the Pyrenean passes, past the shallow graves of so many of their comrades, from captivity in Spain and Portugal, and across the Saxon plain from scenes of victories and defeats. They tramped westward from Silesia, from Bohemia, from the Baltic coast, and northward from Italy, and sometimes they met and mingled with groups of hollow-eyed men who had survived the retreat from Moscow and the Siberian captivity reserved for men of the 1812 Grand Army who had refused to die. Ghosts of an era that was already receding into history they gazed with astonishment at the festive preparations in French frontier towns awaiting courtesy visits by a Bourbon prince. The former prisoners had heard of the Bourbons but few among them had ever looked on one. Their mental horizons were bounded by more recent memories, of half-armed volunteers triumphing at Jemappes and Fleurus and of a long roll of Imperial victories from Lodi to Borodino. They had, for the most part, a surfeit of glory but they found it difficult to applaud the aristocratic popinjays now masquerading as the Royal Guard, successors to the Imperial Guard, or respond with enthusiasm to the invitations of the bourgeois to wear a white cockade and salute men who had been playing whist in English spas when they were entering every capital in Europe. Soon many of them were in trouble and not a few in jail for openly voicing Bonapartist preferences. They could not and would not adjust to a way of life that had been dying when their fathers raided the arsenal at the Invalides and stole thirty thousand muskets to make the Revolution. From now on they were to form the hard core of those who rejected absolutism, not only here in Paris but also in Vienna, Munich, Warsaw and, ultimately, in Moscow. Without knowing it they had conceived and brought forth nationalism and laid their hands on bellropes that were to ring the knell of kings. But before that happened there was to be a short and noisy epilogue.

One contingent of these Imperialists, moving slowly southwest through the Low Countries, entered their homeland by way of Brussels and Charleroi, and may have stopped to buy fruit and skimmed milk at one of the two farms adjacent to the high road, La Haye Sainte and Hougomont. Some of them were to leave their bones in the orchards and furrows about here for, within a few minutes' walk of either farm, was a low plateau called by local men Mont St. Jean. It screened a hamlet known as Waterloo.

Notes

CHAPTER 2

Note 1. Macdonald's Advice to Napoleon. Many times during the next twelve months Marshal Macdonald was to urge his chief to concentrate. Only when it was too late was this advice taken. It is interesting to recall that Napoleon, in his younger days, had been the apostle of concentration and was now seen to be inferior in overall strategy to some of his pupils. Only two of Napoleon's twenty-six marshals, Davout and Masséna, were capable of winning large scale battles in their own right. Soult was also an excellent strategist but only in the defensive sense. The others were good tacticians but were seen as inferior generals when in command of more than a corps.

Note 2. Captain Roëder, of the Hessian Lifeguards, a survivor of the retreat from Moscow, was detained in Stralsund for several weeks on his escape from Russia. A sadistic garrison captain made a habit of thrashing his men with a stick and the flat of his sword outside the prisoner's door. It would seem that service in the Swedish Army was as cruel and degrading as in that of Prussia, where rankers were treated by their officers as serfs.

CHAPTER 4

Note 1. Bessières as a Royalist. Bessières was the only one of Napoleon's marshals who actually took up arms on behalf of the Bourbons against the Paris mob. In the attack on the Tuileries in August, 1792, he was a member of the royal garrison. Too obscure to be proscribed on this account he emerged from hiding after a month and joined the Republican army in the Pyrenees. He first met Napoleon while serving as a cavalry captain in the Army of Italy.

Note 2. Gustavus was killed in the battle but the engagement was a turning point in the Thirty Years' War that had ravaged central Europe in the first half of the seventeenth century.

Note 3. Latour-Maubourg was a typical soldier of the period. Later in the campaign he lost his leg and when his servant commiserated with him, he remarked, "You stupid idiot! From now on you will only have one boot to polish."

CHAPTER 5

Note 1. It may seem odd to the civilian that a commander-in-chief could retire to rest when engaged in a struggle of this nature but the practice is not unusual. Field Marshal Montgomery did precisely this at the opening of El Alamein, retiring to sleep in his trailer. To direct a battle, he later claimed in a broadcast, a man must have a clear mind and a period of rest is absolutely essential. Plans having been made there is nothing more he can do but wait for subordinates to put them into operation. In the forty-eight hours preceding May 21st, Napoleon had not had more than an hour or so of undisturbed rest.

CHAPTER 6

Note 1. Junot's friendship with Napoleon went back to the storming of Toulon, in 1793, when he had been a sergeant and Napoleon was commanding the artillery. He accompanied Napoleon on most of his campaigns, including the expedition to Egypt. When the new nobility was created Napoleon contemplated making Junot the Duke of Nazareth, in honor of his victory over the Turks in the Holy Land, but changed his mind because he was told the soldiers would call him "Junot of Nazareth." Junot, a loyal friend and valiant soldier, was one of the unluckiest generals in the Grand Army. Time and again he came within reach of the coveted marshal's baton but always some failure on his part would cause it to be withheld. He was the first of Napoleon's personal friends to come into collison with Wellington during the French descent on Portugal in 1808. This resulted in the British victory at Vimeiro, and an armistice under which the French were obligingly shipped home by British vessels. Soon after his return to France, in 1813, Junot died by his own hand.

CHAPTER 8

Note 1. The same thing happened at Ligny, two days before Waterloo where d'Erlon's Corps, strong enough to turn either Quatre Bras or Ligny into decisive victories, marched back and forth from dawn to dusk in obedience to commands and countermands from his superiors. Curiously enough Ney was commanding at the first of these engagements.

Note 2. Poniatowski's baton had been well earned. A nephew of Stanislaus, the last king of Poland, he enlisted with the French when the Grand Army captured Warsaw in 1806. Although Napoleon had not yet freed Poland, as Poniatowski and all patriotic Poles hoped he would, he remained loyal and the troops he led were among the most efficient and daring in the French army. They had shared in every campaign made by Napoleon during the last seven years. Thirty-six thousand of them had crossed the Niemen into Russia in June, 1812.

Note 3. This did not prevent Bernadotte from issuing his own bulletin (a grave breach of military discipline) praising their conduct. For this he was disgraced and sent from the field.

Note 4. Invented by Colonel (later Sir William) Congreve the rocket was introduced into the Peninsula War at the insistence of the Prince Regent but the conservative Wellington never had the slightest faith in them on account of their unpredictability. "I don't want to set fire to any town and I don't know any other use for rockets," he wrote in his dispatches.

Note 5. Lieutenant Strangeways rose to the rank of general. Ironically he was killed at Inkerman, fighting against the Russians in the Crimea forty-one years later.

Note 6. It is interesting to compare the casualty rate among Grand Army senior officers with that of World Wars I and II. A fatal casualty among men of high ranks at Ypres or El Alamein was comparatively rare on both sides. In the campaigns of Napoleon the chance of getting killed, wounded or taken prisoner increased after promotion to the rank of colonel. More than a score of generals fell in a single day's fighting at Borodino in September, 1812.

CHAPTER *9*

Note 1. This picture of Jerome in flight comes to us from the pen of Beugnot, his Minister of Finance, but it is fair to add that Beugnot also wrote of him: "Better prepared, he would, I have no doubt, sustained the burden of his name, heavy though that was." A more pleasing aspect of Jerome's unstable character emerges from accounts of Waterloo, eighteen months later. At Hougomont he fought with great gallantry. He was the only member of the original family to survive to enjoy reinstatement that accompanied the establishment of the Second Empire in the middle of the century.

Note 2. General Drouot, of the Guard Artillery, is not to be confused with General Drouet, Count D'Erlon, a famous divisional general in the Grand Army. Drouot, whom Marshal Macdonald describes as "the most upright and honest man I have ever known, well-educated, brave, devoted and simple in manner," bore a charmed life throughout the Napoleonic Wars. It was Napoleon's habit to send his artillery well forward and Drouot would always dismount and advance on foot with his men wearing his full regimentals likely to attract special fire. Yet he never received a scratch and when, after Waterloo, his loyalty to Napoleon seemed likely to mark him down for the fate of Ney, he refused to flee but marched up to the door of the Abbaye prison in Paris and offered to stand trial. Subsequently he was acquitted.

Note 3. After the death of Napoleon's father Napoleon made himself responsible for the care and education of his ten-year-old brother Louis and took him back to France to share his lodgings. Napoleon, then twenty-one, was living on his lieutenant's pay and on arrival in the garrison town the brothers had eighty-five francs between them. Later, when Napoleon got a command, he took Louis on his staff.

Note 4. King of Bavaria's Message to Eugène. The letter from his father-in-law was carried through the lines by a young officer calling himself Major Eberle who was, in fact, Prince Augustus Thurn and Taxis, an aide-de-camp of the king.

Note 5. Hairy Knapsacks. The phrase "hairy knapsacks" derives from the untanned goatskins of which the French infantry knapsacks were made.

Note 6. In *Wellington's Peninsular Victories* (B. T. Batsford, Ltd.) Michael Glover gives some interesting facts on the lethal power of the muskets employed on both sides. The British and Portuguese, he says, used a smooth bore flintback weapon thirty-nine inches long and throwing a ball weighing just over an ounce. It could be lethal up to three hundred yards but a trained soldier was liable to miss at eighty yards and the rate of misfire was about two in thirteen shots. He could reload in twelve to fifteen seconds. The unreliability of firearms on both sides dictated tactics and that is why armies fought in close order and the infantry relied upon square formation to defend themselves against cavalry. A minority of British soldiers, however, were armed with a Baker rifle, thirty inches long and having a quarter turn of rifling, and this was accurate up to three hundred yards. Sir John Moore, killed at Corunna in 1809, gave great attention to rifle practice during a recruit's training and this fact, added to the presence of a number of rifles in the British divisions, gave Wellington a decided advantage in skirmishing. Napoleon could have enjoyed the advantage of the rifle but withdrew it in 1807 because it took thirty seconds to load.

CHAPTER *10*

Note 1. The case of Colonel Viriot affords an interesting sidelight on the injustice that can crush an honest man involved, all unknowingly, in affairs of state. In 1800 a senator was kidnapped by disguised agents of Fouché who were raiding his house in search of compromising documents. The senator returned home unharmed, only too happy to make light of his experience but Napoleon, furious at this cavalier treatment of one of his civic representatives, instructed Fouché to make stringent inquiries and some arrests, which he did, selecting as his victims two innocent scapegoats who were summarily "tried" for the crime of abduction. Viriot, knowing them to be guiltless, happened to be one of their judges and went to extraordinary lengths to save them from the executioner. When this failed he continued in his efforts to clear their names. As a result he himself became the object of relentless police persecution and remained in disgrace and unemployed until the nation was in such danger that even the swords of scapegoats were in demand.

Viriot tried for sixty years to clear his name but was unsuccessful and died in 1860 without ever knowing the facts that had blighted his life. They came to light after Cretineau-Joly, historian of the La Vendée insurrection, had examined all his papers and Lenôtre, the patient explorer of all the bypaths of the Revolution and Empire, had applied himself to the task of proving not only Viriot's innocence but that of the poor wretches for whom he suffered.

Note 2. General Dupont's surrender at Baylen, in 1808, was a blow that inflicted immense damage on the morale of the Grand Army and was, in fact, the first disaster of its kind to occur. Eighteen thousand men were involved and Dupont was court-martialed and imprisoned by Napoleon.

Note 3. Viscount Castlereagh, a political opportunist in his younger days (his election, at the age of twenty-one, to Parliament as representative of County Down, cost £60,000) was nonetheless an exceptionally intelligent and forward looking statesman, cast in the conservative mold of Metternich. In the years following the fall of Napoleon, in which he played such a vital part, he ignored the rising tide of nationalism and became unpopular at home. He committed suicide in the year following Napoleon's death, aged fifty-three.

CHAPTER *11*

Note 1. Marmont's Conscripts: In describing the conduct of his raw troops in this engagement Marmont wrote in his memoirs, "Conscripts who had arrived the day before went into the line and behaved, as regards courage, like old soldiers. Oh, what heroism there is in the blood of France!" He then quotes the story of the two recruits at the battle of Champaubert.

CHAPTER *13*

Note 1. Astyanax, son of Hector. After the fall of Troy the victorious Greeks threw him from the walls in order that Troy should never be re-established.

Note 2. The original copy of this vital dispatch has never been found for Blucher, having read it, let the rider go. The text is from a German translation made at the time and there seems no reason to doubt its authenticity.

Note 3. Chateaubriand's pamphlet: At the time this was written Chateaubriand was residing with his wife in the Rue de Rivoli and lived in fear of Napoleon's secret police. At night the papers were concealed under the author's pillow and by day they were carried about by Madame de Chateaubriand in one of her petticoats. During the Allied advance on Paris it was printed sheet by sheet under conditions of great secrecy but made its appearance the day the Allies entered the city. Its full title was *From Buonaparte to the Bourbons.*

CHAPTER *15*

Note 1. Cabanis, Pierre Jean (1757–1808) was a physician who had also been a politician and had played an important part in the Revolution. He was known to be deeply interested in toxicology. He died under mysterious circumstances, reputedly from sampling one of his own potions. If the poison was the same brew as that given to Condorcet, who used it to commit suicide in prison in 1794, it was probably too old to be effective.

Note 2. The battle of Mount Tabor was fought near Acre during the Egyptian expedition 1798–9. General Kléber (later to command the French and die at the hands of an assassin) was cut off with 2,000 men and fought all day in the desert against 25,000 Turkish horsemen. He was rescued by Napoleon in person and the Turks suffered great slaughter.

CHAPTER *16*

Note 1. Caroline Columbier wrote to Napoleon shortly before he assumed the title of Emperor in 1804, and reminded him of their youthful idyll. She asked if something could not be done for her brother. Always extremely generous to old friends Napoleon replied at once, notwithstanding the fact that Caroline was then the wife of a man called Bressieux. Soon Bressieux was President of an Electoral College, Caroline's brother was a lieutenant, and Caroline herself became a lady-in-waiting in the household of Napoleon's mother. In addition, all the relatives of the Columbiers who had been prescribed during the Revolution were removed from the list of emigrés.

INDEX